GW00367483

HARRAP'S

English Idioms

John O.E. Clark

HARRAP

London Paris

First published in Great Britain 1990
by HARRAP BOOKS Ltd
Chelsea House, 26 Market Square, Bromley,
Kent BR1 1NA

Reprinted: 1990; 1991

ISBN 0-245-60041-8

By the same author:
Word Perfect
Word for Word
Word Wise

Typeset by Action Typesetting, Gloucester
Printed in England by Clays Ltd, St Ives plc

Preface

Idioms are words or phrases whose meaning cannot be taken literally – they defy logical or grammatical analysis. They are characteristic of a language, but because they are illogical they have to be learned. Thus "dark horse" and "queer fish" are established English idioms that may be used to describe a person, whereas "dark fish" and "queer horse" are not.

It can be argued that the idiomatic use of a single word is merely an extension of that word's meaning. For instance, once the word *battle-axe* (a formidable weapon) is employed also for a formidable woman, the idiomatic use becomes a secondary meaning. For this reason, *English Idioms* confines itself to idioms of two or more words. Even so it lists more than 10,000 current English idioms and sayings. Each is listed under a key word that forms part of it, and cross-referenced under any other significant words it contains. Thus "mad as a March hare" is defined under "hare", but included also as a cross-reference under "mad" and "March". Idioms are listed in alphabetical order under the key words. Alternative words or phrases are separated by an oblique stroke; optional words or phrases, in brackets, are ignored for the purposes of alphabetization.

J.O.E.C. – London, 1990

A

aback
to be taken aback = surprised

abeyance
be in/fall into abeyance = be waiting or in suspense

abide
abide by = comply with, remain faithful to
abide by the consequences = endure the result
cannot abide = cannot tolerate

about
about to = just going to
how about?/what about? = what do you think about?
out and about = active, moving around out of doors
up and about = out of bed (after any illness)
  See also: be (about) the **size** of it.

above
above all = most important, more than anything else
above and beyond = in addition, more than necessary
above asking = too proud to ask
above oneself = self-satisfied, conceited
above suspicion = known to be too honest to be suspected of
  wrong-doing
not above = not too honest/proud to
  See also: above **board**; above one's **station**; above **par**; **rise** above
  oneself.

abuse
terms of abuse = bad/uncomplimentary language

accent
accent you could cut with a knife = strong, noticeable accent (in
  speaking)
  See also: **broken** accent/English.

accident
accidentally on purpose = deliberately but underhandedly
chapter of accidents = succession of misfortunes/mistakes

accommodate
accommodate with = supply, lend

accord
according to = as said by
of/on one's own accord = voluntarily
with one accord = unanimously, with everyone's agreement, simultaneously

account
account for = explain
an account to settle = grudge to avenge
be accountable for = be responsible for
by all accounts = according to popular opinion
by one's own account = according to what one says
call to account = require someone to justify his or her actions
give a good account of (oneself) = do/perform well
keep an account of = keep a (written) record of
no accounting for taste = a preference the speaker does not agree with
of no account = worthless, of no importance
on account = towards (in part payment of) a debt
on account of = because of
on no account/not on any account = in no circumstances
on one's own account = for oneself
on somebody's account = on behalf of somebody, for somebody's sake
on that account = for that reason
put/turn to (good) account = use to (personal) advantage
settle/square an account (with somebody) = settle a real or figurative debt, avenge oneself
take account of/take into account = include (in one's judgement)
    See also: **blow**-by-blow account.

ace
ace in the hole = resource or riposte held in reserve
it's ace! = it is the best!

play one's ace = use one's most powerful resource

trump somebody's ace = counter an opponent's move by an even
   more powerful one

(come) within an ace of = (be) very close to
   See also: **black** as the ace of spades; have an ace up one's **sleeve**; **hold**
   all the aces.

ache
   See: one's **heart** aches/bleeds for somebody.

Achilles
   See: Achilles' **heel**.

acid
acid test = crucial test or trial

come the old acid = (try) to deceive somebody

acquaint
acquaint one with = make one aware of

be acquainted with = know

acquaintance
have a nodding acquaintance with = know somebody/something only
   slightly

make the acquaintance of = to get to know or meet

scrape up an acquaintance with = deliberately try to make friends
   with somebody (usually for one's own advantage)

acquire
acquired taste = liking/preference for the unusual, obtained gradually

acquit
acquit oneself = behave (as required/expected)

across
get/put something across = make one's (possibly difficult) meaning
   clear
   See also: across the **board**.

act
act a part = hide one's real feelings

act

act a part = hide one's real feelings

act of God = unforeseen and damaging event, or favourable divine intervention

act on/upon = take action because of (something known)

act up = misbehave or malfunction

catch somebody in the act = come across somebody while he/she is doing something wrong

get in on the act = intrude, or copy somebody, for a hoped for advantage

get/put one's act together = become organized

old pal's act = favouritism to a friend (especially in business)

put on on an act = pretend (ostentatiously)

See also: act/be one's **age**; play/act the **fool**; **read** the riot act.

action

actions speak louder than words = deeds are more effective than mere talk

action stations = be prepared immediately

go into action = start working (vigorously)

out of action = not working (of a machine), indisposed (of a person)

piece of the action = part in (an undertaking)

actress

as the actress said to the bishop = emphasizing a (usually suggestive) double meaning

Adam

Adam's ale = water

Adam's rib = woman(kind) (equated with Eve)

not known from Adam = completely unknown

See also: (sweet) **Fanny** Adams.

add

add up = make sense

See also: add **insult** to injury.

addition

in addition (to) = as well as

address
address oneself to = direct one's effort/attention to
address the ball (at golf) = line up the club before making a shot

admiration
See: **lost** in admiration.

advance
in advance of = before (in time)
make advances to = try to establish a friendship with

advantage
have the advantage of = be in a better/superior position than, or
  know something that somebody else does not
something to one's advantage = something that benefits one (usually
  finanacially)
take advantage of somebody = profit by somebody else's
  ignorance/innocence
to advantage = in a beneficial way
turn to advantage = make beneficial
  See also: **set** something off to advantage.

advocate
See: **devil**'s advocate.

affair
affair of the heart = love affair
have an affair with = have an emotional/sexual relationship with
hole-and-corner/hole-in-the-corner affair = secret (and possibly
  sordid) relationship

afoot
something afoot = planned (secretly)

afraid
be afraid = be sorry

after
after all = in spite of everything
be after somebody = pursue, want to catch
be after something = desire, want to obtain

again
come again? = pardon? (what did you say?)
now and again = occasionally

age
act/be one's age = behave in an adult manner
age before beauty = older people should take precedence over
  younger ones (meant sarcastically)
age of consent = 16 years for a girl in Britain (over which age a man
  can legally have sexual relations with her)
ages since = a long time
an age/for ages = for a long period (of time)
at an advanced age = very old
at an awkward age = at any difficult stage of life, usually adolescence
  or the menopause
come of age = reach the age of being legally responsible for one's
  actions (18 years for most purposes in Britain)
look/show one's age = appear to be as old as one really is
of tender age/years = young/immature
ripe old age = very old
under age = below a legally required age

agony
agony column = letters to a newspaper/magazine from readers with
  problems that are answered by the publication's resident expert
pile on the agony = deliberately make somebody's pain, discomfort
  or disappointment seem worse

agree
agree to differ = agree (amicably) to a difference of opinion
one-sided agreement = agreement that favours one party but not the
  other
  See also: **gentleman**'s agreement.

aid
in aid of = for the help/benefit of

air
airs and graces/put on airs = affectation/adopt an affected manner
airy-fairy = dreamy but impractical

(you could) cut the air with a knife = there was an atmosphere of tension/resentment

dance/walk on air = be in a state of ecstasy

give oneself airs = show off, try to impress/claim to be what one is not

go up in the air = become very angry

have a hangdog air = appear to be shame-faced

hot air = bluster, unsubstantiable claim

(up) in the air = undecided/unresolved

into thin air = emphasizes disappearance

make the air turn blue/turn the air blue = swear, blaspheme

out of thin air = (apparently) from nowhere

something in the air = rumour/suspicion that something is about to happen

take the air = go/walk out of doors

See also: air a **grievance; clear** the air; **free** as the air/wind/a bird; fresh-air **fiend; walk** on air.

Aladdin

Aladdin's cave = repository of expensive/good things

alarm

false alarm = something that does not happen although expected/an unnecessary warning

ale

See: **Adam**'s ale.

Alec(k)

smart Alec(k) = somebody who claims (conceitedly) to know everything

alert

on the alert = prepared and ready for anything

alive

alive and kicking = aware and active

alive with = crowded/infested with

be alive to a situation/the fact that = be aware of something

all
all along = all the time/from the beginning
all and sundry = everyone
all at once/all of a sudden = suddenly
all for something = be enthusiastically in favour of something
all for the best = ultimately for the good
all in = exhausted, or inclusive (of extras)
all in all = taken as a whole
all of = at least, fully
all one = immaterial, makes no difference
all out = with maximum effort
all over the place = to many destinations, or drunk/incompletely done
all round = various
all rounder = somebody with various skills
all set = in a state of readiness
all the best = farewell (i.e. may you fare well)
(not) all there = (not) clever/sane
all the same = nevertheless
all the same to = makes no difference to
all things considered = after everything has been taken into account
all told = in total
all up with = ended (of life/prospects)
all very well = as far as something goes
at all = in the smallest way
for all I care/know = as if I care (expressing indifference or ignorance)
for all that = nevertheless, despite the circumstances
get away from it all = escape from everyday responsibilities
not all that = not as believed/expected/suggested
not at all = not (emphatically)
on all fours = on hands and knees
one and all = everyone
when all's said and done = when everything is taken into consideration
See also: **above** all; all **ends** up; all in a **day**'s work; all in good **time**; all of a **sudden;** all **over;** all ship-shape and **Bristol** fashion; at all **costs; be** all and end all; on all **fours.**

alley
blind alley = something with no prospects or likelihood of a result

allowance
make allowance(s) for = take into account

alone
go it alone = act on one's own, independently of others
let alone = without even considering
leave/let well alone = add/do nothing else (for fear of spoiling something)

along
all along = all the time
along with = together with
go along with = agree (but perhaps deceitfully)
   See also: all along the **line**.

also
also-ran = loser

amends
make amends (for) = make up (for), compensate

angel
guardian angel = protector (who seeks no reward)
like an angel = with purity and/or innocence
on the side of the angels = in favour of what is correct/moral
   See also: angel of **mercy; fools** rush in where angels fear to tread.

anger
   See: more in **sorrow** than in anger.

angle
angle for = try to obtain something using hints

animal
rare animal = somebody of unusual ability/talent, or with an unusual combination of abilities
behave like an animal = (of people) behave in an inhuman or very antisocial way

dumb animals = animals, emphasizing their non-human status and inability to speak for themselves
lower/worse than animals = (of people) inhuman or very antisocial

answer
answer back = reply cheekily
answer for (something) = be responsible/blamed for (something)
answer to the name of = acknowledge the name of, be called
be answerable for = accept responsibility for
know all the answers = be adept/well informed (possibly in a conceited way)
straight answer = unambiguous reply, without being devious
the answer's a lemon = a non-answer to a long, involved/boring question
  See also: answer by **return**; not to take **no** for an answer.

ants
  See: have ants in one's **pants**.

anybody
anybody's guess = uncertain/cannot be predicted

anything
anything but = not in the least, far from

apart
tell apart = distinguish (between)
  See also: **joking** apart.

apology
an apology for = poor example/sample of

appear
appear for = represent in court
keep up appearances = outwardly maintain a status that may not be genuine
make/put in an appearance = attend
to all appearances = apparently, seemingly

appetite
  See: put an **edge** on one's appetite.

apple
apple of one's eye = favourite person, one who is loved best
apple-pie bed = bed with the sheet folded in such a way that one
  cannot get in it
apple-pie order = neat and tidy
rotten apple (in the barrel) = bad person among many good ones
upset the apple-cart = spoil somebody's plans

approval
on approval = returnable if not satisfactory

April
April fool = somebody on whom a joke is played on 1 April (before
  noon)

apron
tied to one's mother's apron strings = totally dependent on one's
  mother

area
no-go area = place that is unsafe (because of military, terrorist or
  criminal acitivity/presence)
  See also: **grey** area.

argue
argue somebody down = reduce somebody to silence through
  vigorous argument
argue something out = keep talking until agreement is reached
argue the toss = questioning (often unreasonably), argumentative

ark
out of the ark = very old

arm
arm of the sea = narrow inlet
arm twisting = pressurizing (by persuasion or threat)
chance one's arm = take a (calculated) risk
give one's right arm (for) = pay any price, make a sacrifice (for)
keep/hold at arm's length = keep remotely formal, distant
long arm of coincidence = however unlikely, coincidences can happen
long arm of the law = inescapable police detection or justice

(my) right arm = good friend and supporter

take up arms = become involved in a conflict

twist somebody's arm = bring pressure on/persuade somebody to force him/her to do something

up in arms = angrily protesting

with one arm tied behind one's back = very easily

with open arms = enthusiastically and without hesitation

  See also: babe/**baby** in arms; **brothers** in arms; one-armed **bandit**; **strong**-arm tactics.

armchair
armchair traveller = somebody who reads or watches films about overseas places but does not actually visit them

armour
  See: **chink** in somebody's armour.

army
you and whose army? = you and who else?

around
to have been around = to be experienced, worldly-wise
  See also: (all) around/round the **houses**.

arrears
in arrears = behind with payment(s)

arrest
(under) house arrest = being compelled (by official order) to remain in one's home
under arrest = in police custody

arrive
arrive at = reach by a process of thought, deduce

art
off to a fine art = (be able to do something) to perfection
  See also: **black** art/magic; **state** of the art; **work** of art.

article
article of faith = deeply-held conviction

as
as for one = as far as one is concerned
as it is = in the present circumstances
as it were = metaphorically speaking
as you were = return to your previous position/state
  See also: as **yet**.

ascendant
(one's star is) in the ascendant = increasing in influence/popularity

ash
  See: **rake** over the ashes

ask
ask after somebody = enquire about somebody's health/happiness
ask for it = deserve/invite unpleasantness
asking price = price/value put on something by the seller
for the asking = freely available
if you ask me = in my view/opinion
  See also: **above** asking; ask a silly **question**; ask for **trouble**.

askance
  See: **look** askance at.

ass
make an ass of oneself/somebody = make oneself/somebody look
  foolish

astray
go astray = become misplaced/stolen
  See also: **lead** somebody astray.

at
at it = doing something
at that = thus far and no further, or as well
  See also: at a (single) **stroke**; not at **all**.

attach
  See: with no **strings** attached.

attack .
blunt the attack = reduce the effect of an aggressive act

make a full-blooded attack (on) = attack strongly/wholeheartedly

attendance
See: **dance** attendance on.

attention
call/draw attention to = bring to somebody's notice
pay attention (to) = be attentive (to)
rivet one's attention = apply/hold all one's attention

attitude
holier-than-thou attitude = (unjustified) stance of being better/more
  virtuous than everyone else

auction
  See: **Dutch** auction.

aunt
Aunt Sally = deliberate target of abuse/ridicule (to make a point)
my giddy/sainted aunt = exclamation of surprise

autumn
autumn of somebody's life = past the age of maturity, after
  somebody's "best" years

avail
avail oneself of = make use of
of/to little/no avail = with hardly any/no result

avenue
explore every avenue = make every possible enquiry

aversion
pet aversion = somebody/something specially disliked

awakening
rude awakening = sudden unpleasant discovery

away
do away with = dispose of, abolish, or kill
get away with = do without being discovered or, if discovered,
  without being punished
  See also: **edge** away; **get** away from it all; **straight** away.

axe

have an axe to grind = pursue a personal and private aim (often
  leading to a biased point of view)
to be axed = to lose one's job

B

baby

babe/baby in arms = somebody who is immature/naive

cry baby = somebody who weeps or complains for the most trivial of causes

left holding the baby = left to take the blame for something

throw out the baby with the bath water = lose something that is very useful when getting rid of something that is apparently of no use

wet the baby's head = celebrate the birth of a baby by having a drink (with the parent)

back

at the back of = ultimately responsible

back and forth = from one place to another and back again

back-breaking task/work = demanding or exhausting task/work

back down = give in, relinquish any claim to something

back-fire = go wrong (resulting in the opposite of what was intended/required)

back number = out-of-date issue of a newspaper or magazine, or something that is outmoded

back of beyond = remote, inaccessible

(at the) back of one's mind = remaining (but not prominently) in one's thoughts

back out (of) = withdraw (from an agreement/contract/promise)

back-pedal = withdraw (after having expressed interest in something)

back-room boys = anonymous people who develop/plan a project

back to the drawing-board = return to the beginning (and re-plan)

back to the wall = in difficulties with no retreat

back up = support somebody/something

behind one's back = without one's knowledge

break the back of = complete the larger part of

by the back stairs = in an unofficial way, indirectly

get off somebody's back = stop harassing somebody

get one's back up = anger/annoy one

get/put somebody's back up = provoke somebody to anger, annoy *glad to see the back of somebody/something* = be pleased when somebody/something leaves or finishes

go back on = change one's mind, contradict

hang back = be reluctant to go forward

have a broad back = be able/willing to accept blame for the errors of others

have no backbone = lacking courage

like the back of a bus = ugly

like the back of one's hand = intimately

make a rod for one's own back = cause trouble for oneself by one's actions

on one's back = harassed by, or bedridden (through illness or disability)

pat on the back = congratulate/praise (mildly)

put one's back into = make a strenuous effort

see the back of = be finished with

stab in the back = betrayal

take a back seat = adopt an inconspicuous/inferior position or role

talk through the back of one's neck = talk nonsense

through the back door = in an unofficial way, indirectly

to the backbone = absolutely, unquestioningly

turn one's back on = abandon, deliberately ignore

when one's back is turned = when one is not looking or absent

with one hand tied behind one's back = very easily

you scratch my back and I'll scratch yours = you do me a favour and I will do you one in return

See also: **answer** back; back-/left-handed **compliment**; back the wrong **horse**; fall off the back of a **lorry**; **fed** up (to the back teeth); **get** one's own back; **go** back to square one; in by the back **door**; like water off a **duck**'s back; **scratch** somebody's back.

background

keep/remain/stay in the background = be deliberately inconspicuous

back seat

take a back seat = remove oneself from a position of authority/power

See also: back-seat **driver**.

backward
bend/lean over backwards = take great trouble to be accommodating or helpful
not backward in coming forward = attention-seeking, not shy
See also: **know** something backwards.

bacon
bring home the bacon = succeed in a (difficult) enterprise
save somebody's bacon = rescue somebody (who is in a difficult situation)

bad
bad blood (between people) = ill feeling
bad debt = money owing that is written off (and never paid)
bad egg/hat/lot = somebody of bad character/reputation
bad language = swearing, blaspheming
bad light/odour = bad/unfavourable reputation
badly off = poor, not wealthy
bad patch = difficult/unfavourable situation
come to a bad end = finish in unpleasant/criminal circumstances (possibly by dying)
go from bad to worse = deteriorate (gradually)
in a bad way = critically ill (of a person), or in a very poor state (of a thing)
in bad taste = ill-mannered/offensive
in somebody's bad books = be in disfavour with somebody
not (so/too) bad = comparatively good
too bad = unfortunate
See also: bad **faith**; good/bad **form**; in bad **odour**; **look** bad; (using) bad/strong **language**; with bad/good **grace**.

badger
badger somebody = pester, make continual demands

bag
bag and baggage = with all one's possessions
bag of bones = very thin (person or animal)
bag of tricks = complete set of accessories/equipment
in the bag = successfully concluded, or as sure as if concluded
mixed bag = varied collection

pack one's bags = leave (in anger)
  See also: bag/bundle of **nerves**; let the **cat** out of the bag

bait
jail bait = precocious young (under age) woman
rise to the bait = to react in a hoped-for way to a hint or stimulus

baker
  See: baker's **dozen**.

balance
in the balance = unresolved
(catch) somebody off balance = at a disadvantage
on balance = considering every aspect
strike a balance = compare things to find their worth
  See also: **tip** the balance.

bald
bald as a billiard ball/coot = completely bald

ball
ball of fire = somebody who is very energetic
ballpark figure = rough estimate
have a ball = have a very enjoyable time
have the ball at one's feet = be in a position to make the next move
have the ball in one's court = have to make the next move
keep one's eye on the ball = be alert, continue to pay attention to
  something
keep/set/start the ball rolling = continue/begin doing something
new ballgame = totally different set of (competitive) circumstances
on the ball = alert, well informed
play ball with somebody = co-operate with somebody
  See also: **address** the ball; **crystal** ball.

balloon
(when) the balloon goes/went up = moment of crisis/trouble

bamboo
  See: bamboo **curtain**.

banana
banana republic = small, unstable and underdeveloped nation

be/go bananas = lose one's temper

band .
beat the band = be extreme (in some respect)
one-man band = work by oneself (with no helpers)
 See: climb/jump onto the **bandwagon**.

bandit
one-armed bandit = fruit machine (gambling)

bandwagon
climb/jump on (board) the bandwagon = support
 somebody/something that looks like being a success (for personal
 gain)

bang
bang goes something = something has suddenly gone
bang on = exactly what is required
go with a bang = go very well
 See also: **gang** bang.

bank
bank on = depend on
break the bank = use all one's available funds, or have a landslide
 win at gambling

banner
carry the banner for = support

baptism
 See: baptism of **fire**.

bar
all over bar the shouting = finished apart from the final throes or
 official announcement
bar none = without exception
called to the bar = made a barrister
colour bar = (unlawful) regulation that excludes coloured people
 from certain activities
prop up the bar = frequent a particular pub

bare
bare bones = essential/most important features
bare-faced lie = shameless/impudent lie
with one's bare hands = without using a tool or weapon

bargain
bargain for = prepare for, expect
drive a hard bargain = insist on harsh terms in an agreement
into the bargain = as well, in addition
make the best of a bad bargain/job = cheerfully accept bad
  luck/adversity
strike a bargain = finally reach an agreement

bargepole
wouldn't touch somebody/something with a bargepole = would avoid
  at all costs

bark
bark up the wrong tree = suffer under a misapprehension
one's bark is worse than one's bite = the (apparent) threat is worse
  than the (real) action
See also: don't keep a **dog** and bark yourself.

barrack-room
barrack-room lawyer = somebody (typically a serviceman) who quotes
  the rule book to annoy/discomfit his superiors

barrel
over a barrel = in an undefendable position, helpless
scrape the (bottom of the) barrel = be forced to use the (poor)
  remnants of something
See also: bad/rotten **apple** (in the barrel).

base
get to/make first base = successfully complete the first stage

bash
have a bash at something = make an attempt at

basinful
have a basinful (of) = endure (more than enough of) something
  unpleasant

basket
put all one's eggs in one basket = commit all one's
   expectations/resources to a single plan

basting
give somebody a (thorough) basting = thoroughly beat

bat
be/have bats in the belfry = mad
blind as a bat = totally blind
carry one's bat = be present for the whole of an activity, right to the
   end
like a bat out of hell = at high speed
off one's (own) bat = independently, without help/prompting
play a straight bat = be honest, undeceitful
   See also: not bat an **eyelid**.

bated
   See: with bated **breath**.

bath
blood bath = carnage, bloody battle

battle
battle of the bulge = slimmer's fight against being overweight
battle royal = intense fight involving everyone
fight a losing battle = continue to resist, even though the outcome will
   inevitably be unfavourable
half the battle = good way towards achieving success, great help
pitched battle = contest with both sides totally committed
running battle = drawn-out dispute or contest

bay
at bay = cornered (by enemies) and made to defend oneself
hold/keep at bay = hold off, keep at a distance

be
be-all and end-all = whole of something
be that as it may = yet, even so
let it be = leave it alone

bead
  See: **draw** a bead on.

beam
broad in the beam = having wide hips
off (the) beam = lacking precision, off course
on one's beam ends = in a desperate situation

bean
full of beans = energetic, lively, high-spirited
haven't a bean = penniless
know how many beans make five = be worldly wise, shrewd
not worth a bean = worthless
spill the beans = be indiscreet, confess

bear
bear/lead a charmed life = be very lucky (in avoiding misfortune)
bear down on/upon = approach purposefully or in a threatening way
bear enquiry/investigation = favourably withstand close examination
bear in mind = remember (with caution)
bear on/have a bearing on = be relevant to
bear oneself = behave
bear out = confirm
bear up = tolerate difficulty/pain with fortitude
bear with = be patient/sympathetic towards somebody
(like a) bear with a sore head = bad-tempered
bear witness = be a witness to something, prove
grin and bear it = (cheerfully) endure difficulty/hardship
  See also: bear a **grudge**; bear **fruit**; bear **garden**; bear one's **cross**;
  bear the **brunt** of; **grin** and bear it.

bearings
find/get one's bearings = locate/orientate oneself
lose one's bearings = get lost, become disorientated

beard
  See: beard the **lion** in his den.

beat
beat about the bush = prevaricate, avoid a direct answer
beat a path to somebody's door = repeatedly visit somebody

beat a (hasty) retreat = run away
beat down = force/persuade somebody to lower the price of
  something
beat hollow = completely defeat
beat it = run away
beat one's brains out = think very hard to (try to) solve a problem
beat somebody to it = do something first (before anyone else can)
beat to a pulp = badly injure through beating
if you can't beat them, join them = if they will not change their
  minds, you must change yours
off-beat = unusual, unconventional
off the beaten track = difficult to get to, away from main roads
take a lot of/some beating = difficult to better
  See also: beat the **band**; beat the **drum** for; beat the living **daylights**
  out of somebody; **dead** beat.

beauty
beauty is in the eye of the beholder = preference (in terms of
  somebody's appearance) is a personal one
beauty is only skin deep = somebody/something that is superficially
  attractive is not necessarily all good
the beauty of it (is) = the best/most satisfying aspect (is)
  See also: **age** before beauty; beauty is only **skin** deep; get one's
  beauty **sleep**.

beaver
beaver away = work long and industriously
  See also: **eager** beaver

beck
at somebody's beck and call = constantly dominated by somebody

become
become of = happen to

bed
bed of nails/thorns = annoying, embarrassing or painful situation
bed of roses = easy/luxurious situation
bed sitter = single room used as a bedroom and a living room
get into bed with = enter into a business agreement/contract with

get out of bed (on) the wrong side = be disagreeable/grumpy
good bedside manner (of a doctor) = way of dealing with a patient
  that reassures and inspires confidence
go to bed with = have sexual intercourse with
make one's bed and (must) lie in it = face the consequences of one's
  actions
  See also: **apple**-pie bed; **feather** bed.

bee
bee in one's bonnet = obsessive idea
bee-line = straight line between two points
bee's knees = the best (person), expert
busy as a bee = very (and continuously) busy

beef
beef about = complain

beer
all beer and skittles = amusing, lacking seriousness
small beer = something that is unimportant

before
before long = soon

beg
beg, steal or borrow = obtain by any means
beg the question = assume the truth of something that can in fact be
  disputed
beg to differ = disagree
go begging = left because unwanted

beggar
beggars can't be choosers = the needy have to take what is available
  See also: beggar **description**.

begin
to begin with = firstly

behalf
on behalf of = representing, in place of

behind
behind the scenes = privately, secretly
behind the times = old-fashioned, out-of-date
come from behind = achieve success although initially at a
  disadvantage
get/fall behind = become late, get in arrears
put something behind one = deliberately try to forget (something
  unpleasant)
  See also: behind one's **back**.

being
for the time being = temporarily

belfry
  See: **bats** in the belfry.

belief
beyond belief = unbelievable
to the best of one's belief = in one's honest view

believe
believe one's ears/eyes = accept as true what one hears/sees
make believe = imagine/pretend

bell
clear/sound as a bell = in excellent health/condition
ring a bell = remind one
saved by the bell = rescued from unpleasantness at the very last
  minute

belly
belly-ache about = complain naggingly
have a bellyful = have more than enough
have eyes bigger than one's belly = overeat, be greedy

belt
below the belt = unfair
belt along/away = travel fast
belt up = stop talking
pull one's belt in/tighten one's belt = spend less, make economies
under one's belt = to have as an achievement or experience

bench
on the bench = serving as a judge or magistrate

bend
bend the rules = cheat, or ignore a regulation
catch someone bending = have an advantage over somebody by surprising him/her
on one's bended knees = in a very submissive way
round the bend = insane, mad
See also: bend/lean over **backwards**; bend somebody's **ear**; lift/bend the **elbow**.

beneath
beneath contempt = not even worth an expression of disapproval

benefit
benefit of the doubt = assumption of innocence, without proof

bent
bent upon = determined
hell bent (on) = very determined

berth
give a wide berth (to) = avoid

beside
beside the point = irrelevant
beside oneself = irrational, very emotional

best
at best = the best that can be expected in the circumstances
at the best of times = even when circumstances are better
(the) best part (of) = most
do one's (level) best = try hard
(all) for the best = leading to a favourable outcome, if unpromising now
get/have the best of both worlds = have the advantages from two different situations
have the best of it = win an argument/contest
make the best of (a bad job) = obtain the best result possible in difficult circumstances, compromise

past it/past one's best = too old (for a particular activity)
put one's best foot forward = make an extra effort, walk quickly
(come off) second best = (be) loser in a contest between two
six of the best = six strokes of the cane
Sunday best = best clothes
to the best of one's ability/belief/knowledge = as well as one is able/knows
(up) with the best = as good as anyone else
See also: **all** for the best; may the best **man** win; to the best of one's **belief**.

bet

bet one's bottom dollar/bet one's life = be almost certain
hedge one's bets = reduce the chances of being wrong by opting for two different choices simultaneously
I/you bet = I am/you can be certain

better

better half = wife, partner
better late than never = more satisfactory that something happens, even if late, than that it never happens at all
better off = more wealthy/more advantageous
for better or (for) worse = whatever happens
get the better of = beat
go one better (than) = supersede (with an improvement)
have seen better days = worn, showing its age
know better = be less foolish
no better than = the same as
think better of somebody = think of somebody in a more favourable way
think better of something = reconsider
See also: best/better **part** of

between

between the devil and the deep blue sea = with a choice between two equally undesirable alternatives
between these four walls = confidentially (and privately)
between two stools = failing to meet either of two (conflicting) requirements

between you and me/ourselves = confidentially
between you, me and the bedpost/gatepost = confidentially (and
    privately)
betwixt and between = midway, neither one nor the other
few and far between = rare, scarce
read between the lines = detect an unstated but implied meaning

bewitched
bewitched, bothered and bewildered = totally confused

beyond
beyond compare/measure = inestimable, very much
beyond one's grasp/reach = unattainable
beyond one's ken = outside one's experience/knowledge
beyond the pale = unacceptable (socially), ill-mannered
  See also: **above** and beyond; **back** of beyond; beyond **belief**; beyond
  price; beyond **recall**.

bias
on the bias = obliquely, diagonally

bib
best bib and tucker = best clothes

bid
bid fair = look promising
bid farewell/welcome (to) = say goodbye/hello (to)
make a bid for freedom = try to escape
straw bid = worthless bid

bide
bide one's time = wait for a good chance

big
be big of somebody = generous (often sarcastic)
Big Apple = New York
Big Brother = dictatorial authority
big fish/noise/shot/wheel = important person
big guns = most important/senior people (in a particular group)
bighead = somebody who is conceited
big time = best/highest reaches of an activity

go down/over big with = be impressive
in a big way = enthusiastically
talk big = boast
too big for one's boots/shoes = conceited
  See also: big **daddy;** big **deal;** big **hand.**

bile
full of bile = bitter and resentful
get one's bile up = arouse bitterness/resentment in one

bill
bill and coo = caress and talk in a loving way
clean bill of health = declared completely fit
fill the bill = be exactly right for what is needed
foot the bill = pay for (somebody else)
top the bill = be the best
  See also: bill of **fare.**

bind
in a bind = in difficulty or trouble

bird
able to/can charm the birds from the trees = be very persuasive, so
  charming that almost anybody complies with one's wishes
a little bird told me = I will not say who told me
bird brain(ed) = fool(ish)
bird has flown = person has disappeared/escaped
bird in the hand (is worth two in the bush) = actual possession is
  better than mere promises
bird of ill omen = carrier of bad news
bird of passage = somebody who is passing through and has no
  permanent home
birds and the bees = fundamental knowledge about (human) sexual
  relations
bird's eye view = view from a high vantage point
birds of a feather = people of similar temperament/views
early bird = somebody who gets up or arrives early
for the birds = trivial, of little worth
free as a bird = completely free and without responsibilities

give somebody the bird = show disapproval vocally (by hissing or booing)
kill two birds with one stone = obtain two results with a single action
like a bird = problem-free
odd bird = strange person
rare bird = unusual person (with two conflicting interests)

birthday
in one's birthday suit = nude

biscuit
take the biscuit = be the worst/most extreme possible

bishop
See: as the **actress** said to the bishop.

bit
bit between one's teeth = eager but out of control
bit by bit = little by little, gradually
bit much = more than one would like, excessive
(a) bit of = some, rather
bit of a lad = man who is somewhat lecherous
bit of all right = attractive/pleasing person or thing
bit of skirt/stuff = young woman (regarded sexually)
bit on the side = extramarital partner
bits and bobs/pieces = odds and ends
champing at the bit = eager to go/start
do one's bit = make a contribution
every bit as = equally as, just as
not a bit (of it) = not at all
thrilled to bits = very pleased
See also: a bit of the **other**.

bite
biter bit = deceiver deceived
bite off more than one can chew = undertake more than one can accomplish
bite one's lip = fail to talk or suddenly stop talking (through embarrassment or annoyance)

bite the hand that feeds one = be very ungrateful (to a benefactor)
once bitten, twice shy = be extra cautious after having had an
  unpleasant experience
put the bite on = borrow money from
what's biting somebody? = what is upsetting somebody?
  See also: bite/snap one's **head** off; bite the **bullet**; bite the **dust**;
  (mere) **flea** bite; one's **bark** is worse than one's bite; take two bites of
  the **cherry**.

bitter
bitter as gall = very bitter
bitter pill (to swallow) = something that is difficult/painful to accept
  See also: to the bitter **end**

black
black and blue = badly bruised
black art/magic = devil worship
black as the ace of spades = completely black
black box = small piece of electronic equipment
blacken somebody's name = spoil/ruin somebody's reputation
black goods/services = refuse to deal with goods/services on the
  instruction of a trade union
black-leg labour = extra (non-union) workers brought in by an
  employer during a strike
black list = list of names of non-favoured/unsuitable people
black look = angry/bad-tempered expression
black market = source of illicit goods (which should be rationed or
  unobtainable)
black mood = angry/ill-tempered disposition
black out = lose consciousness
black sheep (of the family) = somebody who does not conform to the
  family's wishes
black spot = place that is notorious (for accidents/crime)
in black and white = printed
in somebody's black books = out of favour
in the black = in credit (at the bank)
little black book = confidential/private record (of names)
not so black as one is painted = better than one is reputed to be
swear black is white = tell a gross lie

two blacks don't make a white = a second wrong does not remedy the
  first
See also: black **day**; black **economy**; black **eye**; black **ice**.

blame
shoulder the blame/responsibility = accept the total
  blame/responsibility

blank
blank look/stare = empty facial expression
mind be a blank = have no memory of
See also: blank **cheque**; **draw** a blank.

blanket
blanket bath = all-over wash given to a bed-ridden patient
blanket term = all-embracing description
on the wrong side of the blanket = out of wedlock, illegitimate
wet blanket = somebody who spoils one's amusement (by being
  miserable)

blarney
full of blarney = talking in a flattering, persuasive way

blast
at full blast = at maximum speed/strength

blaze
blaze a trail = pioneer, be first to do something
go like blazes = go very quickly

bleed
bleed (somebody) white = extort all of somebody's money
one's heart bleeds for somebody = one is very sorry for somebody
  (often sarcastically)

blessing
blessing in disguise = hidden benefit (thought at first to be unlucky)
count one's blessings = recognize favourable factors (among
  unfavourable ones)
give one's blessing to = approve of
mixed blessing = something with both good and bad aspects

blind

blind drunk = very drunk

blind impulse = sudden, irrational/illogical act

blind somebody with science = deliberately confuse somebody by talking about technicalities

in the country of the blind (the one-eyed man is king) = in a situation where somebody has a little ability/knowledge (he/she has an advantage over people with no ability/knowledge)

none so blind (as those who cannot see) = nobody is less persuadable than somebody who refuses to listen to argument

swear blind = be adamant (even if lying)

the blind leading the blind = the uninformed attempting to inform others

See also: a nod is as good as a wink to a blind **horse**; blind **alley**; blind as a **bat**; blind **date**; blind **spot**; **rob** somebody blind; turn a blind **eye** to.

blink

in the blink of an eye/eyelid = instantly

on the blink = (of machine) with an intermittent fault

block

mental block = obstruction to a thought process

put one's head on the block = deliberately make oneself vulnerable

See also: **chip** off the old block; **stumbling** block.

blonde

dumb blonde = pretty but unintelligent girl

blood

after/out for one's blood = seeking revenge on one

blood and thunder = melodramatic/sensational (of an entertainment medium)

blood brother = very close friend

blood is thicker than water = relations come before (mere) friends

blood letting = disagreement in which someone suffers badly

blood money = favour/reward made to somebody who betrays somebody else

blood on one's hands = be guilty of harming somebody

blood relation/relative = somebody ultimately descended from the same man or woman as oneself
blood sport = sport in which an animal is deliberately killed
blood sucker = blackmailer/extortionist
blood will tell/out = inherited tendencies will eventually make their presence known
blue blood(ed) = (of) aristocratic or noble origin
cause bad blood between people = make people dislike each other
draw blood = hurt/injure
first blood = first success/win
fresh/new/young blood = new member(s) of a group
get blood out of a stone = try to do the impossible
having one's blood up = being angry/excited
in cold/hot blood = calmly and coolly or angrily and bad tempered
in the blood = inherited/innate
make one's blood boil = make one very angry
make one's blood run cold = frighten, make one apprehensive
out for blood = determined to beat somebody/to succeed
runs in one's blood = is inherited
shed/spill blood = injure or kill
sweat blood = work very hard
taste blood = be encouraged/stimulated by an initial success
young blood = (new) younger members of a group
  See also: **bad** blood; blood **bath**; bloody somebody's **nose**; **chill** one's (the) blood; **let** blood; make a full-blooded **attack**; **new** blood; one's own **flesh** and blood; **red**-blooded; **stir** the blood.

bloom
(first) bloom of youth = youthful beauty
past one's bloom = past one's best (in age)

bloomer
make a bloomer = make a silly mistake

blossom
blossom out into = finally develop into

blot
blot on the landscape = eyesore

blot out = obliterate
See also: blot one's **copy** book.

blow

blow a gasket/one's top = lose one's temper
blow-by-blow account = detailed sequential description
blow hot and cold = be alternatively enthusiastic/friendly and then the reverse
blow/let off steam = release pent-up feelings
blow one's own trumpet = boast
blow one's top = lose one's temper
blow out = large or expensive meal
blow over = subside, fade away
blow someone's mind = cause hallucinations
blow the expense = never mind the cost
blow the gaff/whistle on somebody = reveal somebody's guilty secret
blow up = exaggerate
strike a blow for/against = lend one's support/act to oppose
See also: blow something wide **open**; blow up in somebody's **face**; see which way the **wind** blows.

blue

blue film/magazine/video = pornographic film/magazine/video
(in a) blue funk = afraid like a coward
(until one is) blue in the face = without result indefinitely
blue one's money = be (uncaringly) extravagant
blue pencil = (figurative tool of) censorship
blue stocking = prude, woman who values learning above amusement
(scream) blue murder = (create an) angry/violent scene
feel/look blue = be sad
have the blues = be depressed
once in a blue moon = very seldom
out of the blue = unexpectedly
See also: **black** and blue; blue **blood**ed; blue-eyed **boy; bolt** from the blue; make the **air** turn blue; till one is blue in the **face**; true blue **Conservative**.

bluff

call somebody's bluff = challenge somebody whom one thinks is lying

blush

at (the) first blush = on first consideration
spare somebody's blushes = withhold praise so as not to embarrass
 somebody

board

above board = honest, in the open
across the board = in every way, affecting everyone equally
go by the board = be forgotten/ignored
stiff as a board = rigid/very stiff
sweep the board = win everything
take on board = accept an idea/proposal

boat

burn one's boats/bridges = take an irrevocable step
(all) in the same boat = in similar (difficult) circumstances
miss the boat = miss an opportunity
push the boat out = celebrate (with drinks)
rock the boat = interfere in an undertaking so as to jeopardize its
 success

Bob

Bob's your uncle = that is what was wanted

body

body and soul = completely
body-blow = damaging/severe set-back
have/have no body = have/lack substance
keep body and soul together = sustain life
 See also: **dog**'s body; over my **dead** body; **own** somebody body and
 soul.

bog

get bogged down = become stuck, reach a deadlock/impasse

boil

boil down to = amount to
boil over = lose one's temper
come to the boil = reach a critical/significant state
 See also: a watched **pot** never boils; make one's **blood** boil; **off** the
 boil.

bold

See: bold as **brass**; **make** so bold as to.

bolster

bolster up = give (moral) support

bolt

bolt from the blue = total surprise
bolt upright = exactly perpendicular
shoot one's bolt = commit irrevocably and unsuccessfully
  See also: **nuts** and bolts.

bomb

come as a bombshell = come as a complete (unpleasant) surprise
cost a bomb = be very expensive
go down (like) a bomb = be very popular/successful
go like a bomb = move very fast, or sell very well
light/put a bomb under somebody = to stimulate/urge somebody (to
  do something)
  See also: **earn** a bomb.

bone

bone dry = completely dry
bone-headed (from the neck up) = stupid
bone idle = very lazy
bone to pick (with somebody) = issue to accuse somebody of
bone up on = learn or revise a subject
cut to the bone = minimize, make as little as possible
dry as a bone = totally dry
feel in one's bones = intuition/premonition
lazy bones = idle person
make no bones about it = be candid/frank
make old bones = live to a great age
near the bone = bordering on indecency/risqué
  See also: **bag** of bones; **bare** bones; bone of **contention**.

bonnet

See: have a **bee** in one's bonnet.

book

booked for speeding (of the driver of the vehicle) = stopped by the
  police and charged with exeeding the speed limit

book in = register (at a hotel)

bring somebody to book = find evidence to arrest/try/punish somebody

by/according to the book = following the rules (often strictly or fastidiously)

closed book = something of which one is ignorant

in one's bad/good books = disliked/liked

in one's book = in one's own opinion

one for the book = something worth noting/recording

open book = something that is easily understood, unconcealed

read somebody like a book = be fully aware of somebody's unexpressed thoughts

suit one's book = agree with one's own interests

take a leaf out of somebody's book = copy somebody's example

throw the book at = make as many accusations as possible

See also: **cook** the books; **turn** up for the book(s).

boot

(car) boot sale = sale of small secondhand items that the sellers take in the boots of their cars

(tough as) old boots = resilient and hard to harm

die with one's boots on = die at work

hang up one's boots = retire

have one's heart sink into one's boots = be in despair/dismay

lick somebody's boots/shoes = fawn, flatter somebody for personal gain

like old boots = vigorously

order of the boot = sack (from a job)

pull oneself up by one's bootstraps = make a conscious effort to improve one's situation (unaided)

put the boot in = further harm somebody who is already distressed or harmed

the boot's on the other foot = the other person now has the advantage

to boot = also/in addition

See also: too **big** for one's boots.

bore
bore somebody stiff/the pants off somebody/somebody to tears = be very boring

born
be born before one's time = anticipate later ideas/opinions
born with a silver spoon in one's mouth = born with inherited privilege/wealth
in all one's born days = ever
not born yesterday = not a fool/inexperienced person

borrow
borrowed plumes = inappropriate or unofficially used symbols of position/status
borrowed time = unexpected extension of life
  See also: **beg**, steal or borrow

bosom
bosom friend/pal = very close friend
bosom of one's family = immediate family (parents, brothers and sisters)

both
be unable to have something both ways = be unable to make two (equally attractive) choices when only one is actually possible
play both ends against the middle = risky sharp practice (in which one person tries to take advantage of two other participants by setting them against each other and hopes to profit from their conflict)

bottle
be on the bottle = be a regular drinker
bottle up = hold in (emotions/feelings)
hit the bottle = drink excessively
  See also: **crack** a bottle; **lose** one's bottle.

bottom
at the bottom of = ultimately responsible for
bottom fall out of = collapse
bottomless pit = hell
from the bottom of one's heart = very sincerely
get to the bottom of = discover the truth about

knock the bottom out of = demonstrate that something has no value
rock bottom = lowest point possible
touch bottom = reach the lowest point
  See also: **bet** one's bottom dollar; bottom **drawer**.

bound

bound for = going towards
bound to = sure to/must
bound up in = involved with
bound up with = associated with
I'll be bound = I'm sure
out of/within bounds = outside/inside permitted limits
within the bounds of possibility = possible (just)

bow

another/two string(s) to one's bow = additional attribute/talent
bow and scrape = fawn/be servile
bowed down with = troubled/worried by
bow to somebody's better/superior judgement/knowledge = accept
  that somebody knows better
bow to the inevitable = accept that something is unavoidable
bow out = resign
shot across the bows = warning

bowl

bowl a fast one = trick/be deceitful
bowl along = go at a fast, easy pace
bowl of cherries = ease and luxury
bowl over = surprise completely

box

box clever = be crafty
box number = number that identifies an advertiser (in a newspaper
  etc.) who does not want to reveal his address; replies sent to the box
  number at the paper are passed on to the advertiser unopened
box the compass = name the (32) points of the compass in correct
  sequence
  See also: **black** box; box somebody's **ears**; get on one's **soap** box.

boy

blue-eyed boy = a favourite

boy racer = teenager on a small mortorcycle or in an old (slow) car

boys in blue = policemen

boys will be boys = childish behaviour (in men and boys) is to be
  expected

golden boy = young man showing exceptional promise, and idolized
  because of that

jobs for the boys = favours for friends/relations

mother's boy = spoiled son

nancy boy = man who is effeminate/gay

new boy = new employee

old boy network = informal association of professionals, typically ex-
  public school or ex-army

one of the boys = accepted member of a group

  See also: **back-room** boys; **fancy** boy; **happy** as a sandboy; **man** and
  boy; **old** boy/girl; **whipping** boy.

brace

brace yourself = be prepared for unpleasantness

brain

brain child = one's own idea

brain drain = drift of graduates (particularly scientists/technicians)
  from Britain to the United States

brains trust = discussion group of experts

have a brainstorm = have an uncontrolled emotional outburst

have a brainwave = have a sudden inspiration

have something on the brain = be obsessed/preoccupied with
  something

hare-brained (scheme) = impractical/stupid (plan)

make one's brain hurt/reel = be very difficult to grasp (mentally), or
  be incredible

pick somebody's brains = seek particular information from somebody
  with the necessary knowledge

rack one's brains = try very hard to remember/think of something

scatter brain = somebody who is careless/disorganized in thinking

turn one's brain = make one go mad

  See also: **beat** one's brains out; **cudgel** one's brain.

branch
branch out = develop into/become independent of
offer/hold out an olive branch = want to make peace

brass
brass hat = high-ranking officer/official
bold as brass = shamelessly self-assured
get down to brass tacks = reduce an argument/discussion to the fundamental issues
have the brass neck to (do something) = be bold/shameless enough to (do something)
top brass = senior management/officers

brave
put on a brave face = pretend that the situation is better than it really is
See also: brave the **elements**.

breach
fill/step into the breach = deputise for somebody/substitute for something
heal the breach = end a serious disagreement

bread
best thing since sliced bread = something (new) that is very well liked
bread and butter = living, basic daily work
breadwinner = wage-earner for a family
cast one's bread on/upon the waters = speculate (with little hope of reward/success)
have one's bread buttered on both sides = have an easy/effortless existence
know which side one's bread is buttered = be aware of where one's best interests lie
on the breadline = extremely poor
take the bread out of somebody's mouth = prevent somebody from earning a living
See also: one's **daily** bread.

break
bad/lucky break = bad/good luck

break a fall = prevent injury (in a fall)

break a habit = cease to do something habitually

break a journey = interrupt a journey

break a leg = good luck/do well (in a performance)

break a/the record = do better than a/the previous performance

break cover = to suddenly emerge from hiding

break down/up (emotionally) = lose control of one's emotions

break even = make neither a profit nor a loss

break in on = interrupt

break in the weather = change (for the better) in the weather

break into = begin vocalizing, or force an entry, or make an abrupt start

breakneck speed = very fast pace

break new ground = pioneer, make a discovery

break of day = dawn

break off = stop suddenly

break one's neck (for) = be in a great hurry (to do something)

break/keep a promise = fail to keep a promise

break out (in a rash) = appear (suddenly)

break out into a cold sweat = be suddenly afraid/apprehensive

break ranks = move out of position (in disorder)

break service = win a point against the server (in tennis etc.)

break somebody's heart = cause somebody (deep) distress

break something down = separate something (into its components)

break the ice = strike up an acquaintance after overcoming initial shyness

break the news = convey information

break the thread = interrupt a line of reasoning/thought

break through = force an opening in an obstruction

break wind = release gas from the stomach or bowel

break with = sever connections with

make a/the break = leave

See also: break/get out of the **habit**; break/keep one's **word**; break one's **duck**; break the **back** of; **break** the bank; **make** or break.

breakfast

   See: **donkey**'s breakfast

breast
beat one's breast = greatly regret an error
make a clean breast of = confess fully

breath
breath of fresh air = refreshing development
hold one's breath = wait (in anticipation) for something to happen
in the same breath = simultaneously
out of/short of breath = breathless
save your breath (to cool your porridge) = I do not want to hear your
   comments
take one's breath away = astonish/give intense pleasure to/surprise
   one
under one's breath = in a whisper
waste one's breath = talk when nobody heeds or is listening
with bated breath = anxiously, in anticipation of something
   (unpleasant)
with one's last breath = while on the point of death

breathe
breathe again = recover/relax
breathe down somebody's neck = watch somebody (too) closely
breathe easily/easy/freely = to be relieved
breathing space = pause (for recovery)
breathe life into = provide the inspiration/vital force
breathe one's last = die
not to breathe a word = not to tell
take a breather = take a rest (from vigorous activity)

brick
a (gold/regular) brick = a (very good) friend
like a ton of bricks = firmly/heavily
like talking to a brick wall = wasting time trying to convince
   somebody who is bigoted/obstinate
make bricks without straw = make something without the essential
   materials
See also: bang/knock one's **head** against a brick wall; **drop** a
brick/clanger.

bridge
burn one's boats/bridges = make an irrevocable decision
cross that bridge when one comes to it = do not worry unnecessarily
   about a difficulty that may never arise
   See also: **water** under the bridge.

brief
hold no brief for = have nothing to say in favour of

bright
bright and breezy/bright-eyed and bushy-tailed = cheerful and happy
bright and early = very early in the morning
bright idea = clever original thought (sometimes used sarcastically)
bright lights = entertainment district
bright spark = clever person
look on the bright side = be optimistic
   See also: bright as a **button**

bring
bring about/to pass = make happen
bring back to life = revive
bring down = cause something to end
bring down the curtain on = put an end to
bring forth = produce
bring home to one = make one realize
bring in = introduce, or yield
bring into line = cause to conform
bring into play = cause to start functioning
bring into the world = give birth to/be a parent of
bring off = succeed in doing something
bring on = cause
bring oneself to = persuade oneself
bring out = demonstrate/reveal, or publish
bring round/to = restore somebody to consciousness
bring somebody down to earth = make somebody aware of
   practicalities (rather than dreams/fanciful ideas)
bring somebody up short = make somebody stop what he/she is
   doing
bring something to a head = precipitate a crisis in order to get action

bring something to light = ensure that something is noticed, or to reveal something

bring the house down = gain an audience's whole-hearted approval

bring to a close = conclude (formally)

bring to bear = employ/put to use

bring to light = reveal

bring to mind = cause to recall

bring to pass = cause to happen

bring up = raise (a topic), or rear (a child), or vomit

bring up the rear = come in last place/position

bring word = convey information/news

See also: bring down/fall about somebody's **ears**; bring home the **bacon**; bring into **contempt**; bring (carry) into **effect**; bring somebody down to **earth**; bring to **book**.

bristle

bristle with = be full of

Bristol

all ship-shape and Bristol fashion = properly organized and tidy

broad

as broad as it's long = either way is as good as the other

See also: broad **hint**; broad in the **beam**; have broad **shoulders**; in broad **daylight**.

broken

broken accent/English = imperfect speech/English

broken home = family in which the parents no longer live together

broken reed = supporter who has failed

broken-winded (horse) = breathless/exhausted

See also: **stony** broke.

broker

honest broker = trustworthy and impartial intermediary

broom

new broom = somebody (eager) who is newly appointed

brother

brotherhood of man = whole of human society

brothers in arms = comrades (in adversity)
See also: **Big** Brother; **blood** brother.

brow
by the sweat of one's brow = through one's own hard work
See also: **knit** one's brows

browned
browned off = bored/disenchanted

brunt
bear the brunt of = receive (and withstand) the main thrust of an
attack

brush
brush aside/to one side = ignore (objections to something)
brush up on = revise/refresh one's memory about
brush with danger/death/the law = come close to/into conflict with
danger/death/the law
give somebody the brush-off = terminate a friendship with somebody
tarred with the same brush = assumed to have the same (bad)
qualities as one's associates
See also: brush/sweep something under the **carpet**/rug; **daft** as a
brush.

brute
brute force = (excessive) physical force

buck
buck up = hurry
pass the buck = pass on responsibility (for something one does not
want to be held responsible for)
the buck stops here = I/we are ultimately responsible

bucket
kick the bucket = die
rain (in) buckets = rain very heavily
See also: **cry**/**weep** buckets.

buckle
buckle down/under = get down to hard work/submit

bud
budding talent = emerging ability
nip in the bud = forestall/frustrate a scheme/plan (before it can be implemented)

bug
bitten by a bug = become addicted to/enthusiastic for something
bugged room = room having electronic devices that detect and transmit (to an outsider) any conversation
bug somebody = (deliberately) annoy somebody
computer bug = error in a computer program
debug a (computer) program = find and remove an error in a computer program
litter bug = somebody who (knowingly) drops/scatters litter
See also: **snug** as a bug in a rug.

build
big build-up = accumulation of interest/resources before an event

bulk
in bulk = in large quantity
the bulk = most

bull
like a bull at a gate = very forcefully
like a bull in a china shop = in an awkward/clumsy manner
like a red rag to a bull = certain to anger/very provocative
score a bull's eye = have a spectacular (but unlikely) success
take the bull by the horns = take bold action to overcome a difficulty

bullet
bite the bullet = take on a challenge, or persevere (unwillingly)
bullet with one's name on = inevitable hit
give somebody the bullet = to dismiss somebody (from employment)

bump
bump into = meet unexpectedly
bump off = kill
bump up = increase/raise

bun
have a bun in the oven = be pregnant

bunch
bunch of fives = punch (with a clenched fist)

bundle
bundle of energy = full of vigour
bundle of nerves = very nervous
go a bundle on = be enthusiastic about

bunk
do a bunk = abscond/go away suddenly

buoy
buoy up = give (encouraging) support to

burden
burden of one's song = (repeated) main point/message
white man's burden = colonial responsibility

burglar
cat burglar = thief who climbs up the outside of a building to gain
access (through a window)

burn
burn a hole in one's pocket = have more money than one is
accustomed to, and be eager to spend it
burning question = vital issue
burn one's fingers/get one's fingers burned = suffer, having made a
bad decision
burn the candle at both ends = be active night and day
burn the midnight oil = work until very late
burn to a frazzle = burn (food) completely
burnt offering = food spoiled by burning
money to burn = have more money than is essential for one's needs
See also: burn one's **boats**/bridges; have one's **ears** burning.

burst
burst a blood vessel = lose control of one's temper
burst at the seams = uncomfortable (over)full

burst into tears/laughter, or burst out crying/laughing = suddenly express extreme sadness/happiness

bury
bury one's head in the sand = deliberately ignore something that is obvious (but unpleasant)
See also: bury the **hatchet**/one's differences; **dead** and buried.

bus
busman's holiday = time off work during which one does much the same as if one were still at work
miss the bus/boat = miss an opportunity
See also: like the **back** of a bus.

bush
beat about the bush = prevaricate
bush telegraph = method of (unofficially) spreading news/rumour by word of mouth
take to the bush = go into hiding

bushel
hide one's light under a bushel = conceal one's talents

business
bad business = troublesome/unsavoury affair
be business-like = be efficient/organized
be in business = be able to proceed
be no business of somebody's = of no concern to somebody
business end (of something) = operative part (of something)
funny/monkey business = dubious/illegal activity
get down to business = reduce (a discussion) to its essentials
go out of business = fail (of a business, because of financial difficulties)
have no business (to) = have no authority/right (to)
like nobody's business = very well
make it one's business (to) = deliberately undertake (to)
mean business = to be taken seriously
mind one's own business = not become involved
send somebody about his/her business = refuse unsolicited offers of advice/help

the business/works = exactly what is required
to mean business = to take something seriously
  See also: **monkey** business.

bust
bust a gut = try one's utmost (to the point of exhaustion)
fit to bust/burst = with utmost vigour
go bust = fail in business

but
anything but = emphasizing the opposite
but for = if it was not for
no buts about it = without (any) doubt
  See also: **all** but.

butt
butt in = interrupt

butter
(fine words) butter (me) no parsnips = don't try to hide the truth with
  clever words
butter somebody up = flatter somebody (while seeking a favour)
butter wouldn't melt in his/her mouth = he/she appears to be
  innocent/naive (although probably is not)
spread the butter too thick = over-flatter somebody
  See also: **bread** and butter; have one's **bread** buttered on both sides;
  know which side one's **bread** is buttered.

butterflies
butterflies in one's stomach/tummy = state of
  anticipation/nervousness

button
bright as a button = clever/intelligent
button-hole somebody = detain somebody for a (private) conversation
button one's lip = remain silent
have something buttoned/sewn up = with all preparations
  made/complete
press the button = activate/give the order to proceed

buy
buy a pig in a poke = buy something unseen

buy somebody off = pay somebody to desist/go away
buy out = purchase a rival's business
buy up = purchase as much as possible
(a) good buy = (a) bargain

by
by and by = soon
by and large = taken as a whole
by oneself = alone
by the by/by the way = incidentally
by the same token = as well

bygones
let bygones be bygones = forget former differences

byword
become a byword = become proverbial/standard

C

Cain
raise Cain = be very angry and likely to cause a scene

cake
go/sell like hot cakes = to sell quickly
have one's cake and eat it = be able to choose both of two desirable,
  but mutually exclusive, options
icing on the cake = additional unexpected perk
piece of cake = easy task
slice of the cake = share of the benefit/profit
that takes the cake! = exclamation of disbelief/incredulity

calculate
calculated to = intended/likely to

calf
calf/puppy love = adolescent love
kill the fatted calf = welcoming hospitality after an absence

call
call a halt = put an end to
call a spade a spade = be blunt/forthright
call a thing one's own = have exclusive possession of something
call away = be asked to attend somewhere else
call down = invoke
call for = to collect, or require as necessary, or demand
call in/into question = express doubts about
call it a day = bring to an end for the time being
call it a night = end an activity in the evening/night
call it quits = the advantage is now even
call names = insult
call off = cancel/postpone indefinitely
call on/upon = require, or appeal to, or visit
call out = cry/shout out loud
call the shots/tune = be in charge of, make the decisions
call to mind = remember

call to order = restore order

call up = summon, or telephone

no call to = no need/reason to

not called for = not necessary (although acceptable)

on call = be available if required

pay a call = to visit somebody

uncalled for = unwanted and unnecessary

See also: call/draw **attention** to; called to the **bar**; call of **nature**; call off the **dogs**; call somebody **names**; call somebody's **bluff**; call something into **question**; call to **account**.

calm

calm before the storm = a period of (relative) peace before a crisis or uproar

See also: calm as a **millpond**.

camel

the last straw that breaks the camel's back = something that exceeds the limit of endurance/tolerance

camp

camp-follower = hanger-on

camp it up = to act in an over-effeminate manner

enter the enemy's camp = enter the premises/inner sanctum of a rival

See also: **strike** camp.

can

(one) can keep it = remark used by somebody who is unimpressed or disgusted

can of worms = troublesome matter

in the can = completed (of a task), or in prison

See also: **carry** the can.

candle

cannot/not fit to hold a candle to somebody = cannot be favourably compared with somebody

not worth the candle = the effort/trouble is not justified by the result

See also: **burn** the candle at both ends; hold a candle to the **devil**.

cannon

cannon fodder = soldiers (of inferior rank) who are deliberately put into the front line to become inevitable casualties in a war

canoe
paddle one's own canoe = be completely unaided

cannot
cannot but/cannot help but = be bound to/must

canvas
under canvas = in a tent

cap
go cap in hand = to beg, ask humbly
if the cap fits, wear it = recognise one's shortcomings
pass/send/take the cap round = ask for donations (by circulating a
  cap or any container)
put on one's thinking cap = think hard/seriously about something
set one's cap at = try to gain the affections of
that caps it all! = exclamation of disbelief/incredulity
to cap/top it all = to better/crown an achievement
  See also: **Dutch** cap; **feather** in one's cap.

capital
make capital of/out of = turn a situation to good account or
  advantage

captain
captain of industry = industrial tycoon

captive
captive audience/market = a lack of choice on the part of the
  consumer

card
(quite) a card = a joker/prankster
ask for/get one's cards = resign/get dismissed from one's
  employment
have a card up one's sleeve = to have something unexpected in reserve
hold all the cards = be in a position of control/power
house of cards = inherently unstable plan/structure
lay/put one's cards on the table = be frank/honest
one's best/leading/trump card = something that one is particularly
  good/strong at

on the cards = very likely to happen/can be foreseen

play one's cards close to one's chest = be secretive about one's (real) intentions

play one's cards right/well = act/behave/plan to one's best advantage

reveal/show one's cards = declare one's intentions

show the red card = dismiss somebody from work

show the yellow card = give a warning

stack the cards against somebody = impede somebody's plans/progress

care

have a care! = be careful!

take care of = look after, or be careful with

See also: for **all** I know/care; not care a tinker's **cuss**/damn; not care **tuppence**.

career

chequered career = work record that includes many changes (for better and worse)

carpet

brush/sweep something under the carpet/rug = deliberately forget/hide something that is to one's disadvantage

on the carpet/mat = being disciplined (by a superior)

(roll out the) red carpet = (give somebody an) elaborate/formal welcome

carrot

a stick or a carrot = a threat or an inducement

carrot to a donkey = inducement/temptation

carry

carried away = lacking self-control

carry all before one = be highly successful/beat all rivals

carry a torch (for somebody) = have (unreciprocated) love for somebody

carry off (a situation) = overcome a disadvantage/succeed

carry on = display emotion out of proportion to its cause

carry on with = have an affair with

carry out = do/execute

carry over = postpone
carry the can = accept blame/responsibility
carry the day = win
carry through = complete (in spite of difficulties)
carry weight = have influence
carry (along) with = persuade
See also: carry **conviction**; carry one's **bat**; carry the **banner** for.

cart

put the cart before the horse = do something in the wrong order
See also: clever as a cartload/wagonload of **monkeys**; upset the **apple**-cart.

case

as the case may be = whichever (of several choices) applies
case in point = pertinent example
(no) case to answer for = action/behaviour that needs (no)
  justification
cast-iron case = irrefutable argument
hard case = somebody who is tough (with criminal/violent tendencies)
in any case = whatever else is considered/happens
in case = as a precaution
in case of = in the event of
in that case = in that event/that being so
is/is not the case = is true/false
make out a case for = provide an argument in favour of
open and shut case = situation of predictable/sure outcome
See also: **meet** the case.

cash

cash and carry = retail outlet that supplies goods (often in bulk) at
  lower than normal prices on condition that the purchaser provides
  carriage (for delivery)
cash down = immediate payment for (possibly part of) goods or
  services
cash in on = take advantage of
cash in one's chips = die
cash on the nail = cash (coins/banknotes) as opposed to cheques,
  credit cards, promissory notes etc.

hard cash = coins/banknotes (as opposed to less negotiable cheques etc.)

cast
cast about = look/seek for
cast adrift = abandon(ed)
cast anchor = end a voyage (lower the anchor)
cast an eye over = make a cursory inspection
cast a shadow over = have a dampening/dispiriting effect on
cast aside = discard (as of no relevance/value)
cast a spell over = exert a controlling influence (by no obvious means)
cast aspersions on = make unfavourable comments about
cast doubts on/upon = introduce doubt about
cast down = miserable/unhappy
casting vote = deciding vote made (by the chairman of a meeting) when a previous vote is tied (with equal numbers of votes on each side)
cast in one's lot = agree to share the fate of somebody else
cast lots = settle an issue by means of a lottery
cast light upon = reveal information about something
cast off = release a vessel's moorings before sailing, or throw away
cast out = expel from
cast the net = make a wide search
See also: cast in the same **mould;** the **die** is cast.

castle
an Englishman's home is his castle = privacy and security are guaranteed in one's own home
castles in Spain/the air = a dream of (non-existent) wealth and happiness

cat
a cat may look at a king = all people are equal, irrespective of their social backgrounds
be a copycat = imitate
bell the cat = risk a confrontation with an opponent for the common good
cat and mouse game = activity involving continuous manoeuvring for supremacy

cat get one's tongue = be rendered speechless
cat's pyjamas/whiskers = the best
cat that swallowed the cream = self-satisfied person
curiosity killed the cat = warning not to be inquisitive/nosy
enough to make a cat laugh = very funny
fight like cat and dog = be continually quarrelling
grin like a Cheshire cat = grin widely
lead a cat and a dog life = continually quarrel
let the cat out of the bag = unintentionally reveal a secret
like a cat on hot bricks = fidgety, restless, uneasy
like something the cat brought in = dishevelled/untidy
make a cat's paw of = dupe/exploit
no/not enough room to swing a cat = confined/cramped for space
not a cat in hell's chance = no chance
put the cat among the pigeons = (deliberately) cause an uproar
run around like a scalded cat = bustle/run around busily (but often unnecessarily)
when the cat's away (mice will play) = people will take advantage of any lack of supervision
which way the cat jumps = probable outcome, dependent on preceding events
See also: **play** cat and mouse with; **rain** cats and dogs.

catch
catch a cold = make a bad choice/purchase
catch a glimpse/sight of = see very briefly
catch cold = become chilled
catch hold of = grasp
catch it = get into trouble
catch on = understand, or become fashionable/popular
catch one's breath = take a brief rest
catch penny = cheap/tawdry
catch phrase = commonly used expression
catch red-handed = discover somebody in the act of doing something wrong
catch somebody bending/napping/on the hop = take somebody unawares/unprepared, or at a disadvantage
catch somebody's eye = gain somebody's attention

catch somebody out = discover somebody making an
   error/misdemeanour, or trick somebody
catch somebody with his/her fingers/hand in the till = discover
   somebody in the act of stealing (money)
catch somebody with his pants/trousers down = discover somebody
   at an extreme disadvantage
catch up = get level with
catch up on = do something that has been postponed
Catch 22 situation = inescapable dilemma
   See also: catch a **crab**; catch **fire**; catch one's **death**; catch somebody
   in the **act**; (catch) somebody off **balance**.

caught
   See: **catch**.

cause
good cause = undertaking that deserves support (because of its
   altruistic/charitable nature)
lost cause = undertaking that is bound to fail

caution
be a (real) caution = be amusing/popular (for flouting convention)
throw caution to the winds = behave with extreme rashness

cave
   See: **Aladdin**'s cave.

cease
   See: **wonders** will never cease.

centre
centre of attraction/attention = somebody/something that holds most
   attention

ceremony
stand on ceremony = behave in an over-formal manner

certain
for certain = assuredly, inevitably
moral certainty = very probable

of a certain age = middle-aged (or older)
  See also: **dead** certainty; in an interesting/certain **condition**.

chain
chain of events = (inevitable) sequence of happenings
chain letter = (usually anonymous) letter requesting the recipient to
  send several copies of it to other people, with a view to bringing good
  luck or obtaining money for the originator.
chain reaction = a result which brings about another similar result
  which, in turn, causes another, and so on
chain store = one of a group of similar shops under the same ownership

chair
address the chair = direct one's comments to the chairman (as is
  required in a formal meeting of, for example, a committee)
appeal to the chair = request the formal protection/support of the
  chairman (of, for example, a committee)
fall off one's chair = be very surprised
take the chair = act as chairman (of, for example, a committee)

chalk
by a long chalk = by a wide margin
chalk something up to experience = accept something unfortunate
  (stoically), while intending to avoid it in future
chalk up = record, score
different as chalk and/from cheese = entirely different

champ
champ at the bit = be (very) impatient

chance
(not a) cat's/snowball's chance in hell = (not) even the remotest
  chance (of all)
chance in a million = very remote change, virtual impossibility
chances are = (the) probability is
chances are even/against it = it is equally possible/unlikely
(no) earthly chance/fat chance = (not even) the remotest chance
even chance = equal probability
eye on/to the main chance = alert for an opportunity for personal
  gain

fancy one's chances = be (over)confident that one will succeed
fighting/sporting chance = fair/reasonable chance
game of chance = dependent on luck (as opposed to choice/skill)
ghost of a chance = even the remotest chance
on the off chance = in case, in the hope
stand a good/fair chance of = be fairly likely to
take a chance/take no chances = risk/not risk something
   See also: chance one's **arm**; **dog**'s chance; **fat** chance.

change
change hands = change ownership
change of air = different environment/climate
change of heart = change in one's feelings (often leading to a change of mind)
change of life = menopause
change one's tune = change one's mind
get no change out of = fail to get help/satisfaction from
ring the changes = vary
small change = low-value coins
   See also: a change is as good as a **rest**; change the **subject**.

chapter
quote chapter and verse = provide evidence for one's statements (often to a boring extreme)
   See also: chapter of **accidents**.

character
in/out of character = as/not as expected from somebody's usual behaviour

charge
charge an arm and a leg = charge very high prices, overcharge
charge with = entrust with/make responsible for
charged with = filled with
in charge of = responsible for
trump up a charge = invent an accusation

charity
charity begins at home = one's family should have first claim to one's kindness/resources

cold as charity = callous/unsympathetic

Charlie
proper Charlie = a fool

charm
go/work like a charm = function very well
lead a charmed life = run risks with impunity

chase
chase (after) rainbows = dream/think about the unobtainable
chase up = try to make something happen more quickly
wild goose chase = useless journey/search

chat
chat up = talk to somebody persuasively for one's own gain

cheap
cheap as dirt/dirt cheap = very cheap
on the cheap = at minimum cost

check
check into/up on = examine for accuracy/truthfulness
check in/out = begin/end one's stay at a hotel
check off = account for items (on a list)
hold/keep in check = restrain
keep a check on = examine/record routinely

cheek
cheek by jowl with = (very) close to
cheek of the devil = (insolent) audacity
give somebody cheek = show lack of respect to somebody
  senior/superior
have a/the cheek to = be impertinent/insolent
turn the other cheek = ignore a slight/violence against oneself
  See also: have/with one's **tongue** in one's cheek.

cheer
cheer up = adopt a happier manner
  See also: **cup** that cheers.

cheese
big cheese = somebody in authority/of importance
cheesed off = bored/disgruntled
hard cheese! = bad luck! (usually meant in sympathy)
cheese paring = mean(ness)

cheque
blank cheque = permission to do anything one likes

cherry
take two bites at the cherry = make two attempts at doing something
  that should be achievable in one attempt

Cheshire
  See: grin like a Cheshire **cat**

chest
get something off one's chest = confess, say something one has been
  suppressing for a time
hold/play one's cards/hand close to one's chest = be secretive
  See also: put **hairs** on somebody's chest.

chestnut
old chestnut = worn-out joke/statement (and thus lacking credibility)
pull the chestnuts out of the fire = to (take a risk to) help somebody
  in difficulty

chew
chew something over = think about something at length
chew the cud = consider carefully, ponder
chew the fat = talk at length (but usually inconsequentially)

chicken
chicken-feed = paltry amount/sum
chicken-hearted/livered = cowardly
chicken out = lose one's nerve
don't count one's chickens (before they're hatched) = don't count on
  the outcome of something before it has happened
no (spring) chicken = no longer young
tender as a chicken = soft

chief
too many chiefs and not enough Indians = too many people in a
   supervisory role, and too few workers to implement their instructions

child
child bride = woman who marries when she is considered to be too
   young (immature) for marriage.
child of nature = somebody with (genuine) naivety
child's play = very easy challenge/task
latch-key child = (young) schoolchild who has a key to the family
   home, to gain access before the parent(s) return after work
love child = child born to a couple who are not married
second childhood = child-like behaviour in middle/old age

chill
cast a chill over = have a saddening/depressive influence on
chilled to the bone/marrow = very cold
chill one's blood = cause terror
take the chill off = make warmer
   See also: **catch** a chill/cold; send chills up somebody's **spine**.

chime
chime in with = inject one's remarks into those already stated

chimney
smoke like a chimney = smoke (cigarettes) excessively

chin
have a chin-wag = have a prolonged conversation
keep one's chin up = remain cheerful (in adversity)
lead with one's chin = make an attack without defending oneself
take (it) on the chin = courageously accept adversity/punishment

China
   See: not for all the **tea** in China.

chink
chink in one's armour = a (little-known) weakness that makes one
   vulnerable (to attack)

chip
blue chips = highly valued (and low-risk) investment

chip in = contribute to, or interrupt
chip off the old block = child that resembles a parent
chip on one's shoulder = embittered/bigoted attitude
have one's chips = be dead/finished
when the chips are down = at the critical/crucial point

chisel
chisel somebody = cheat somebody

chock
chock-a-block = crowded/packed together

choice
Hobson's choice = no choice at all
spoiled for choice = with a wide range of choices

choose
  See: choose/draw the short **straw**.

chop
chop and change = keep changing (one's choice/mind)
for the chop = about to be dismissed/disposed of
give somebody the chop = dismiss/get rid of somebody
give something the chop = destroy/discontinue/dispose of something
lick one's chops = relish (in anticipation of
  food/pleasure/satisfaction)

chord
strike a chord = trigger a memory
touch a chord = stimulate an emotion

chorus
chorus of approval = general/unanimous approval
in chorus = in unison

chuck
chuck away = carelessly throw away
chuck something in = stop doing something
chuck out = expel, throw away/out
chuck up = vomit

chum
chum up with = make (close) friends of

chump
off one's chump = mad

church
go into the church = become a priest
poor as a church mouse = very poor

Cinderella
Cinderella of something = least admired/favoured person

circle
come full circle = return to the starting point
dress circle = balcony immediately above the stalls in a cinema or
  theatre
go round in circles = keep moving (literally or figuratively) but make
  no progress
run round in (small) circles = be very busy (but often ineffectively)
square the circle = attempt the impossible
vicious circle = sequence of problematic events in which the result of
  one only worsens the course of the next, and so on, until the final
  outcome exacerbates the first

circumstance
circumstantial evidence = evidence which gives an indication of
  somebody's involvement (in a crime, for example), but which does
  not constitute direct proof
extenuating circumstances = acceptable excuse
in/under the circumstances = taking into account the conditions or
  the situation
victim of circumstances = somebody who suffers through no fault of
  his/her own
  See also: in **easy** circumstances.

circus
three-ring circus = noisy confused place

civil
civil tongue (in one's head) = politeness

Civvy Street
in Civvy Street = not in the armed forces

claim
stake a claim = (make a) claim

clamp
clamp down (on) = impose (even more stringent) restrictions (on)

clam
clam up = become silent

clanger
drop a clanger = make a blunder

clap
clap eyes on = see, catch sight of
clapped out = worn out
clap-trap = inconsequential/worthless talk
like the clappers = very fast

class
class of one's/its own = without equal
bottom/top of the class = best/worst in a group

claw
get one's claws into = display jealousy (through sarcasm/insult), or
   entrap (into marriage)

clay
feet of clay = weakness of character in somebody previously thought
   to be worthy of respect

clean
clean as a whistle = very clean(ly)
clean bill of health = fit
clean cut = sharply/unambiguously defined, or of healthy appearance
clean down = rub/scrub until totally clean
clean out = empty something, or take all of somebody's money
clean sheet/slate = unblemished record (of behaviour)
clean through = right through, without obstruction
clean up = make a substantial gain

come clean = confess
keep one's nose clean = stay out of trouble
live a clean life = be blameless/moral
make a clean breast of = confess
make a clean sweep = dispose of (everything)
one's hands are clean = one is blameless/innocent
show a clean pairs of heels = outrun (one's pursuers)

cleaners
taken to the cleaners = have all one's money taken (through gambling or deception)

clear
clear as crystal/crystal clear = perfectly clear/plain
clear as mud = obscure
clear away = remove
clear conscience = feeling of blamelessness/innocence
clear cut = clearly/unambiguously defined
clear of = free from
clear off = go away
clear out = clean/empty, or go away
clear the air = have a frank discussion to eliminate any misunderstanding
clear the way = remove obstructions
clear up = tidy, or become fine (of weather), or make plain
coast is clear = there is nobody to observe
in the clear = free from debt/suspicion
steer clear of = avoid
  See also: clear/sound as a **bell**; clear somebody's **name**; clear the **decks**; see one's **way** clear.

cleft
cleft stick = dilemma

clever
  See: clever **dick**.

cliff
cliff-hanger = happening/story with an unpredictable ending

click
click into place = suddenly become clear (in understanding)
click with somebody = spontaneously become firm friends or lovers

climb
climb down = withdraw (an untenable opinion/statement)
social climber = somebody who advances his/her position by
  associating with people of influence
  See also: climb/jump onto the **bandwagon**.

clinch
clinch a deal = finalize an agreement

cling
cling on like a limpet/grim death = hold on to something with
  determination

clip
clipped speech = staccato way of talking
clip somebody's wings = curtail/limit somebody's powers
clip somebody's ear = slap somebody on the side of the face (literally
  or figuratively)

cloak
cloak and dagger = secret/surreptitious (with implications of
  espionage)
under the cloak of = under the pretence of

clock
against the clock = under time pressure
beat the clock = finish a task earlier than expected
clock on/off = record the time of arrival at/departure from work
like clockwork = smoothly, without a hitch
put/set/turn the clock back = return to former (often outmoded)
  ways
round the clock = without break for 24 hours
watch the clock = keep a close watch on the time so as not to work
  any longer than absolutely necessary
  See also: **regular** as clockwork.

close
at close quarters = near
close call/shave = near miss
closed book = unknown, undiscovered
close down = shut (for good)
close-fisted = mean
closed shop = place of work at which employees have to belong to a trade union as a condition of employment
close in (up)on = surround
close on = very nearly
close ranks = act together defensively
close season = time during which fishing/hunting for certain species is not allowed, extended to mean also the period of the year during which a particular sport is not played
close up = move nearer together, or shut (as a verb); or near (hyphenated, as an adjective)
close with = grapple with
See also: behind closed **doors**; close the **door** to; close to **home**.

cloth
cloth ears = said of somebody who ignores/refuses to listen
respect for the cloth = respect for the clergy
man of the cloth = member of the clergy
sackcloth and ashes = state of remorse/penitence

clothing
wolf in sheep's clothing = somebody who appears to be harmless but is in fact dangerous

cloud
cloud cuckoo land = ideal/perfect dream world
be/have one's head in the clouds = day-dreaming
cast a cloud over = have a depressing influence on
every cloud has a silver lining = consolation can always be found in every misfortune
on cloud nine = in a state of euphoria/happiness
under a cloud = under suspicion/distrusted
wait till the clouds roll by = wait until circumstances improve

clover
in clover = happy and prosperous

club
club together = combine finances/resources
in the (pudding) club = pregnant
join the club! = expression of sympathy in mutual adversity/bad luck

clue
have no/not a clue = have no idea/inkling

clutch
clutch at a straw/straws = make a desperate (and usually
  unsuccessful) attempt

coach
drive a coach and horses through = discredit/evade easily
slow coach = somebody who is reluctant/tardy

coals
carry coals to Newcastle = take something to where it is superfluous
haul over the coals = discipline/rebuke for a wrongdoing

coast
    See: coast is **clear**.

coat
be dragged by one's coat tails = be forced to do something
  (reluctantly)
cut one's coat according to one's cloth = do only what one has the
  resources for
hang on somebody's coat tails = associate with a successful colleague
  in order to further one's own progress
trail one's coat = try to pick a quarrel with somebody

cobwebs
blow the cobwebs away = refresh oneself (in the open air)

cock
be cock-a-hoop = exultant/triumphant
cock and bull story = unbelievably exaggerated account
cock a snook = disdainfully defy

cock-eyed = illogical/impractical

cock of the rock/walk = somebody who (arrogantly) dominates others

cocksure = (over)confident

cock up = bungling error

go off at half cock = begin before everything is ready

knock into a cocked hat = be much better than

live like fighting cocks = live well (on good food)

take a cockshot at = make a wild throw at

See also: cock an **eye** at.

cockles

warm the cockles of one's heart = make one feel warm (emotionally or physically)

cocktail

Molotov cocktail = (home-made) petrol bomb

coffin

coffin nail = cigarette

nail in one's/somebody's coffin = one of several cumulative mistakes that contributes to one's/somebody's downfall

cog

cog in the machine = somebody who make an apparently insignificant contribution to a large scheme/organization

coil

shuffle off this mortal coil = die

coin

coin a phrase = invent an expression, or more usually to draw attention to a well-worn one

coin it = make (much) money quickly

other side of the coin = opposite aspect/point of view

pay back in the same coin = reply/retaliate in the same manner

coincidence

See: long **arm** of coincidence.

cold

cold all over/cold sweat = fright

blow hot and cold = alternate between enthusiasm and disinterest
cold comfort = little or no satisfaction
cold light of day = commonsensical/logical analysis
cold shoulder = deliberately avoid
cold steel = edged weapons
cold storage = safe keeping
cold war = non-violent but hostile relationship between nations
in cold blood = deliberately
leave one cold = be unaffected by (emotionally)
left out in the cold = excluded/ignored
pour/throw cold water onto something = be unenthusiastic about
   something
stone cold = very cold
   See also: get cold **feet**; make one's **blood** run cold; **out** in the cold.

collar
collar somebody = detain somebody
feel somebody's collar = make an arrest
hot under the collar = angry
white-collar worker = office worker/professional
   See also: **dog** collar.

collision
head-on collision = collision in which a vehicle runs into the front of
   a vehicle approaching it

colour
false colours = pretence
give/lend colour to = corroborate/support
local colour = background knowledge
nail one's colours to the mast = commit publicly (to a point of view)
off colour = unwell
paint in glowing colours = exaggerate the advantages/benefits of
   something
see the colour of (somebody's) money = insist on a down payment or
   proof that money is available before supplying goods/services
show oneself in one's true colours = reveal oneself as one really is
with flying colours = in triumph/very successfully
   See also: colour **bar**.

column
dodge the column = avoid duty/work
fifth column = group of collaborators/saboteurs
  See also: **agony** column.

comb
go through something with a fine-tooth comb = thoroughly
  examine/search something

come
come about = happen/occur
come across = find/meet (accidentally)
come again = pardon
come along = hurry up
come away = break off/dislodge
come away empty-handed = achieve nothing
come back = remember, or return
come-back = return to fame/prominence
come by = acquire/obtain
come down = reduce (verb), or loss of position/status (noun)
come down on = discipline/rebuke
come forward = volunteer
come good = prove (eventually) to be helpful/talented/successful
come hell or high water = no matter what happens
come hither = flirtatious/seductive
come in for = become subject to/receive
come in handy = prove to be useful
come into = inherit
come into force = become operational
come into one's own = show at one's best
come of = result from
come off = succeed
come off badly/well = fail/succeed
come off second best = lose
come on to = begin/start to
come out with = say
come over = affect, or become, or make an impression, or visit
come right = have a happy/successful outcome
come round/to = regain consciousness

come to an arrangement = agree
come to blows = fight
come to grief = meet a disaster
come to light = be discovered/revealed
come to pass = happen
come to terms with = accept
come true = actually occur
come under = classified with, or subordinate to
come unstuck = fail, or encounter an unexpected problem
come upon = find
come up to = equal
come up to scratch = meet a standard
come up with = get level with, or produce/suggest
come what may = no matter what
have it coming to one = deserve what is about to happen
how come? = how did that occur?
if it comes to that = in that event
it comes to this = summarized
not know whether one is coming or going = be confused
   See also: come back to **earth**; come **down**; come home to **roost**; come
   of **age**; come out in the **wash**; come out on **top**; come to **nothing**;
   come to **rest**; come/turn up **trumps**; **easy** come, easy go.

comedy
black comedy = drama/story that has a comic treatment of a tragic
   theme

comfort
comfort station = public lavatory
creature comforts = food, clothing, and other providers of physical
   (as opposed to emotional) well-being
crumb of comfort = slight consolation

comforter
Job's comforter = somebody whose advice/comments make one feel
   worse rather than bringing comfort in adversity

coming
have something coming to one = about to experience something
   (deserved/inevitable)

not know whether one is coming or going = be in a state of great confusion/uncertainty

command
at one's command = within one's grasp/knowledge

comment
no comment = I do not wish/refuse to say anything

commentary
running commentary = "live" account/commentary made while a (sporting) event is actually taking place

commission
kick-back commission = (monetary) reward given as an inducement for placing a contract/work with an associate
in/into commission = functional/operational
on commission = (earnings) for sales made/services rendered
out of commission = not operational

common
by common consent = by a majority agreement
common as muck = with very poor manners
common ground = area of agreement/mutual interest
common knowledge = something that is generally/widely known
common or garden = very ordinary
common origin = single source
common parlance = ordinary manner of speaking
common touch = behaviour similar to that of ordinary people
in common = of mutual interest, or similarity
in common with = like/in agreement with

company
bad company = disreputable associates
good company = somebody who is entertaining/pleasant to be with
having company for dinner = entertaining guests for a meal
in company with = like/in agreement with
keep company with = be the regular (sexual) partner of
keep somebody company = remain with somebody
know a person by the company he/she keeps = judge somebody by his/her associates

part company = leave/separate
present company excepted = excluding those present
  See also: **two**'s company (but three's a crowd).

compare
beyond compare = unequalled
compare notes (with) = talk to somebody else about matters of
  common interest
in comparison with = compared with

complete
complete with = including

complex
Oedipus complex = sexual love of a boy/man for his mother

compliment
back-/left-handed compliment, or a two-edged compliment = ironical
  comment that sounds like a compliment but is not
complimentary tickets = free tickets (to a theatre, etc.)
compliments of the season = Christmas greetings
fish for compliments = solicit favourable comments
give one's compliments = express one's good wishes
pay a compliment = praise, or show appreciation/respect
return the compliment = offer back a favour in return for one
  received

compound
compound the felony = make a difficulty even worse

computer
  See: computer **bug**.

concern
as far as I am concerned = in my opinion, which I know you will
  ignore/not take into account
going concern = fully operational business

conclusion
arrive at/come to the conclusion = decide (having weighed the
  evidence)
foregone conclusion = predetermined outcome (but often only in the
  opinion of the speaker)

jump to a conclusion = prematurely decide the outcome/significance
  of something

condition
in condition = fit/healthy
on condition that = based on the agreement/restriction that
out of condition = unfit
  See also: in a **delicate** condition; in **mint** condition.

conference
round-table conference = discussion that involves everybody with a
  relevant point of view

confess
I must confess = I freely admit

confidence
confidence trick = deception that takes advantage of somebody's
  belief in the honesty of the deceiver
in (strict) confidence = on condition that one does not reveal what
  one is told
take into one's confidence = trust somebody with a secret
  See also: **vote** of confidence.

conjure
conjure with = become involved with/consider/conceive
name to conjure with = name of somebody important

connection
in connection with = concerning
in that connection = referring/relating to something (specified)
fail to make/miss the connection = fail to appreciate an association
  (of ideas/thoughts)

conscience
conscience money = payment/reward given to somebody who has
  betrayed a principle/trust
have on one's conscience = retain guilt about
in all conscience = to be completely honest

consent
  See: **age** of consent.

---

consequence
of little/no consequence = unimportant
of some consequence = important
take the consequences = accept the blame/results
  See also: **abide** by the consequences.

Conservative
true-blue Conservative = somebody committed (to the point of
  bigotry) to the politics/policies of the Conservative Party

consideration
in consideration of = taking into account
small consideration = insignificant fee/bribe
take into consideration = allow for/take account of
under consideration = being thought about

construction
put a false construction on = lie about/misinterpret (deliberately)

contact
come in(to) contact with = encounter/meet

contempt
bring into contempt = fail to show (due) respect for
contempt of court = failure to obey, or interference with the running
  of, a court of law
familiarity breeds contempt = a long friendship can develop into
  acrimony/disrespect
hold in contempt = show a disrespectful attitude towards

content
to one's heart's content = as much as one desires

contention
bone of contention = subject that always leads to an argument

contractor
cowboy contractor = tradesman who uses unskilful methods and
  substandard materials

contradiction
contradiction in terms = conflicting/illogical statement

contrary
contrary to expectations = not what was expected
on/to the contrary = it is the opposite

convenience
at one's convenience = whenever it suits one
at one's earliest convenience = as soon as it suits one
make a convenience of = take advantage of/use (for selfish purposes)
public convenience = public lavatory

conversation
conversation piece = unusual object that stimulates discussion

converted
preach to the converted = put a point of view to somebody who
  already holds it

conviction
carry conviction = be convincing/persuasive
have the courage of one's convictions = have unshakeable belief in
  one's point of view

cook
cook somebody's goose = spoil somebody's chances of success
cook the books = falsify the accounts
cook up = invent
what's cooking? = what is happening?

cookie
that's the way the cookie crumbles = that is the inevitable
  (undesirable) result

cool
cool as a cucumber = calm/self-assured
cool, calm and collected = in total control of one's feelings
cool down = become less angry/emotional
cool it = become less angry/emotional immediately
cool one's heels = be kept waiting
keep a cool head/keep one's cool = remain calm
  See also: cool **customer**; cool **hand**; **lose** one's cool/rag/wool; **play** it
  cool.

coop
fly the coop = escape

cop
cop it = get into trouble (for a misdemeanour)
cop shop = police station
fair cop = just arrest/discovery (of a wrongdoer)
not much cop = not very good/not worthy of its reputation

copy
 See: **fair** copy.

copybook
blot one's copybook = make a serious blunder (which affects one's
 record/reputation)

core
hard core = unshakeable central group
to the core = thoroughly

corn
tread on somebody's corns = usurp (somebody's authority/position)

corner
all the corners of the earth = everywhere
corner the market = buy/control the major source of supply of a
 commodity
cut corners = achieve a required result by making economies in
 materials/time
drive somebody into a corner = force somebody into a situation from
 which he/she cannot retreat
in a tight corner = in an awkward situation (from which it is difficult
 to escape)
knock the corners off somebody = show somebody how to correct
 his/her ineptitude/inexperience
out of the corner of one's eye = (looking at something)
 indirectly/surreptitiously
round the corner = nearby
turn the corner = begin to improve
 See also: hole-and-corner/hole-in-the-corner **affair**.

corner-stone
lay the corner-stone = establish

corrected
stand corrected = admit a mistake

cost
at all costs = no matter what the price
at the cost of = at the expense/loss of
count the cost = estimate the likely cost (in terms of risk/time, etc.)
  of an undertaking
to one's cost = to one's loss
  See also: cost a **packet**.

cottage
cottage hospital = small (country) hospital with very limited facilities
cottage industry = small-scale manufacturing/production (typically in
  somebody's home)

cotton
cotton on to = understand
wrap somebody (up) in cotton wool = be overprotective

cough
cough up = pay (a debt)
cough it up = speak out
cough to = admit (a misdemeanour/mistake)

counsel
keep one's own counsel = keep one's views to oneself

count
count against = be disadvantageous
count for = be worth
count me in/out = include/exclude me
count on = rely on
does not count = should be/is excluded/ignored
out for the count = deeply asleep/unconscious
  See also: count for **nothing**; count one's **blessings**; count the **cost**;
  stand up and be counted.

countenance
keep one's countenance = not betray one's feelings/remain calm

counter
over the counter = from stock at a retailer/shop
run counter to = disagree with
under the counter = secretly/surreptitiously (of something not openly available)

country
appeal/go to the country = seek re-election (of a government)
country cousin = (unsophisticated) person who lives in the country
in one's line of country = within one's competence/experience

courage
muster/pluck/screw/summon up one's courage, or take one's courage in both hands = force oneself to attempt something (that one feels incapable of doing or that involves danger/risk)
See also: **Dutch** courage; have the courage of one's **conviction**s.

course
adopt a course (of action) = commit to (a way of) doing something
change course = alter one's direction
continue/embark on a course (of action) = pursue/decide on a way of doing something
crash course = intensive programme of training
in (the) course of = being/in process of
in due course = eventually
run its course = proceed to its inevitable/logical conclusion
stay the course = endure/persist
See also: as a **matter** of course; **par** for the course; **steer** a middle course.

court
laughed out of court = ridiculed
hold court = converse with less important people
pay court to = solicit attention/favours
put oneself out of court = take an action that excludes one from consideration
See also: have the **ball** in one's court; **kangaroo** court; **rule** something out of court.

cousin
  See: **country** cousin.

Coventry
send somebody to Coventry = refuse to speak to somebody (as a
  punishment for a misdemeanour)

cover
cover one's tracks = hide/remove incriminating evidence
cover up = hide (something incriminating)
take cover = seek protection
under cover = indoors/protected
  See also: **break** cover; cover a lot of/the **ground**; cover/include a
  multitude of sins.

cow
milch cow = source of easy profit
sacred cow = something held in high esteem and beyond criticism
till the cows come home = for ever

crab
catch a crab = make a clumsy rowing stroke by dipping the oar too
  deep in the water

crack
crack a bottle = open a bottle and drink the contents
crack a crib = break into a house to steal
crack of doom = end of the world
crack the whip = apply authority (severely/vigorously)
crack up = break down/deteriorate mentally, or praise highly
drive somebody crackers = make somebody go mad
fair crack of the whip = fair opportunity/share
get cracking = hurry up (and start)
have a crack at = make an attempt (to)
not what it's cracked up to be = not as good as is claimed
paper over the cracks = make a temporary/insubstantial repair (only
  to obvious defects)
  See also: crack a **joke**.

cradle
cradle snatcher = somebody who has as a partner or who marries
  somebody much younger than himself/herself

from the cradle = since early childhood

cramp
cramp somebody's style = restrict somebody's room to demonstrate his/her ability

crash
crash out = fall (deeply) asleep
  See also: crash **course**.

crazy
be crazy about = like very much

cream
cream off = take the best part
the cream of = the best of

create
create a stink/merry hell = make a (big) fuss

credit
a credit to = somebody whose achievements reflect favourably on somebody else
get/take the credit for = be held (favourably) responsible for
give credit for = acknowledge somebody's ability
give credit to = acknowledge somebody's contribution to/praise

creek
up the creek (without a paddle) = in difficulties

creeps
give one the creeps = make one feel abhorrent/fearful
make one's flesh creep = cause a feeling of abhorrence

crest
on the crest of a wave = euphoric/successful

crew
skeleton crew = minimum number of people to perform a task (that normally requires more)

crib
  See: **crack** a crib.

cricket
not cricket = dishonourable/unfair
chirpy/merry as a cricket = very lively/jaunty

crock
crock of gold = unattainable reward
old crock = battered old car, or an old person

crocodile
crocodile tears = insincere sorrow/sympathy

Croesus
  See: **rich** as Croesus

crop
crop up = happen/occur (unexpectedly)
come a cropper = have an accident (involving a fall), or suffer a
  misfortune

cross
bear one's cross = tolerate sorrow/suffering
have one's cross to bear = carry a heavy responsibility/sorrow
  See also: cross one's **mind**; cross-**purposes**; cross somebody's **palm**
  with silver; cross somebody's **path**; cross **swords** with somebody;
  get/have one's **wires** crossed; keep one's **fingers** crossed.

cross-roads
at the cross-roads = at a point of decision

crow
as the crow flies = in a direct line
crow about/over = boast
crow's feet = lines round the eyes
  See also: **stone** me/the crows.

crowd
follow the crowd = do what everybody else does

crown
crown it all = finally/in addition to everything

cruel
be cruel to be kind = help somebody by using unpleasant methods

crumpet
bit of crumpet = sexually attractive young woman

crunch
come to the crunch = reach the testing point

crush
have a crush on somebody = be infatuated by somebody

crust
earn a crust = earn a living
upper crust = aristocracy/high ranks of society

cry
be crying out for = be in obvious need of
cry down = speak badly of, disparage
far cry = long way
cry for the moon = wish for the unattainable
crying need = something needing urgent attention
crying shame = great shame
cry off = cancel a previous commitment
cry one's eyes/heart out = cry copiously
cry out for = appeal (passionately) for/need (desperately)
cry over spilt milk = continue to regret something that cannot be
  reversed
cry stinking fish = speak unfavourable about one's associates
cry/weep buckets = cry profusely
cry wolf = call for help unnecessarily
for crying out loud! = exclamation of annoyance/surprise
in full cry = at the most vigorous part of the action
  See also: cry **baby**; **hue** and cry; **voice** crying in the wilderness.

crystal
crystal ball = something that enables one to predict the future
  See also: **clear** as crystal.

cuckoo
cuckoo in the nest = interloper, somebody who takes advantage of a
  friendship for personal gain
  See also: in **cloud**-cuckoo-land.

cucumber
  See: **cool** as a cucumber.

cudgel
cudgel one's brains = think very hard (in an attempt to remember something)
take up the cudgels = lend strong support to (a cause)

cue
take one's cue from = follow somebody else's example

cuff
off the cuff = unrehearsed

cup
another cup of tea = a totally different matter
cup that cheers = alcoholic drink
in one's cups = drunk
nice (old) cup of tea = difficult situation
not one's cup of tea = not what one likes/prefers
one's cup is full = one is feeling very emotional/happy

cupboard
cupboard love = simulated affection for personal gain
skeleton in the cupboard = shameful secret

cupid
play cupid = introduce a couple in the hope that they will become close friends/fall in love

curate
  See: like the curate's **egg**.

cure
kill or cure = take extreme action that either resolves a difficulty or makes it much worse

curiosity
  See: curiosity killed the **cat**.

curl
curl up = recoil in abhorrence

have somebody by the short and curlies = put somebody in an
  indefensible position
  See also: make one's **hair** curl.

currency
acquire/gain/obtain currency = become widely known

curry
curry favour = be obsequious in order to gain approval

curtain
bamboo curtain = barrier to diplomatic relations/trade between
  China and the Western world
curtains for somebody = somebody's death/demise
curtain-raiser = short preliminary to the main event
draw a curtain over = hide/make secret
iron curtain = barrier to diplomatic relations/trade between the
  Soviet Union and the Western world
ring down the curtain = bring to an end/conclude

cuss
not to care a tinker's cuss = not to care at all

customer
cool customer = somebody who is aloof/self-assured
queer/rum customer = somebody who is strange/unpredictable
rough/ugly customer = somebody with an aggressive/threatening
  manner
slippery customer = somebody who is elusive or reluctant to make a
  commitment
tough customer = somebody with great emotional/physical strength,
  or who is difficult to deal with

cut
be cut, or half cut = drunk, or nearly drunk
cut above the rest = superior
cut across = contradict
cut a dash/figure = have an (ostentatiously) elegant/fashionable
  appearance
cut and dried = predetermined/unalterable
cut and run = abandon something/escape/leave hurriedly

cut and thrust = competitive aspects of a situation

cut back = make economies

cut both ways = affect both aspects of something equally

cut down to size = reduce somebody's arrogance/superiority

cut fine = complete just in time

cut in = interrupt, or take over somebody else's dancing partner

cut it out! = stop doing that!

cut off = break in a telephone conversation (because of equipment malfunction)

cut off without a penny/shilling = disinherit

cut one's own throat = take self-damaging action

cut one's teeth on = learn about initially/have fundamental knowledge of

cut out = exclude, or stop working (of a machine)

cut out for = have a natural ability for

cut somebody dead = deliberately ignore somebody (in public)

cut short = curtail/interrupt

cut the ground from under somebody/somebody's feet = anticipate/refute an opponent's arguments, so leaving him/her with no case

cut the (Gordian) knot = take quick, bold action to resolve a difficulty

cut to the quick = very hurt (emotionally)

cut up = feeling great sorrow

cut up nasty/rough = become aggressive/angry

short cut = more direct/quicker way

See also: cut a long **story** short; cut **corners**; cut **loose**; cut no **ice**; cut off in one's **prime**; cut one's **coat** according to one's cloth; cut one's **losses**; cut off one's **nose** to spite one's face; cut somebody to the **quick**; cut the **air** with a knife; cut to the **bone**.

cut-off

cut-off point = point (usually in time) beyond which no further action is taken

cut-throat

cut-throat competition = viciously aggressive/restrictive

cylinder

firing on all cylinders = functioning perfectly

D

dab
be a dab hand at = be adept/expert at

dabble
dabble in = take a passing interest in

daddy
daddy of them all = best/largest example
big daddy = authoritarian father/leader
sugar daddy = mature/elderly man who lavishes attention/gifts on a young woman

daft
as daft as a brush = very silly/stupid

daggers
at daggers drawn = prepared for a confrontation/fight
look daggers at = look with a piercing and disapproving stare

daily
daily dozen = regular (daily) physical exercises
one's daily bread = one's living

daisy
push up the daisies = be dead
  See also: **fresh** as a daisy.

damage
what's the damage? = how much do I owe you? (to pay for goods/services)

damn
damn all = nothing at all
damn well = expression used for emphasis
damn with faint praise = disguise criticism/disapproval with insincere praise
do one's damnedest = do one's best
I'll be damned if = I won't

not care/give a damn = not care at all
not worth a damn = totally worthless

damp
damp down = discourage/suppress
damp squib = expected success that turns out to be a failure
put a/the damper on = discourage/counteract an (expected) effect

dance
dance attendance on = fawn on/pamper
lead somebody a (merry/pretty) dance = deliberately mislead
  somebody/waste somebody's time
  See also: dance/walk on **air**; make a **song** and dance about
  something.

dander
get one's dander up = become (very) angry

Darby
Darby and Joan = devoted and elderly married couple

dare
dare-devil = somebody who takes excessive (and unnecessary) risks
how dare you! = how can you say that/be so rude
I dare say = I suppose/venture to say
(just) you dare = do not (with great emphasis)

dark
dark horse = somebody of unknown (and possibly dubious) character
in the dark = in ignorance/not knowing
keep it dark = keep it secret/to yourself
leap/shot in the dark = an attempt that has little chance of success/a
  guess
whistle in the dark = encourage with (false) optimism
  See also: dark **days**.

darling
mother's darling = spoiled (male) child

dash
cut a dash = impress by one's dress
dash off = hurry away, or do something quickly/superficially

dash somebody's hopes = disappoint/disillusion somebody

date
blind date = prearranged meeting between strangers (usually a man and a woman)
date somebody = arrange to go out with somebody (of the opposite sex)
make a date with somebody = arrange to meet somebody
out of date = behind the times/out of fashion
up to date = modern/in fashion
to date = up to now

daughter
See: daughter **language**.

daunted
nothing daunted = irrespective of any difficulty

David
David and Goliath situation = confrontation in which the person with less ability/experience/strength wins

Davy Jones
Davy Jones' locker = the (bottom of the) sea

dawn
dawn on = become aware/enlightened

day
all day long = continuously/without a break for a whole day
all in a day's work = within one's duties/obligation
any day (now) = soon
any day of the week = at any time
as happy as the day is long = very happy
black day = bad/disastrous event
carry/win the day = gain a victory
dark days = troubled times
day after day/day in day out = continuously (and monotonously) for several days
day-dream = lose oneself in one's imagination
day of reckoning = time when one has to account for past actions

days of old/yore = in (distant) historical times

days to come = the future

every dog has its day = eventually everyone achieves (temporary) success

fall on evil days = suffer unfortunate circumstances

for days on end = for many consecutive days

from day to day = as time progresses (daily)

good old days = earlier times (remembered with fondness)

have one's day = have a time when one is prosperous/successful

livelong day = all day long

make a day of it = spend all day doing something enjoyable

make somebody's day = give somebody a welcome surprise

name the day = announce the date of a forthcoming wedding

not one's day/one of those days = time when things do not go as planned

not to have all day = to have only a limited time

off-day = day when things do not go well/to form

old/olden days = distant past

one of these (fine) days = at some time in the future

one's days are numbered = one's time is limited

open as the day = totally honest

palmy days = time of prosperity

red-letter day = memorable date/event

salad days = time of youthful inexperience

save the day = prevent a failure

the other day = one day recently

to have seen better days = to be past its best/have outlived its usefulness

that will be the day! = that is very unlikely!

See also: at the **end** of the day; **call** it a day; daily **round**; **day's** grace; **dog** days; **early** days; every **dog** has its day; have a **field** day; have seen **better** days; in all one's **born** days; in **broad** daylight; (a bit) **late** in the day; **man** of his day; **nine** days' wonder; one of these **fine** days; **pass** the time of day; **roll** on the day; **save** something for a rainy day; **tomorrow** is another day.

daylight

beat the living daylights out of somebody = beat severely/knock senseless

daylight robbery = flagrant overcharging
frighten/scare the living daylights out of somebody = terrify
　somebody
in broad daylight = in full view during the day
see daylight = perceive an eventual solution to a problem

dead

dead and buried = (long) forgotten
dead as a dodo = extinct/obsolete
dead as a doornail/mutton = (emphatically) dead
dead beat = exhausted
dead certainty = absolute certainty
dead drunk = very drunk (to the point of unconsciousness)
dead from the neck up = foolish/stupid
dead heat = race/competition in which two (or more) contestants are
　exactly level at the finish
dead loss = total loss/useless
dead man's shoes = job opportunity provided by somebody's death
　or retirement
dead of night = darkest part of the night
dead-pan = lacking any expression
dead ringer (for somebody) = a double/somebody who looks exactly
　the same
dead to the world = fast asleep/unconscious
dead wood = useless appendage/person
drop dead! = go away!
enough to wake the dead = very loud
go dead = cease working
make a dead set at = purposefully attack/approach
over my dead body = only if my most vigorous opposition fails
refuse to/wouldn't be seen dead in = be too ashamed/embarrassed to
　do something
　See also: be in (deadly) **earnest**; **cut** somebody dead; dead **duck**; dead
　end; dead-end **job**; dead to **rights**; dead **men** tell no tales; **play**
　dead/possum; **stone** dead; **stop** dead.

deadline

meet a deadline = have something ready on time

deaf
deaf as a post = (very) deaf
turn a deaf ear to = deliberately ignore
  See also: fall on deaf **ears**; **stone** deaf.

deal
big deal! = I'm totally unimpressed
fair deal = a substantial amount/quality, quite a lot
it's a deal = it is agreed
raw deal = unfair treatment
square deal = fair/reasonable agreement

dear
oh dear! = expression of (anxious) surprise

death
be the death of (somebody) = be the cause of (somebody's) death, or
  cause great amusement, or annoyance/trouble
catch one's death = catch a chill/very bad cold
death trap = place in which one is in danger of being seriously
  injured/killed
do to death = overdo/overexpose
feel like death warmed up = feel exhausted/ill
in at the death = present at the very end
pale as death = very pale
sick to death of = thoroughly fed up
sign somebody's death warrant = commit an action that results in
  somebody's death or downfall
tickled to death = highly amused
to the death = until somebody is defeated or killed
work something to death = force something to work excessively, or
  overexpose something
  See also: at death's **door**; **cling**/hold on like **grim** death; **dice** with
  death; **fate** worse than death; **jaws** of death; **kiss** of death.

debt
be in somebody's debt = owe somebody (often gratitude)
get into debt = owe money
  See also: **bad** debt.

deck
clear the decks = prepare for action
sweep the deck = beat everybody and win all the stakes

declare
declare war = give formal notice of intent to fight

deep
in deep water = in trouble
  See also: deep **game**; dive/throw somebody in at the deep **end**; still waters run deep.

default
in default of = in the absence of
win by default = win because the opponent does not compete

defensive
on the defensive = in a state of defence
throw somebody on the defensive = put somebody in a situation in which he/she has to defend himself/herself

deference
in deference to = because of respect for

degree
by degrees = gradually
one degree under = unwell
third degree = persistent/brutal interrogation
to a degree = to some extent/in a way

delicate
in a delicate condition = pregnant

deliver
  See: deliver the **goods**.

delusion
have delusions of grandeur = believe one is more important than one actually is

demand
in demand = (very) popular

make demands on = continually require/put pressure on
on demand = when(ever) asked

demon
demon for = very enthusiastic/have a deep commitment for
the demon drink = habitual drinking/alcohol(ism)

den
den of thieves = group of criminals, or derogatory term for a group of like-minded people
lion's den = enemy territory/dangerous situation

dent
make a dent in = reduce/lessen

depart
new departure = change of course/method
the (dear) departed = somebody who is dead

depend
depend upon it = be sure/beyond doubt
that depends on = is conditional on

depth
out of/beyond one's depth = in difficulty (because of overstretching one's ability/knowledge)
plumb the depths = reach the lowest level
in depth = in great detail/thoroughly

description
beggar description = be indescribable (because of its greatness)

deserts
receive one's just deserts = get what one deserves

deserve
richly deserve = be (rightly) entitled to

design
by design = according to a plan/deliberately
have designs on = wish to take/own

desire
See: leave a **lot**/much to be desired.

desk
desk general = commander with no battle experience

despair
give way/yield to despair = give up hope

device
leave somebody to his/her own devices = leave somebody alone

devil
be a devil = be bold/take a risk
be a devil for = be very fond of
better the devil you know = the bad thing you are aware of is better
   than another of which you are unaware
between the devil and the deep blue sea = in a dilemma/with a choice
   between two equally unpleasant alternatives
devil-may-care = wildly reckless
devil in disguise = somebody/something apparently good but actually
   bad
devil take the hindmost = I do not care what happens to others
devil's advocate = somebody who ensures that the unfavourable
   aspects of a decision/situation are taken into account as well as the
   favourable ones
hold a candle to the devil = play safe by keeping on good terms with
   both sides in a dispute
play the very devil with = make worse/misbehave
speak/talk of the devil = said of somebody who appears just as
   he/she is being talked about
the devil looks after/takes care of his own = bad people seem to
   succeed (in preference to good ones)
the very devil = mischief-maker/nuisance
   See also: **dare** devil; give the devil his **due; needs** must (when the
   devil drives); the devil/hell to **pay**; the devil's own **job**.

dialogue
dialogue of the deaf = discussion in which neither side
   acknowledges/agrees with the opinions of the other

diamond
diamond cut diamond = contest between equally determined and well-matched opponents
rough diamond = somebody who is (apparently) brash/unsophisticated but is nevertheless good-hearted

diarrhoea
verbal diarrhoea = wordy but insubstantial speech

dice
dice with death = take a (severe) risk
no dice = definitely not
the dice are loaded = the odds are against/there is no chance of success

dick
clever dick = a know-all
  See also: any/every **Tom**, Dick and Harry.

die
be dying for = have a great desire for
be dying from/of = be approaching death because of
be dying to do something = be very keen to do something
die away/down = fade/gradually diminish
die in harness/with one's boots on = die while still at work
die laughing = be highly amused/laugh to the point of exhaustion
die off = die one by one
die out = become extinct
never say die = do not give in
straight as a die = totally honest
the die is cast = the outcome is inevitable/it is too late to change one's mind
  See also: die like a **dog**; **do** or die; what did your last **servant** die of?

differ
  See: **agree** to differ; **beg** to differ.

difference
make all the difference = have a great effect on
sink one's differences = forget past disagreements

split the difference = compromise between two close
  amounts/quantities
  See also: **bury** the hatchet/one's differences.

dig
dig in = begin energetically
dig oneself in = secure one's position
dig one's feet/heels/toes in = be resolute/stubborn
dig somebody in the ribs = poke somebody in the side of the chest
  See also: dig one's **grave**; **gold**-digger.

dignity
stand on one's dignity = be pompous/insist on respect

dilemma
on the horns of a dilemma = faced with two equally unpleasant
  alternatives

dim
take a dim view of = disapprove of, or be unimpressed

din
din into = force somebody to accept/learn something (by repeating it)

dinner
dog's dinner = an (untidy) mess

dint
by dint of = by means of

dip
dip into = examine superficially, or use part of a reserve
dip into one's pocket = spend money

diplomacy
wrist-slap diplomacy = demonstration of a minor disagreement
  between countries at diplomatic level

direction
  See: **step** in the right direction.

dirt

pay dirt = soil (from a mine) containing precious metal or precious stones

See also: dirty **game; eat** dirt; **treat** somebody like (a piece of) dirt.

dirty

dirty look = disapproving/hostile stare

dirty money = money obtained dishonestly

dirty trick = dishonest/unfair means

dirty weather = stormy/wet weather

dirty weekend = weekend spent together by an unmarried couple or one having an illicit (extramarital) affair

dirty work = criminal activity, or unpleasant task

do the dirty on = betray/play a mean trick on

See also: dirty **dog;** dirty/rough **end** of the stick; dirty **game;** dirty old **man;** dirty/soil one's **hand**s.

discount

at a discount = at a reduced price

discretion

discretion is the better part of valour = it is wiser to be safe than to indulge in risky heroics

reach the age of discretion = (of a woman) be legally old enough to have sexual intercourse

discussion

open to discussion = arguable/negotiable

disguise

See: **blessing** in disguise.

dish

dish out = give out/distribute

dish up = present food/information

what a dish! = what an attractive girl!

disorderly

disorderly house = brothel

dispose

be disposed to = be willing to

---

be indisposed = be unwell
be well disposed towards somebody = think well of/be friendly with
  somebody
dispose of = get rid of/kill, or complete/deal with

distance

keep one's distance = not be too familiar/personal
within spitting/striking distance = very close

ditch

last-ditch effort = final attempt
last-ditch stand = final resistance (from a point of no retreat)
  See also: **dull** as ditchwater.

dive

  See: dive/throw somebody in at the deep **end**.

divine

divine right = God-given privilege (of kings/queens to rule)

do

anything doing? = is anything happening?
could do with = need
do away with = abolish/destroy/kill
do duty for = act on behalf of/substitute for
do for = cause harm to somebody
do me a favour! = I do not believe you!
done in = exhausted
done to a turn = cooked to perfection
do or die = be determined to succeed at all costs
do somebody in = kill somebody
do something for = improve the appearance/appeal of
do up = make improvements/repairs
have done with = finish/have no further connection with
have to do with = have relevance, or be associated with
it (just) isn't done = it is socially unacceptable
that will do = that is enough
that's done it! = it has happened and there will be trouble
well done! = congratulations!

you do that! = you carry on (I don't care)
  See also: do **justice** to; do one's **bit**; do one's **nut**; do somebody
  proud; do the **dirty** on; do the **trick**; do to **death**; **hard** done by;
  (well) I **never** did; **make** do; **nothing** doing.

dock
in dock = undergoing repair, or in hospital
put somebody in the dock = on trial/under examination

doctor
doctor something = interfere with/modify something
family doctor = general practitioner
have an animal doctored = have a male animal castrated
(just) what the doctor ordered = exactly what is required
  See also: doctor the **accounts**.

dodo
  See: **dead** as a dodo.

dog
call off the dogs = end a search
die like a dog = have a shameful/undignified death
dirty dog = somebody who is underhanded/unscrupulous
dog collar = (priest's) clerical collar
dog days = hottest time of the year
dog-eared = with frayed/tattered edges
dog eat dog = ruthless competition
dog fight = aerial combat between fighter aircraft, or general mêlée
(in the) dog house = (in) disgrace (particularly a husband with whom
  his wife is displeased)
dog in the manger = somebody who spoils somebody else's pleasure
  (although not wanting to participate himself/herself)
dog Latin = incorrect Latin
dog's body = general assistant/helper
dog's breakfast/dinner = a mess
dog's chance = remote chance of success
dog tired = exhausted
don't keep a dog and bark yourself = do not employ somebody to do
  a job and then do it yourself

every dog has its day = everyone eventually gets a favourable
  opportunity
gay dog = somebody who is overtly carefree
give a dog a bad name = a bad reputation is remembered
go to the dogs = decline/be ruined
hair of the dog (that bit you) = drink similar to that which gave one a
  hangover
lead a dog's life = have an unpeaceful/worrying life
let sleeping dogs lie = do not disturb a situation that is finally calm
  after being troubled
let the dog see the rabbit = give the participants a chance
lie doggo = remain in hiding
like a dog with two tails = ecstatic/very happy
lucky dog = somebody who has good fortune (often said with envy)
shaggy dog story = drawn-out joke (with a weak ending)
sly dog = somebody who is crafty/secretive
tail wagging the dog = minor factor controlling a major one
throw somebody to the dogs = condemn somebody to an unpleasant
  fate
top dog = champion/somebody in the most superior position
treat somebody worse than a dog = behave towards somebody with
  total insensitivity/no respect
underdog = somebody who is inferior/on the losing side
work like a dog = work very hard (for little reward)
you can't teach a old dog new tricks = elderly/experienced people
  find it difficult to adjust to new ideas
  See also: dog's **dinner**; every dog has his **day**; have a hangdog **air**;
  love me, love my dog; **rain** cats and dogs; **sick** as a dog; there's **life**
  in the old dog yet.

doing
  See: **do**.

doldrums
in the doldrums = in a state of (enforced) inactivity

doll
doll up = dress in one's finery

dollar
feel/look like a million dollars = feel/look very attractive
the 64 thousand dollar question = a very difficult/unanswerable question
See also: **bet** one's bottom dollar.

done
See: **do**.

donkey
donkey's breakfast = straw-filled mattress, or wood-chip wallpaper
donkey work = menial/routine tasks
for donkey's years = for a very long time
talk the hind leg off a donkey = talk incessantly (to the point of boredom)

doom
See: **crack** of doom.

doomsday
till doomsday = for ever

door
at death's door = on the point of death
behind closed doors = in secret
close the door to = exclude
have a foot in the door = gain access to a (difficult-to-enter) group/organization
in by/through the back door = secretly/without (formal) permission
keep the wolf from the door = ensure that one has enough money for basic necessities (such as food and shelter)
lay at somebody's door = blame somebody
leave the door open = provide a possibility for the future
lock the stable door after the horse has bolted = take precautions after the event
next door to = almost the same as
on one's doorstep = close to where one lives
show somebody the door = ask/tell somebody to leave
shut/slam the door in somebody's face = refuse to talk to somebody
See also: **open** door policy; **open** the door to.

dose
like a dose of salts = very quickly
  See also: dose/taste of one's own **medicine**.

dot
dot the i's and cross the t's = pay attention to/complete the details
on the dot = exactly on time
sign on the dotted line = write one's signature (on a binding/formal
  document)
  See also: the **year** dot.

double
be somebody's double = to resemble somebody very closely
double-back = retrace one's steps
double-barrelled name = hyphenated surname
double-cross = betray a trust/break a promise
double-dealing = using deceptive/underhanded business practices
double-dyed = stained with guilt
double-edged = dual/double-purpose
double-quick = very quick
double talk = ambiguous statement (intended to mislead)
double time = fast marching pace, or twice the usual rate of pay
double up = increase twofold, or do duty for two things
in double harness = in partnership with
seeing double = having double vision (usually through the action of
  alcohol), or mistaking two very similar things as being the same
  See also: double **Dutch**.

doubt
beyond/without (a shadow of a) doubt = certainly
doubting Thomas = somebody who always expresses doubt
give somebody the benefit of the doubt = accept somebody's word if
  it cannot be proved wrong
in doubt = questionable/uncertain
no doubt = certainly

dove
dove of peace = symbol of peace
  See also: **gentle** as a dove.

down

be/feel down = feel depressed

do somebody down = abuse/slander somebody

down and out = knocked down and unconscious/with no fight left, or (somebody) with no means of (financial) support

down-at-heel = poor/poverty-stricken

down-hearted = dispirited/depressed

down in the mouth/dumps = miserable/unhappy

down under = Australia (and New Zealand)

down with! = away with!

have a down on somebody = treat somebody unfairly/wish somebody harm

See also: down on one's **luck**; down-to-**earth**; down **tools**; go down the **drain**; **hit** somebody when he/she is down; **run** somebody down; suit somebody down to the **ground**; **talk** down to somebody.

dozen

baker's dozen = thirteen

dozens of = many

talk nineteen to the dozen = talk rapidly

See also: **six** of one and half-a-dozen of the other.

drab

See: **drib**s and drabs.

drag

be in/wear drag = (of a man) wear women's clothes

drag in/up = bring an unnecessary/unwanted topic into a discussion

drag on = go on so long as to cause boredom

drag out = prolong (unnecessarily), or to extract information (from somebody who is reluctant to give it)

drag somebody through the mire/mud = dishonour/shame somebody

See also: drag one's **feet**.

drain

go down the drain = go to waste/be lost

See also: **brain** drain; **laugh** like a drain.

draught

on draught = available from a barrel (as opposed to being in bottles or cans)

See also: **feel** the draught/pinch.

draw

draw a bead on = aim at

draw a blank = fail to find something

draw a veil over = say no more about something

draw away/back = recoil/retreat

draw in = shorten, or arrive/stop

draw lots = take part in a lottery (to select somebody for something)

draw on = take from (reserve)

(long) drawn out = extended/prolonged

draw near = approach

draw off = decant/siphon or divert the flow of (a liquid)

draw on = allure/entice, or take from

draw out = extend/prolong, or extract information, or withdraw money

draw somebody aside = take somebody from a group for a private conversation

draw somebody's fire = tactically allow oneself to be attacked

draw to an end = bring/come to a conclusion

drawn game = contest that ends with both sides even

draw up = compile, or arrive

draw upon/on = take from reserves/resources

good draw = popular attraction

on the drawing-board = at the design/planning stage

quick on the draw = quick to react

See also: call/draw **attention** to; **back** to the drawing-board; choose/draw the short **straw**; draw a **parallel**; draw **blood**; draw/pull in one's **horns**; draw the **line** (at).

drawer

bottom drawer = household articles collected by a girl before she gets married

(not) out of the top drawer = (not) of a high social position

dream
beyond one's wildest dreams = much better than one could
 expect/imagine
dream up = devise/invent
(go) like a dream = work perfectly, as hoped/planned
not dream of = not occur to one
sweet dreams = sleep well
 See also: **day** dream.

dress
dress down/give a dressing down = give somebody a severe reprimand
dress to kill/up to the nines = dress to attract attention
dress up = wear one's best clothes, or don a costume, or decorate
 something (to improve its appearance)

dribs
dribs and drabs = small, scattered amounts/quantities

drift
catch/get the drift of = understand

drink
drink like a fish = drink heavily/to excess
drink in = absorb (eagerly)
drink on the house = complimentary drink (from the
 landlord/proprietor)
drink to = to toast
in/into the drink = in/into the water
 See also: drink (take) one's **fill**; drink somebody under the **table**;
 spike a drink; the **demon** drink.

drive
back-seat driver = somebody who offers unwanted advice to the
 person in charge
drive at = imply/suggest
drive away/off = repel/discourage
drive somebody mad/round the bend/round the twist/to drink =
 severely anger/annoy/frustrate somebody
in the driver's seat = in control

what are you driving at? = what are you implying/trying to say?
  See also: drive a hard **bargain**; drive somebody up the **wall**;
  drive/hammer something **home**; **pure** as the driven snow.

drone
drone on = talk incessantly and monotonously

drop
drop a brick/clanger = make a blunder (in conversation)
drop a hint = make a subtle suggestion
drop a line = write a letter
drop behind = get farther (back) from the leader
drop in = call on/visit
drop in the bucket/ocean = insignificant amount/quantity
drop off = fall asleep, or decline
drop out = reject convention (and join the alternative society)
fit/ready to drop = exhausted
have a drop too much = be drunk
have the drop on somebody = have the advantage over somebody
  See also: at the drop of a **hat**; drop **dead**; drop/give/throw a **hint**.

drown
drown one's sorrows = drink in order to (temporarily) forget one's
  troubles

drug
  See: drug on the **market**.

drum
beat the drum for = be an enthusiastic supporter of
drum up = assemble/organize
drummed out = expelled in disgrace
drum something into somebody = make somebody learn something
  (by repetition/indoctrination)
  See also: **jungle** drums.

drunk
  See: **blind** drunk; **dead** drunk.

dry
dry as dust = parched/very dry, or very uninteresting

dry up = be unable to talk/stop talking, or dry dishes (after washing them)

dry out = stop drinking (alcohol)

See: **bone** dry; **cut** and dried; **high** and dry; dry **run**.

duck

break one's duck = score/succeed (after having failed previously)

dead duck = something that is finished/over with

lame duck = something that needs (financial) support

like a dying duck (in a thunderstorm) = sad and weak

like water off a duck's back = without having any effect

lovely weather for ducks = wet weather

make a duck = score zero (at cricket)

sitting duck = easy target

take to something like a duck to water = be completely at ease in a new situation

ugly duckling = somebody who is unattractive/unpromising when young

due

give somebody his due = give somebody the credit he/she deserves

give the devil his due = acknowledge a good aspect in somebody one dislikes

dull

dull the edge of = make less effective

dull as ditchwater = very dull

dumb

our dumb friends = animals (stressing their non-human nature)

See also: dumb **animals**; dumb **blonde**.

dummy

like a tailor's dummy = lacking animation

dumps

(down) in the dumps = depressed/miserable

duration

for the duration = for as long as something lasts

dust

bite the dust = die/cease to exist

like gold dust = extremely rare

not so dusty = quite good

not to see somebody for dust = unable to see somebody because he/she has left in a hurry

shake the dust from one's feet = move away

throw dust in somebody's eyes = confuse/mislead somebody

when/after the dust has settled = when the situation is calm again

See also: **dry** as dust.

Dutch

double Dutch = nonsense

Dutch auction = auction at which the bidding starts with a high price, which is gradually reduced until somebody is willing to pay it

Dutch cap = (contraceptive) diaphragm

Dutch courage = confidence that results from having an alcoholic drink

Dutch treat = occasion on which everybody pays for himself/herself

go Dutch = share the cost (equally)

I'm a Dutchman if... = phrase that emphasizes the improbability of a statement

talk to somebody like a Dutch uncle = give severe but friendly advice

duty

duty bound = have a moral/personal obligation

See also: **do** duty for; in the **line** of duty.

dwell

dwell on = talk about at length

dye

dyed-in-the-wool = fixed/inflexible (in one's views)

of the deepest dye = extreme/fanatic (in one's views)

See also: **double**-dyed.

dying

See: **die**.

E

eager
eager beaver = somebody who is enthusiastic/overzealous

eagle
eagle eye = keen/vigilant sight

ear
about one's ears = all around one
an ear for = an appreciation of
be all ears = listen attentively
bend somebody's ear = talk (boringly) to somebody
box somebody's ears/give somebody a thick ear = slap somebody on the side of the head
cauliflower ear = injury caused by repeated blows/pressure to the ear
come to/reach one's ears = be made aware of
coming out of one's ears = in great excess
ear-splitting = excessively loud/shrill
flea in the ear = a scolding
gain the ear of = get somebody to listen to one
give ear to = listen/pay attention to
give one's ears for = make great personal sacrifice for/pay any price for
grate on the ear = sound harsh/unpleasant
have a word in somebody's ear = speak to somebody privately
have long ears = be inquisitive/nosey
have one's ear to the ground = be alert to the situation
have one's ears burning = be the subject of conversation
have the ear of = have access to a (higher) source of information
I'm all ears = I am listening intently
in one ear and out of the other = not remembered/ignored
lend an ear = listen (attentively)
no ear for music = non-musical
play by ear = play a musical instrument without using printed music
play it by ear = see how a situation develops and react accordingly/improvise

prick up one's ears = suddenly start listening carefully
throw somebody out on his/her ear = forcibly eject somebody
unable to believe one's ears = amazed/astounded
up to one's ears in = overwhelmed with/submerged in
reach somebody's ears = come to somebody's attention/notice
set somebody by the ears = lead to disharmony among people
wet behind the ears = inexperienced/naive
within earshot = within hearing distance (that is, relatively near)
   See also: **dog**-eared; **fall** on deaf ears; make a **pig**'s ear of something; make a **silk** purse out of a sow's ear; **pin** back one's ears; turn a **deaf** ear to; **walls** have ears.

early
bright and early = first thing in the morning
early days/early in the day = too soon to be sure
   See also: early **bird**.

earn
earn a bomb = earn much money
   See also: earn a crust; earn an honest penny.

earnest
be in (deadly) earnest = be very serious

earth
bring somebody down to earth = make somebody face up to reality
come back to earth = face reality
down-to-earth = basic/practical
ends of the earth = remotest parts of the world
go to earth = go into hiding
have not an earthly = have no chance whatever
like nothing on earth = incomparably/indescribably bad
move heaven and earth = go to any lengths/do everything possible
no earthly good/use = useless
no earthly reason for = no justification for
pay the earth for = pay a very high price for
run somebody/something to earth = find somebody/something that is
   elusive/hidden
salt of the earth = somebody who is very good/worthy
what on earth? = exclamatory question of surprise

wipe off the face of the earth = destroy completely
   See also: all the **corners** of the earth; **how** on earth?; like **heaven** on
   earth.

ease
ease up = slow down/relax
put/set somebody's at his/her ease = make somebody feel relaxed

easy
easier said than done = harder to do than to talk about
easy as pie = very easy
easy come, easy go = something (e.g. money) that is easily obtained
   can be lost/parted with casually
easy-going = relaxed/undemanding
easy meat/touch = somebody who is easy to dupe/take advantage of
easy money = money obtained with little effort
easy on the eye = pleasant to look at
go easy on somebody = be lenient with somebody
go easy on/with something = do not be (over)generous with
I'm easy = I don't mind/I'm agreeable
in easy circumstances/on easy street = financially secure/well off
on easy terms = easily/in a relaxed manner, or on credit/hire
   purchase
take it easy = relax/slow down
   See also: **ill** at ease.

eat
eat away/into = erode/consume gradually
eat dirt = tolerate insults/humiliation
eat humble pie = apologise meekly (when proven wrong)
eat like a horse = eat a lot
eat one's head off = eat greedily
eat one's heart out = make one envy/grieve/pine
eat one's words = deeply regret what one has said
eat somebody out of house and home = eat more than one's host can
   afford/provide
have somebody eat out of one's hand = gain somebody's complete
   confidence/have control over somebody

---

make somebody eat his/her words = make somebody
 retract/withdraw a statement
what's eating you? = what are you bothered/worried about?
 See also: **dog** eat dog; eat one's **hat**; have one's **cake** and eat it; the
 proof of the **pudding** is in the eating.

ebb
 See: at (a) **low** ebb.

economy
black economy = unofficial business ventures that evade tax
suit-case economy = economic system that is subject to high inflation

edge
edge away = gradually move away
edge somebody out = gradually get rid of somebody
give somebody the rough edge of one's tongue = scold/reprimand
 somebody
have the edge on = have the advantage
not get a word in edgeways = be unable to interrupt somebody who is
 talking continuously
on edge = nervous/tense
put an edge on one's appetite = make one hungry
set one's teeth on edge = make one cringe/feel uncomfortable (as a
 result of a grating sound)
take the edge off = make less severe/stringent
 See also: **dull** the edge of; on the **razor's** edge; **thin** end of the
 wedge.

educate
educated guess = answer given on the basis of knowledge/past
 experience

eel
slippery as an eel = difficult to catch/pin down

effect
bring (carry) into effect = put into operation
for effect = in order to impress
in effect = in fact/effectively
of/to no effect = useless(ly)

take effect = happen/come about
to that effect = confirming that
to the effect that = that states/confirms
with effect from = to commence on/from

effort

Herculean effort = maximum (physical) effort
  See also: last **ditch** effort.

egg

don't put all one's eggs in one basket = do not commit all one's
  resources in one place
egg-head = somebody of superior intellect
egg somebody on = encourage somebody
good egg = somebody who is likeable/popular (usually because
  he/she is accommodating/amenable)
have egg on one's face = be embarrassed/humiliated
kill the goose that lays the golden egg = forgo/relinquish a source of
  income/wealth (through greed)
like the curate's egg = good in parts
nest egg = savings (for the future)
sure as eggs is eggs = absolutely certain
tread on eggs = proceed with great caution
  See also: **bad** egg/hat/lot; put all one's eggs in one **basket;** teach
  one's **grandmother** to suck eggs.

ego

ego trip = self-indulgent activity

eight

  See: **figure** of eight; **one** over the eight.

elbow

at one's elbow = close at hand
elbow grease = manual effort/energy
elbow one's way = force one's way (through a crowd)
elbow room = enough space to move in
give somebody the elbow = get rid of somebody
lift/bend the elbow = drink (regularly)
more power to his elbow = may he succeed/good luck to him

out at the elbows = tattered/worn out
up to one's elbows = very busy
  See also: up and down like a **fiddler**'s elbow.

element
brave the elements = go out in bad weather
in one's element = doing what one best likes doing/at home
out of one's element = in an unknown/unnatural situation

elephant
memory like an elephant = very good memory
pink elephants = hallucinations symptomatic of dipsomania (chronic
  alcoholism)
rogue elephant = an elephant which splits away from the herd and
  becomes a dangerous nuisance, hence somebody who is
  rebellious/anti-authoritarian
white elephant = useless/unwanted object

eleven
eleventh hour = very last minute

else
or else = or you will regret it

empty
empty-handed = carrying/with nothing
empty-headed = not very bright (mentally)
on an empty stomach = without having eaten

end
all ends up = completely
at an end = completed/exhausted/over
at one's wit's end = out of patience/in a state of despair
at the end of one's rope/tether = limit of one's patience
at the end of the day = finally, when everything has been taken into
  account
be the end of = cause the demise/death of
come to a sticky end = die/end in a very unpleasant situation
dead end = situation from which no progress can be made
dive/throw somebody in at the deep end = tackle a new situation in
  its most difficult aspect

end for end/end over end = in a reverse position

end it all = commit suicide

end of the line/road = enforced conclusion/limit

end on = with the end facing (rather than the side)

ends of the earth = any extreme

end up = finally arrive/become

in the end = finally

keep one's end up = do one's share

make (both) ends meet = have enough money to live on

no end of = a lot/very much

not know one end of something from the other = know nothing about something

not look beyond the end of one's nose = make only a superficial search

not see beyond the end of one's nose = be narrow-minded, with no imagination/vision

not the end of the world = the situation is not as bad as it seems

on end = continuously/without a break

on the receiving end = get something (usually unpleasant)

put an end/stop to = destroy/finish

the (absolute) end = the ultimate limit

the end justifies the means = the method employed is acceptable if the result is what is desired

thin end of the wedge = the (insignificant in itself) beginning of something that eventually leads to a major difficulty

tie up the loose ends = put the finishing touches to something

to no end = with no result/without success

to the bitter end = to the finish, regardless of the cost or consequences

(get hold of the) wrong end of the stick = misunderstand

See also: at a **loose** end; be-**all** and end-all; **come** to a bad end; dead-end **job**; **dirty**/rough end of the stick; **draw** to an end; **fag** end; for **days** on end; go off the **deep** end; in at the **deep** end; make one's **hair** curl/stand on end; **never** hear the end of something; **no** end of; **odds** and ends/sods; on one's **beam** ends; see the **light** at the end of the tunnel; **think** no end of.

enemy

be one's own worst enemy = contribute to one's own failings

how goes the enemy? = what is the time?
sworn enemies = irreconcilable opponents

English
broken English = English spoken by somebody with an incomplete
  knowledge of the language
plain English = straightforward/uncomplicated language

enlarge
enlarge on = expand an explanation

enough
curiously/remarkably/strangely/oddly enough = actually (although
  you would not expect it to be true)
enough and to spare = more than is needed
enough is enough = I can tolerate no more
enough to wake the dead = very loud/noisy
fair enough = I'm in agreement
sure enough = as expected
that's (quite) enough = that is sufficient/stop
  See also: enough is as good as a **feast**.

enquiry
searching enquiry = in-depth investigation

enter
enter a protest = make a protest
enter into = involve oneself/engage in, or sympathize with, or form
  part of
enter (up)on = begin
enter somebody's head = occur to somebody

entry
make an entry = record in a log/register etc., or arrive in a
  ceremonious manner

envy
be the envy of somebody = be envied by somebody
green with envy = very envious

equal
all/other things being equal = everything being taken into
  consideration and found not to matter

be/feel equal to = feel adequate for

err
err on the right side = deliberately overestimate a requirement

errand
  See: **fool**'s errand.

error
clerical error = mistake in typing/writing
  See also: **trial** and error.

escape
  See: **narrow** escape/squeak.

estate
the fourth estate = the press

esteem
hold in high esteem = regard with (great) respect

estimate
rough estimate = broad indication/calculated guess

eternal
eternal city = Rome
eternal triangle = sexual association of two women and a man (or two
  men and a woman)

eternity
for (an) eternity = for ever/a very long time

even
be/get even with = take revenge on
even so = all things considered
even Stephen(s) = equal/level
even up = equalize
  See also: **break** even; even **chance**; even **keel**; even **money**.

event
at/in all events = whether or not that is so
be wise after the event = know too late what one should have done
happy event = birth of a baby

in any event = anyway/regardless of what happens
in the (normal) course of events = as things (usually) happen
in the event = as things transpired
in the event of = if something should happen

ever
am/do I ever = emphatically yes
did you ever? = expression of puzzled surprise
ever so = very
ever such a = a very
for ever and a day = for ever/a very long time
for ever and ever = eternally

every
every man jack (of them) = all (of them)
every now and again/then, every so often = occasionally
every other = alternate
  See also: at every **turn**.

everything
everything but the kitchen sink = an (unnecessarily) large number of
  objects
hold everything! = stop everything (you are doing)!
  See also: everything comes to he/him who **waits**.

evil
put off the evil hour/moment = postpone something unpleasant
  See also: fall on evil **days**; give somebody the evil **eye**.

example
make an example of somebody = reprimand/punish somebody as a
  deterrent to others
set somebody a (good) example = behave in a way that encourages
  others to copy

exception
take exception to = be offended by/object to
the exception that proves the rule = a general principle is not proved
  to be invalid if it cannot be applied to a particular instance

exchange
exchange words = argue/quarrel
(fair) exchange is no robbery = nobody loses if things exchanged have the same value

excuse
lame excuse = unconvincing reason

exercise
exercise one's power = use one's authority
object of the exercise = aim/purpose

exhibition
make an exhibition of oneself = behave in a (very) foolish manner

expect
be expecting = pregnant
expect me when you see me = be unable/unwilling to specify when one will be somewhere

expense
at one's/somebody's expense = to one's/somebody's disadvantage
at the expense of = by causing harm to
go to the expense of = spend money (to impress/achieve something)
put somebody to expense = cause somebody to spend money
See also: **blow** the expense.

explain
explain away = give a satisfactory excuse

explore
See: explore every **avenue**.

expression
holier-than-thou expression = facial expression that is self- satisfied, smug, superior

extent
to a certain extent, to a considerable/large extent = partly, mostly

extreme
go to extremes = do more than is necessary
go to the other extreme = take an opposite view/course of action

eye
all eyes = very attentive
before one's (very) eyes = in one's direct vision
black eye = bruising of the eye socket caused by a blow to the eye
cast/run an eye over = look at quickly/superficially
clap/set eyes on = see/notice
cock an eye at = give a knowing glance
eye for an eye = take revenge by doing to an enemy what he/she did
  to you
eye-opener = revelation
eye somebody (up and down) = view somebody with doubt/suspicion
eye-wash = nonsense
get one's eye/hand in = become familiar with a situation
give somebody the evil eye = give somebody a threatening/malicious
  look
give somebody the glad eye = flirt with somebody
have a (good) eye for = be a good judge of something's qualities
have/keep an eye on the main chance = take a mercenary view/be
  alert for ways of turning things to one's own advantage
have a roving eye = habitually look at (and try to form associations
  with) attractive women
have/keep an eye on = keep a close watch on
have eyes bigger than one's belly/stomach = greedy
have eyes in the back of one's head = be aware of something that one
  should apparently not know about
have one's eye on = notice/take a liking to
have one's eyes about one = be alert/watchful
in one's mind's eye = in one's imagination
in the eyes of = from the point of view of (the church/law etc.)
in the public eye = famous/well-known, subject to public scrutiny
keep an eye open/out for = watch out for
keep a weather eye open = be alert for any changes
keep one's eye in = remain in form/practice
keep one's eyes open/peeled/skinned = remain alert
make (sheep's) eyes at = flirt/make appealing glances at
meet somebody's eyes = look at somebody face to face
more than meets the eye = more than is immediately obvious
naked eye = unaided vision (without the use of an optical instrument)

not to be able to take one's eyes off somebody/something = be unable to stop looking at somebody/something

not to believe one's eyes = doubt the credibility of something unusual

one in the eye for = a come-down/rejection

out of the corner of one's eye = at the edge of one's vision

private eye = private detective

pull the wool over somebody's eyes = deceive somebody

score/hit a bull's eye = achieve sudden success

see eye to eye = agree/share the same point of view

see with (only) half an eye = notice something that is obvious

see with one's own eyes = witness personally

sight for sore eyes = pleasant surprise

through the eyes of = from somebody else's viewpoint

turn a blind eye to = deliberately ignore/pretend not to see

up to one's eyes = very busy

view with a beady eye = observe with caution

with an eye to = with an eventual aim

with one's eyes open = fully aware of the likely consequences

with one's eyes closed/shut = very easily

worm's eye view = very low viewpoint

See also: **apple** of one's eye; **bird**'s eye view; **catch** somebody's eye; **cry** one's eyes/heart out; **eagle** eye; **easy** on the eye; eye **witness**; **hawk**-eyed; in the **blink** of an eye; in/a **twinkling** of an eye; keep one's **eye** on the **ball**; **lynx**-eyed; **open** one's eyes to; remove the **scales** from somebody's eyes; **shut** one's eyes to; smack in the eye; throw **dust** in somebody's eyes; **twinkle** in somebody's eye.

eyeball
eyeball to eyeball = in direct conflict

eyebrow
raise one's eyebrows = be mildly shocked/surprised

eyelid
not bat an eyelid = be impassive/show no reaction

F

face
blow up in somebody's face = be violently changed/ended
face down = with the front or upper surface downwards
face (the) facts = acknowledge the truth
face it out = maintain a falsehood
face the music = submit to discipline/punishment
face to face = in the presence of, or person to person
face up = with the front or upper surface upwards
face up to = accept (a challenge) without weakening
face out = defy/refuse to admit a mistake
face value = apparent worth
face with = confront
fall flat on one's face = make a blunder
fly in the face of = vigorously oppose
give something a face-lift = improve the (outward) appearance of
  something
have a red face = be embarrassed
have the face to = be bold enough to
his/her face fell = he/she expressed disappointment
in the face of = when confronted by
keep a straight face = not show one's feelings (especially when
  amused)
let's face it = let us be honest
long face = gloomy/miserable expression
look somebody in the face = look unflinchingly at somebody
look/stare one in the face = be very obvious
lose face = lose respect
make faces = grimace
not just a pretty face = somebody who is more intelligent than it
  might appear
one's face is one's fortune = one's good looks are one's chief
  advantage
on the face of it = apparently/based on the available evidence
poker/straight face = expression that reveals no emotion

put a brave/bold/good face (up)on it = remain outwardly cheerful in adversity

put a new face on it = alter the situation

put one's face on = apply make-up

save face = retain respect

set one's face against = refuse to accept

show one's face = attend/be present only briefly

shut your face = shut up/be quiet

staring one in the face = very obvious

throw something in somebody's face = forcibly remind somebody of something (disadvantageous to him/her) that he/she would rather forget

till one is blue in the face = endlessly

to one's face = honestly/openly

See also: bare-faced **lie**; **blue** in the face; have a face like a **fiddle**; have/pull a **long** face; have **egg** on one's face; **laugh** in somebody's face; plain as the **nose** on your face; **pull** a face; shut/slam the **door** in somebody's face; was my face **red!**; **wipe** the grin/smile off somebody's face.

fact

facts of life = knowledge of sex, or truth of a situation

facts and figures = data, statistics, and so on

hard facts = undeniable truth

in (actual) fact = actually/in truth

See also: as a **matter** of fact; **face** the facts; **matter** of fact; **matter**-of-fact.

fag

fag end = last part/remnant

fagged out = exhausted

too much fag = too much trouble

fail

failing that = if that does not apply/happen

without fail = for certain

See also: **words** fail me.

failure

(nearly) have heart failure = be very surprised

faint

have not the faintest idea = have no knowledge of whatsoever
  See also: **damn** with faint praise.

fair

all's fair in love and war = vigorous competition is acceptable in
  emotionally-charged situations
fair and square = honest(ly), or exactly on target
fair copy = good likeness, or clean/uncorrected version of a text
fair do's = be fair
fair enough = accepted/agreed
(by) fair means or foul = (by) any method, honest or not
fair sex = women
fair's fair = be fair/honest
fair to middling = average, not good and not bad
go a fair way towards = be nearly enough
  See also: **bid** fair; fair **cop**; fair **deal**; fair **game**; fair-weather **friend**;
  play fair.

fairy

fairy godmother = benefactor
  See also: **airy-fairy**.

faith

bad faith = lack of trust
breach of faith = broken promise
in bad faith = dishonestly
in (all) good faith = honestly (but often with a problematic outcome)
pin one's faith on/put one's faith in = rely (completely) on
shake one's faith = undermine one's beliefs
shatter one's faith = destroy one's beliefs
  See also: **article** of faith.

fall

easy as falling off a log = very easy
fall about (laughing) = laugh uncontrollably
fall astern/behind = get/lag behind
fall away/off = decline
fall back = retreat
fall back on/upon = resort to

fall between two stools = fail to meet either of two requirements (because of a reluctance to commit to one of them)
fall by the wayside = fail to complete something
fall flat = fail to interest/succeed
fall for = become in love with
fall/run foul of = quarrel with
fall into arrears = get behind with payments owed
fall into place = become clear/understandable
fall into line/step = agree with
fall in with = adopt/comply with (something already existing)
fall on/upon = come across, or attack/seize
fall on bad times = become impoverished
fall on deaf ears/on stony ground = be (deliberately) ignored
fall on one's feet = be very lucky (to survive a risk)
fall out = cease to be friends/disagree
fall over backwards = make every effort to do something
fall over oneself = be overeager to please
fall short = fail to meet a specified amount/quantity/standard
fall through = fail to happen
fall to one's lot = become one's duty/responsibility
fall under = be included in/with
fall upon somebody's neck = fawn, be obsequious
fall within = lie between
ride for a fall = take a course that is likely to lead to disaster
See also: come/fall apart at the **seams**; fall flat on one's **face**; fall from **grace**; fall **guy**; fall into the **habit**; fall **off**; fall off the back of a **lorry**; fall **sick**; fall to **pieces**; his/her **face** fell.

false
false pretences = deliberate deception
false start = beginning that falters and has to be repeated
false step = misdemeanour/mistake
strike a false note = appear not to be genuine
See also: false **alarm**; put a false **construction** on.

familiarity
See: familiarity breeds **contempt**.

family

family feud = long-standing family quarrel

family tree = ancestry/genealogy

in the family way = pregnant

person of (some) family = somebody who is high born

run in the family = be an inherited characteristic

  See also: family **doctor**; family **man**.

fan

fan the flames = make a difficulty even worse

fancy

catch/take/tickle somebody's fancy = stimulate somebody's desire
  for/interest in something

footloose and fancy free = carefree, with no responsibilities

fancy boy/man = (male) lover

fancy one's chances = be (over)confident

fancy oneself = be conceited

fancy price = overexpensive

fancy somebody = be sexually attracted to somebody

fancy that! = I am surprised!

fancy woman = (female) lover

just fancy! = just imagine!

take a fancy to = take a liking to

  See also: **flight** of fancy.

Fanny

(sweet) Fanny Adams = nothing at all

far

as far as in one lies = as much as one is able

as/so far as one can tell = apparently

by far/far and away = absolutely/without equal

far and near/wide = over a large area

far be it from me = presumptuous and self-denigrating remark

far-fetched = exaggerated/lacking credibility

far-flung = distant

far from/not far from = distant/close

far from it = by no means/not at all

far gone = in need of repair (of a thing), or not totally conscious through drink/drugs (of a person)

go far = be successful (in one's career)

go too far = be excessive in one's behaviour/be impolite

so far, so good = up to this point everything is satisfactory (although it may not continue to be so)

See also: far **cry** from; far **out**; **few** and far between.

fare

bill of fare = menu, or list of things available/to be done

farm

farm out = make something somebody else's responsibility, to subcontract

farthing

not give a brass farthing = not care (in the slightest)

fashion

after a fashion = in an approximate sort of a way (intended as a veiled criticism)

all the fashion = (very) popular

See also: all ship-shape and **Bristol** fashion; **like** it's going out of fashion.

fast

fast and furious = quick(ly) and vigorous(ly)

not so fast = wait a minute

play fast and loose = deceitfully/selfishly change one's attitudes

pull a fast one = cheat/deceive

stand fast = remain still, unmoving/unyielding

See also: **make** fast.

fasten

fasten on to = grasp

fasten your seat belts! = hold on!/be prepared for a (pleasant) surprise

fat

fat chance = very unlikely

fat lot of = very little

live off the fat of the land = live in luxury
the fat is in the fire = an action has caused trouble
   See also: **chew** the fat; kill the fatted **calf**.

fate

as sure as fate = inevitably
fate worse than death = something that is most undesirable, or (of a
   woman) unwilling participation in sex
seal somebody's fate = guarantee future unpleasantness for somebody
tempt fate = take a risk

father

father and mother of = extreme version of
father figure = man regarded with affection/respect, as a child might
   show to a father
like father, like son = people usually behave like their parents
his father's son = resembles his father
how's your father = improper (often sexual) activity
on the father's side = inherited through the father
the father of = founder/inventor
when father turns, we all turn = father is the absolute authority in
   our family
   See also: **mother** and father of.

fault

fault on the right side = flaw which is to somebody's credit, not
   discredit
find fault with = be (over)critical of
to a fault = to excess

favour

do me/us a favour! = you cannot expect me to believe that!
find favour = receive approval
in high favour = well thought of
in somebody's favour = to somebody's advantage
   See also: **curry** favour.

fear

for fear of = in case
in fear (and trembling) = very apprehensive(ly)/anxious(ly)

never fear = do not worry
no fear! = no I will not!
put the fear of God into = frighten/terrify
there's not much fear of = it is extremely unlikely that (something will happen)
without fear or favour = in a totally fair/unbiased manner

feast

enough is as good as a feast = sufficient is as good as a large amount/quantity
feast one's eyes on = enjoy looking at

feather

be spitting feathers = be very angry/thirsty
feather bed = spoil/cosset
feather-brained = impractical/lacking in common sense
feathered friends = birds
feather in one's cap = attainment/honour
feather one's nest = selfishly (and possibly dishonestly) further one's own interests
in fine feather = happy/healthy
make the feathers fly = provoke a fierce struggle
show the white feather = display cowardice
smooth somebody's (ruffled) feathers = calm somebody down
you could have knocked me down with a feather = I was taken totally by surprise
See also: **birds** of a feather; **ruffle** somebody's feathers.

fed

fed up (to the back teeth) = (very) bored/tired

feed

See: **chicken** feed.

feel

feel for = have (great) sympathy for
feel free = do not hesitate/do as you please
feel like = experience emotionally
feel out of it = feel excluded from something
feel the draught/pinch = experience difficulty (because of lack of money)

feel up to it = be inclined/well enough to do something
get the feel of = become accustomed to
not to feel oneself = to feel unwell
   See also: feel at **home**; feel in one's **bones**; feel/look **blue**;
feel **small**.

feeler
put out feelers = make (discreet) enquiries

feeling
cause/create bad feelings = offend
feeling for somebody = affection for somebody
feeling for something = aptitude for/be in sympathy with something
fellow-feeling = sympathy
get the feeling that = come to the conclusion that, or feel
have mixed feelings about = be ambivalent/have neither good nor
   bad feelings about
I know the feeling = I think/have experienced the same thing
no hard feelings = no offence/no feeling of bitterness
play on somebody's feelings = deliberately manipulate somebody's
   emotions
sinking feeling = feeling of (great) apprehension
vent one's feelings on = release anger/frustration (caused by one
   thing) by attacking something else
   See also: **Monday** morning feeling.

feet
at somebody's feet = under somebody's influence (because of his/her
   attractiveness/talent, etc.)
cut the ground from under somebody's feet = nullify somebody's
   argument/effectiveness
drag one's feet = move slowly
feet first/foremost = dead/unconscious
find one's feet = become accustomed to a new situation
get back on one's feet = return to normal health after an illness, or
   return to prosperity after being in debt
get cold feet = go back on a commitment because of fear/nervousness
have both feet on the ground/keep one's feet on the ground = take a
   practical/realistic view

have one's feet under the desk/table = be settled in a job/somebody else's family

have the world at one's feet = be well-placed to succeed

have two left feet = be inept at anything requiring skilled footwork

keep one's feet = maintain one's balance/upright posture

not let the grass grow under one's feet = waste no time

on one's feet = standing

put one's feet up/take the weight off one's feet = take a rest (by lying/sitting down)

run/rushed off one's feet = very busy

set somebody on his/her feet = provide help in getting somebody established

sit at somebody's feet = remain with an expert/master in order to learn

stand on one's own (two) feet = be independent

sweep somebody off his/her feet = make a very favourable impression, or make somebody fall in love with one

think on one's feet = be mentally agile/think quickly

throw oneself at somebody's feet = ask in a very humble manner/beg for mercy

under one's feet = in one's way

vote with one's feet = move elsewhere to register disapproval

walk off one's feet = tire by excessive walking

with one's feet up = inactive/resting

See also: **foot**; **crow**'s feet; **fall** on one's feet; feet of **clay**; have the **ball** at one's feet; **land** on one's feet; shake the **dust** from one's feet.

fell

at one fell swoop = very quickly/all at once

fellow

hail-fellow-well-met = very (and often insincerely) friendly

See also: fellow-**feeling**.

fellowship

extend the hand of fellowship = wish to make friends

fence

rush one's fences = act carelessly and quickly

right/wrong side of the fence = socially acceptable/unacceptable *sit on the fence* = be undecided/hedge

fend
fend for oneself = look after/provide for oneself

ferret
ferret out = (deviously) seek

fetch
fetch and carry = perform menial tasks for somebody
fetch up at = arrive

fettle
in fine fettle = in good health (mentally and/or physically)

fever
at fever pitch = very excited

few
a few too many = too much to drink
a good few = many
few and far between = extremely rare
have a few = have several (too many) drinks
  See also: a man/somebody of few **word**s; **precious** few/little; **quite** a
  few.

fiddle
be on the fiddle/work a fiddle = do something dishonest for gain
fiddle about = spend time on trifles/mess about
fiddle while Rome burns = be inactive during an emergency/while
  something significant is happening
fit as a fiddle = extremely fit
have a face like a fiddle = be visibly miserable/unhappy
play second fiddle = take a minor/secondary role
up and down like a fiddler's elbow = move repeatedly (and often
  ineffectively)

field
back/play the field = take advantage of every available opportunity
have a field day = derive great pleasure from doing something
field of view/vision = range of sight

take the field = enter a place of competition/contest
  See also: **play** the field.

fiend
fresh-air fiend = somebody who (sometimes antisocially) insists on
  having windows open/taking long walks in the open air

fifty
go fifty-fifty with = share (the cost) equally

fig
not care/give a fig = not care at all
not worth a fig = worthless

fight
fight it out = continue a (not necessarily physical) contest until there
  is a clear winner
fight like cat and dog = quarrel repeatedly and vigorously
fight shy of = avoid/be reluctant to
fight to a standstill = engage in combat/a contest until one is totally
  exhausted
knock/take the fight out of somebody = reduce somebody's
  aggressiveness or will to survive/win
look/spoil for a fight = actively seek an argument/challenge
plenty of fight left in one = with plenty of reserves of energy
put up a good fight = react well to a challenge
running fight = contest that continues for a long time
show fight = react aggressively to a challenge
three-cornered fight = contest between three opponents
  See also: **dog** fight; fight **tooth** and nail; live like fighting **cocks**.

fighting
hand-to-hand fighting = combat not involving weapons
  See also: fighting/sporting **chance**; fighting **fit**; live like fighting
  cocks.

figment
figment of one's imagination = something that is totally imaginary

figure
cut a good/pretty or a poor/sorry figure = make a good/bad
  impression

figurehead = somebody with a high position but no real authority
figure of eight = pattern in the shape of the figure eight
figure of fun = somebody who is ridiculed
figure of speech = usage of words (such as idiom and metaphor)
   which gives them a recognized, but non-literal, meaning
figure out = calculate, resolve a problem
in round figures = approximately, to the nearest round number
that figures! = that is what I would have expected/thought
   See also: **ballpark** figure; **facts** and figures; **father** figure.

file
in Indian file = in a line, one behind the other
rank and file = ordinary people

fill
drink (take) one's fill = drink as much as one wants
fill an office = take up an (official) appointment
fill in for = deputize for
fill out = become fatter
fill somebody in = provide somebody with missing information
fill somebody's shoes = take over somebody else's job/role
   See also: fill the **bill**.

filthy
filthy lucre = money
filthy rich = very wealthy

final
final touch = last contribution (to complete something to perfection)
   See also: have the final/last **word**.

find
find fault with = discover a flaw in
find guilty = convict
find oneself = be (at/in a particular place/situation)
find out = make a conscious effort to discover something
find something heavy going = have difficulty doing something
take us as you find us = accept us as we are if you arrive unexpectedly
   See also: find/get one's **bearings**; find it in one's **heart**; find one's
tongue.

fine

(draw a) fine distinction = (indicate) a slight difference

fine and dandy = satisfactory

get something down to a fine art = be very proficient at something

not to put too fine a point on it = to be candid/frank

one of these fine days = one day soon

finger

at one's fingertips = well within one's competence/knowledge

all fingers and thumbs = clumsy

burn one's fingers/get one's fingers burnt = suffer (as a result of poor judgement)

can count on the fingers of one hand = there are very few

crook one's little finger/snap one's fingers = demand/get attention

green fingers = skill at gardening

hang on by one's fingernails = make a desperate effort to retain something

have a finger in = have an interest in

have a finger in every pie = be simultaneously involved in many activities

have itchy fingers = be very eager

have light/sticky fingers = have a reputation as a thief

have more (of something) in one's little finger than somebody else has in his/her whole body = be much better than somebody else

keep one's fingers crossed = wish for good fortune

keep one's finger(s) on the pulse = remain informed about something

lay a finger on somebody = harm somebody (usually physically)

lift/stir a finger = make an effort to do something

point the finger at = accuse/blame

pull/take one's finger out = stir from complacency/inactivity (and do something)

put one's finger on = identify

put the finger on = inform on somebody to the police

slip through one's fingers = miss an opportunity

twist somebody round one's little finger = get somebody to do anything one wishes

work one's fingers to the bone = work very hard

See also: **catch** somebody with his/her fingers/hand in the till; **snap** one's fingers at.

finish

finish with someone = end an association/friendship
See also: finishing **touches.**

fire

baptism of fire = unpleasant first experience of something
between two fires = being attacked from both/two directions
catch/take fire = begin to burn
fire away = begin
fire bug = arsonist
fire up = become angry and indignant
go through fire and water = tackle any difficulty (to do something)
hang fire = be delayed
have several irons in the fire = be involved with several activities
  (simultaneously)
in the line of fire = at risk because one is between two opposing
  forces
jump out of the frying pan into the fire = move from one difficulty to
  an even worse one
like a house on fire = very quickly/well
play with fire = take an extreme (and unnecessary) risk
pull the chestnuts out of the fire = rescue somebody from a difficult
  situation
set the Thames on fire = cause a sensation
spread like wild fire = spread rapidly
there's no smoke without fire = a rumour is usually based, however
  remotely, on fact
under fire = being criticised/held responsible
See also: **ball** of fire; **baptism** of fire; **draw** somebody's fire; firing on
all **cylinders**; **open** fire; the **fat** is in the fire.

first

at first hand = directly from the source
at first sight = as seen initially (without any detailed examination)
first and foremost = before any other consideration
first and last/from first to last = completely

first class = best/excellent
first come, first served = precedence will be given to the first arrival(s)
first light = dawn
first-night nerves = nervousness felt before doing something for the
   first time
first off = before something else
first thing = as early as possible in the day
first things first = put things in their correct order of priority
get a first = win first prize, or be awarded a first-class degree at a
   university
in the first place = initially/to begin with
of the first magnitude/order/water = of the best quality
   See also: at the first **blush**; first **blood**; not **know** the first thing
   about.

fish

big fish = somebody important
big fish in a small pond = somebody who is important only among a
   small group
cold fish = somebody who is unemotional/unsympathetic
feed the fishes = drown
fish for compliments = seek praise
fish in troubled waters = interfere/get involved in an unpleasant
   situation
have other fish to fry = have alternative/more important matters to
   attend to
like a fish out of water = lacking experience and thus ill-at-ease
neither fish nor fowl = neither one thing nor the other
(fine/pretty) kettle of fish = confused/difficult situation
queer fish = somebody who is eccentric/strange
small fish = somebody who is relatively unimportant
smell something fishy = be suspicious
there are plenty more fish in the sea = there are numerous other
   people to meet
   See also: **cry** stinking fish; **drink** like a fish.

fist

iron fist = firmness, or harsh discipline

mailed fist = military power
See also: **hand** over fist; **shake** one's fist.

fit
fighting fit = in the peak of health
fit in with = be accommodating/comply with
fit like a glove = fit snugly/perfectly
fit of nerves = short period of anxiety/nervousness
fit the bill = meet the requirement
fit to bust = excessively/very much
fit to drop = exhausted
fit to wake the dead = very loud
fit up/out = do/make/supply something to meet a requirement
have/throw a fit = be angry/excited
in fits and starts = intermittently/spasmodically
not fit to hold a candle to = very inferior to
see/think fit = consider sensible/wise

fix
fix on = decide
fix up = arrange for
in a fix = in difficulty

flag
flag down = stop (a vehicle)
flag of convenience = foreign flag of registry of a ship (used as a
  method of tax avoidance)
hang/put the flags out = celebrate
hoist/show/wave the white flag = surrender
keep the flag flying = (work to) maintain the existing situation
show the flag = demonstrate (and defend) one's position

flake
flaked out = exhausted

flame
add fuel to/fan the flames = make a difficulty even worse
old flame = ex-boyfriend or ex-girlfriend
shoot down in flames = discomfit/destroy
  See also: **fan** the flames.

flare
flare up = break out/erupt

flash
flash in the pan = something that is short-lived/unique
in a flash = in a moment
quick as a flash = very quickly

flat
be caught flat-footed = caught unprepared/taken by surprise
fall flat = fail
flat as a flounder/pancake = completely flat
flat broke = having no money
flat denial = complete denial/refusal
flat out = at maximum speed, or asleep/unconscious
flat spin = panic/state of great agitation
that's flat! = that is my final word!

flatter
don't flatter yourself! = don't think so well of yourself!

flea
(mere) flea bite = insignificant amount/quantity
flea market = place that sells only second-hand articles
flea pit = run-down cinema or theatre
sent somebody off/away with a flea in his/her ear = dismiss
  somebody after a rebuff/scolding

flesh
flesh out = expand/extend
have/get one's pound of flesh = be determined to obtain one's total
  entitlement
in the flesh = in person
more than flesh and blood can stand = beyond human endurance
neither flesh/fish/fowl/nor good red herring = neither one thing nor
  the other
one's own flesh and blood = one's family
thorn in one's flesh = persistent source of irritation
  See also: **goose** flesh/pimples; **go** the way of all flesh; make one's
  flesh **creep**.

flies
See: **fly**.

flight
flight of fancy = a dream/imaginary situation
in the first/top flight = among the leaders
put somebody to flight = make somebody run away
take flight = run away

fling
fling oneself at somebody = make an obvious and strenuous attempt to gain somebody's affections/attention
have one's fling = (take a final opportunity to) do as one pleases

flip
flip through = look at in a casual way
flip over = change, or somersault

flit
See: do a **moonlight** (flit).

float
float a company = raise the finance to launch a new company
float an idea = bring an idea to the notice of others

flock
like a flock of sheep = in an easily-led group, with no will of its own

flog
flog a dead horse = persist in doing something that cannot produce the desired result
flog (a topic) to death = persist in discussing something until everybody is bored with it

flood
flood tide = high tide/high water
before the Flood = a very long time ago
See also: **open** the flood gates.

floor
fall through the floor = be extremely surprised
get in on the ground floor = be in at the beginning of something

floor somebody = knock somebody down, or defeat in argument

shop floor = working environment of manual workers, or the workers themselves

sink through the floor = fall steeply and rapidly

sweep/wipe the floor with = defeat convincingly and easily

take the floor = stand up to speak, or begin to dance
  See also: **hold** the floor.

flower

flower people = people who advocate non-violence and oppose materialism/militarism

in the flower of one's youth = at one's physical best
  See also: (as) welcome as the flowers in May.

flutter

cause a flutter = cause excitement/a stir

flutter one's eyelashes at somebody = catch the attention of somebody of the opposite sex

have a flutter = make a (modest) bet

fly

couldn't/wouldn't hurt a fly = very feeble, or very gentle

fly a kite = release an idea/information in order to gauge people's opinions about it

fly at somebody = attack somebody (physically or verbally)

fly-by-night (operator) = operating for only a short time (and then doing so in an untrustworthy way)

fly in the ointment = something that mars/spoils something else

fly off at a tangent = digress

fly off the handle = burst into anger

fly on the wall = eavesdropper

let fly = harangue/scold severely

like flies = in very large numbers

make the fur/sparks fly = precipitate a fierce row

no flies on him/her = he/she is no fool

pigs might fly! = that is most unlikely!
  See also: as the **crow** flies; fly in the **face** of; fly the **coop**; **time** flies.

flying

flying feet = ability to run fast

flying high = (successfully) holding a position of importance/power
flying pickets = secondary pickets brought from elsewhere during a strike to supplement the local pickets
flying start = very good beginning
flying visit = very brief visit
send flying = knock over
with flying colours = with distinction/merit

foam
foam at the mouth = be very angry

fob
fob off = (try to) pass off a substitute for the thing required

fog
in a fog = confused (mentally)
not the foggiest (idea) = not an inkling

fold
fold up = collapse/close
return to the fold = go back to a group (after an absence)

follow
follow one's bent = do what one is best at/use an inborn ability
follow one's nose = go directly ahead
follow one's own devices = improvise
follow suit = copy/do the same as somebody else
follow the dictates of one's heart = do what one instinctively wants to
follow up = take action using information provided/progress already made
follow-up = something that comes after something else/a sequel
See also: follow/tread in somebody's **footsteps**.

food
food for thought = something worthy of careful consideration
off one's food = lacking an appetite

fool
fool around = behave in a foolish way, or have an affair with
fool for one's pains = somebody whose effort/help is rewarded by ingratitude

fool's errand = pointless task

fool's gold = iron pyrites (an ore of iron that outwardly resembles gold)

fool's paradise = illusory happiness

fools rush in (where angels fear to tread) = people take action without thinking through the consequences

make a fool of somebody = make somebody look foolish

more fool you = you behaved foolishly

nobody's fool = somebody who does not lack common sense/intellect

play/act the fool = behave in a foolish manner

not suffer fools gladly = be intolerant with people who lack common sense/are slow to learn

See also: **April** fool.

foot

catch somebody on the wrong foot = catch somebody off balance

follow/tread in somebody's footsteps = do the same as one's predecessor

foot the bill = pay for something

gain a foothold = gain possession of small part of something

get/have a foot in the door = gain acceptance/admission to an organization etc.

get/start off on the right/wrong foot = begin well/badly

have a foot in both camps = deal with both parties in a dispute

keep/miss one's footing = remain upright/stumble

my foot! = certainly not!

not put a foot wrong = never make a mistake

on a firm footing = on a secure basis

on a friendly footing = in a friendly way

one foot in the grave = very ill/old

on foot = walking

put one's best foot forward = begin to do something purposefully

put one's foot down = insist

put one's foot in it = unintentionally do or say something distressing/insulting

set foot on = go somewhere (for the first time)

stamp one's foot = display anger

See also: **feet**; have a foot in the **door**; **tread** under foot; wait on somebody **hand** and foot.

football
political football = issue that is an object of contention between political parties

for
for all one is worth = with the utmost effort
for it = due for a scolding
for what it is worth = if you think it worth anything
  See also: **but** for; for **effect**; for **show**.

forbid
forbidden fruit = unattainable desire
God forbid = I hope not

force
by force of circumstances = by circumstances out of one's control
come into force = take effect
driving force = somebody whose enthusiasm/influence stimulates others to act
force of habit = habitual
force one's way = attain something/reach somewhere by using force
force somebody's hand = compel somebody to do something
force the pace = (bring pressure to bear) to speed something up
join forces = combine with others for a common purpose
join the forces = enlist in military service
use brute force (and ignorance) = try to do something (in an unsubtle way) merely by using force

fore
come to the fore = become prominent

foreign
foreign body/substance = object that should not be present/impurity
on foreign soil = abroad

forget
forget it = never mind
forget oneself = behave in a disrespectful/ill-mannered way

forgive
forgive and forget = discount any previous disagreements/differences

fork
fork in the road = point/moment of decision
fork out = pay
  See also: **speak** with a forked tongue.

forlorn
forlorn hope = undertaking with very little chance of success

form
good/bad form = socially acceptable/unacceptable behaviour
in the form of = taking the appearance/shape of
matter of form = for the sake of convention
off form = not up to one's best
on form = at one's best
(run) true to form = (happen) as expected/predicted

formula
face-saving formula = scheme that prevents somebody from being
  criticized/embarrassed

fort
hold the fort = take care of something while the person responsible is
  absent

forth
hold forth = speak (pompously)

fortune
make a fortune = earn a lot of money
small fortune = a lot of money
soldier of fortune = a mercenary

forty
forty winks = nap/short sleep

forward
look forward to = anticipate with pleasure
  See also: not **backward** in coming forward.

foul
  See: **fall**/**run foul of**; foul one's (own) **nest**; foul **play**.

found
all/*everything found* = (of a job) including food and accommodation
  as well as pay

foundation
foundation garment = corset, roll-on or the like
shake somebody to the foundations = greatly frighten/surprise
  somebody

fountain
fountain head = origin/source

four
four-letter word = obscenity/swearword
four-square to = directly facing
make up a four = join three others to play cards/golf
make a foursome = combine to make four people
on all fours = on hands and knees/on four feet

fowl
dress a fowl = remove the entrails of poultry before cooking

fox
be foxed = be puzzled
cunning as a fox = very cunning
old/*sly fox* = somebody who is cunning
  See also: **run** with the fox/hare and hunt with the hounds.

frame
frame of mind = mental attitude
frame-up = arrest/conviction based on falsified evidence

fraught
fraught with danger = full of risk

fray
in the thick of the fray = at the centre of the action

free
free and easy = relaxed/unhampered by responsibilities

free as the air/wind/a bird = completely free
free-for-all = contest in which everyone has an equal chance of
  winning
free from/of = without
free, gratis and for nothing = totally free
free hand = unrestricted authority to act
free-hand = made without the aid of drawing instruments
free-lance = somebody who is employed for a particular task and not
  as a regular member of the workforce
free translation = approximate interpretation
make free with = make use of somebody else's property
scot free = completely free
set free = release
  See also: **feel** free; give (free) **rein** to.

French
pardon my French = forgive my bad language
take French leave = abscond/go away without permission
  See also: French **letter**.

fresh
fresh as a daisy/fresh as (new) paint = very fresh
  See also: fresh-air **fiend**.

Friday
girl/man Friday = general assistant/helpmate

friend
bosom friend = close friend
fair-weather friend = somebody who is friendly only when one is
  having good fortune
friend at court = associate in a position of importance/power
make friends with = become (closely) acquainted with
our dumb friends = animals
we're just good friends = we have no sexual involvement
your friend and mine = somebody we all/both know and like
  See also: **feathered** friends.

frills
without frills = plain/unelaborate

fringe
lunatic fringe = people with an extreme point of view

frog
frog in the throat = hoarseness
frog-march = manhandle somebody by grabbing his collar and the seat of his trousers

front
in front of = in somebody's hearing
  See also: front **man**.

frown
frown on = disapprove of

fruit
bear fruit = produce (good) results
  See also: **forbidden** fruit.

fry
small fry = somebody who is insignificant

full
be full of oneself = boastful/conceited
in full = complete(ly)
know full well = definitely know
in the fullness of time = eventually
  See also: full **house**; full **steam** ahead; (at) full **tilt**; have one's **hands** full.

fun
for the fun of it = for amusement
fun and games = amusement
like fun = very quickly/vigorously
make fun of/poke fun at = cruelly derive amusement from/ridicule
  See also: **figure** of fun.

funeral
that's your funeral! = you must take the consequences!

funk
in a blue funk = very afraid/terrified

funny
funny business = deceit/trickery, or sexual activity

furniture
part of the furniture = somebody who is unnoticed (because he/she is nearly always present)

fury
like fury = very quickly/vigorously

fuss
make a fuss = complain
make a fuss of = be overattentive/spoil

future
in future = from now on
in the future = some time yet to come

G

gab
gift of the gab = ability to talk convincingly and easily

gaff
blow the gaff = inform (on somebody to the authorities)/reveal a
  (guilty) secret

gall
gall and wormwood = reason for bitterness
have the gall to = have the cheek/impudence to
  See also: **bitter** as gall.

gallery
play to the gallery = show off to gain popularity
  See also: **rogue**'s gallery.

gambit
opening gambit = opening move (seeking an advantage)

game
beat/play somebody at his own game = compete successfully with
  somebody in their own area of expertise
deep game = secret/devious ploy
dirty game = activity in which people do not always act in an
  honest/moral way
fair game = somebody/something that may be justifiably attacked
game of chance = gambling game (usually a card game played for
  money)
game, set and match = total defeat
game to the end = continuing to try (even in adversity) until one can
  continue no more
give the game/show away = inadvertently reveal a secret
know what somebody's game is = discover what somebody's
  (devious) intentions are
losing game = activity which one cannot succeed at
mug's game = activity which only a fool would expect to succeed at

name of the game = crucial/important factor

off/on one's game = not performing/performing at one's best

on the game = earning money as a prostitute

play a waiting game = delay making a commitment until the situation is more advantageous

play the game = behave in an honourable way

put somebody off his game = distract somebody while playing a game

so that's your game = so that is what your intention is

the game is not worth the candle = the result is not worth the effort needed to achieve it

the game is up = you are discovered (committing a crime/deception)

two can play at that game = I can also be as deceitful/unpleasant/etc. (as somebody else)

what's the game? = what is going on?

what's your game? = what are you doing?

winning game = game in a series that decides the overall result/winner

gang

gang bang = multiple rape

gang up on somebody = combine to harm somebody

press-gang somebody = force somebody to do something (against his/her wishes)

garden

bear garden = noisy and chaotic gathering

everything in the garden is lovely = everything is satisfactory

(lead somebody) up the garden path = deceive somebody

gasp

at/on/with one's last gasp = at the point at which one must finish (because of exhaustion or death)

gate

gate-crash = attend a party uninvited

like a bull at a gate = in a clumsy/impetuous way

See also: **open** the flood gates.

gate-post

between you, me and the gate-post = confidentially

gauntlet
run the gauntlet = be exposed to criticism/danger/etc.
throw/fling down the gauntlet = issue a challenge
take up the gauntlet = accept a challenge

gen
gen up on = (fully) inform oneself about

gentle
the gentle sex = women
gentle as a dove = very gentle/tender

gentleman
gentleman's agreement = unwritten agreement kept to because of the integrity of the parties concerned

get
be getting on for = approaching/close to
get about = move/travel
get ahead = succeed (in one's career)
get a load of something = look at something (expressing approval/surprise)
get along with you!/get away (with you!) = you don't say! (= I can hardly believe what you are telling me)
get a move on = hurry up
get at somebody = provoke/needle somebody
get at something = tamper with something
get away from it all = remove oneself from the pressures of everyday life
get away with = not to be caught out (in a crime/deception/mistake)
get by = (just) manage
get cracking/going/weaving = begin doing something (vigorously/with a will)
get down to it = tackle a task in earnest, or reduce something to basics
get even with = take revenge on
get hold of = grasp/obtain somebody/something, or contact somebody
get into = become interested in
get it = understand

get it in the neck = be punished/scolded
get lost! = go away!
get off = avoid a reprimand/punishment
get off to a bad/good start = begin promisingly/unpromisingly
get off with somebody = form a (sexual) relationship with somebody
get on = succeed (in one's career)
get oneself up = dress extravagantly/formally
get one's eye in = attain one's standard of ability
get one's own back = take revenge
get on one's bike = go away
get on one's high horse = take offence (because of hurt pride)
get on with somebody = have a friendly relationship with somebody
get on with something = (start to) do something
get on with you! = I don't believe you! (jokingly)
get out of hand = become out of control
get out of something = avoid blame/a duty/punishment, etc.
get over = recover
get rid of = dispose of
get round = cajole/persuade
get round to = find time to
get something across/over = communicate information/make
  something understood
get something going = begin an undertaking, or start a machine
get the better of = defeat
get the wind up = become afraid
get the wrong end of the stick = misunderstand/miss the point
get through to = make contact with
getting at = insinuating/meaning
get together = meet
get up to = do (in the sense make mischief)
get under somebody's skin/get up somebody's nose = annoy/irritate
  somebody
get well oiled = become drunk
get wind of = hear about
how are you getting on? = how are things progressing/prospering?
tell somebody where to get off = reprimand somebody
  See also: *don't get me* **wrong**; *get away with* **murder**; *get off
  somebody's* **back**; *get somebody's* **goat**.

ghost
ghost of a chance = little or no chance
ghost town = town that is abandoned/very quiet
give up the ghost = die
look like a ghost/as if one's seen a ghost = appear very pale

gift
think one is God's gift to = conceitedly (and mistakenly) believe that one is very highly regarded
   See also: gift of the **gab**.

gild
gild the lily = add unnecessary extra ornament to something that is already beautiful/ornamental

gilt
gilt-edged investment = reliable/safe investment
take the gilt off the gingerbread = remove the attractive part of something

ginger
ginger group = group of activists (within a larger organization)
ginger up = enliven

gird
gird up one's loins = prepare for action

girl
bachelor girl = unmarried woman
bunny girl = scantily-clad hostess at a night club
good-time girl = woman who very much likes to enjoy herself (and is not too concerned how she does it)
   See also: girl/man **Friday**.

give
don't give me that = do not expect me to believe that
give a bad/good account of oneself = perform badly/well
give and take = fair compromise (for mutual benefit)
give as good as one gets = be able to meet an attack with an equally effective counter-attack
give away = betray/reveal

give-away = incontrovertible evidence (of guilt)

give birth to = originate

give chase = chase

give in = surrender/yield

give it a miss = not do something

give it a rest/give it up = take a break from or stop doing something

give me (a) something = I like something best

give off = emit

give oneself away = (accidentally) reveal one's guilt

give oneself up = surrender

give or take = except for/approximately

give out = become exhausted

give rise to = generate/produce

give somebody away = hand over the bride in marriage, or reveal a secret about somebody

give somebody a wide berth = avoid somebody

give somebody/something a miss/the go-by = avoid

give somebody his/her head = allow somebody to do as he/she pleases, without restraint

give somebody what for = thoroughly castigate/punish somebody

give up = surrender, or yield

I give up! = I cannot guess what happens next, or exclamation of frustration

not to give a brass farthing/tuppenny damn = not to care

what gives? = what is happening?

See also: give a **dog** a bad name; give **ear** to; give **ground**; give in one's **notice**; give **notice**; give **place** to; give somebody a piece of one's **mind**; give somebody enough **rope**; give somebody the **elbow**; give somebody the evil **eye**; give somebody the glad **eye**; give somebody the **works**; give the game **away**; give **way** (to).

given

given to = inclined to

gizzard

something that sticks in one's gizzard = something that annoys one intensely

glad
be glad to see the back of somebody = be pleased when somebody leaves
glad rags = best clothes
See also: give somebody the glad **eye**.

glance
at first glance = at the first brief look
glance at/over = look briefly at

glass
glass jaw = weakness that makes a boxer very vulnerable to blows on the chin
people who live in glass houses (shouldn't throw stones) = critics should be wary of criticism
See also: **raise** one's glass to.

globe
four corners of the globe = throughout the world
globe trotters = regular international travellers

glory
glory hole = cupboard or small room containing discarded items
glory in = take pride/self-satisfaction in
in all one's glory = dressed in one's best/finery

gloss
gloss over = deliberately ignore/take only superficial notice of

glove
hand in glove with = in inseparable association with
iron hand/fist in a velvet glove = firmness concealed behind apparent gentleness
with kid gloves = with extreme gentleness
with the gloves off = earnestly and without mercy
See also: **fit** like a glove.

glutton
glutton for punishment = somebody who does not mind difficult/unpleasant tasks etc.

gnomes
gnomes of Zurich = Swiss bankers influential in the world money market

go
at one go = with only one attempt
be on the go = be active/busy
from the word go = from the beginning/start
go after/for = attack, or attempt to get/chase
go against the grain = oppose natural tendencies
go ahead = carry on/continue, or go before
go as you please = do as you wish
go at something bald-headed = do something impetuously
go a long way towards = approach closely to
go along with = agree/comply with
go back on = break (an agreement/promise)
go begging = be left over
go between = intermediary
go bust = become bankrupt/insolvent
go-by = action to avoid something
go by the board = be ignored
go downhill = decline/worsen
go down with = become ill with
go fifty-fifty/halves = share equally
go for a Burton = die/cease to be of any use
go for nothing = be given away (free)
go for somebody = attack somebody
go-getter = somebody who is ambitious/forceful at his/her job
go great guns = perform well
go in for = enter (a competition)/participate in
go into something = investigate something
go it alone = do something without outside help
go off = become bad
go off one's chump/head/rocker = go mad/lose all control (temporarily)
go off somebody = become less friendly with somebody
go off the deep end = become suddenly angry
go on = continue/proceed

go one better = outdo

go on the stage = become an actor/actress

go out of one's way = take extra trouble to do something

go over to the other side = change one's allegiance/loyalty

go over the ground = examine fundamental aspects of something

go phut = cease to function/work

go round = avoid/detour

go straight = be law-abiding (after having broken the law)

go through fire and water = overcome extreme difficulty/hardship (to achieve something)

go through the motions = pretend to do something (without actually doing it properly)

go through with = fulfil a commitment

go together = complement/match

go to one's head = make one become conceited/over-confident

go to pieces = lose control of one's behaviour/emotions

go to pot/to the dogs = deteriorate, or become disorganized/out of control

go to sea = enlist in the navy

go to sleep = become numb

go to the country = seek re-election (of a government)

go to the wall/go under = become bankrupt/insolvent

go to town = be extravagant/lavish

go to war = engage in warfare

go west = cease to exist/die

go with a bang = be a (spectacular) success

go without = have none

go without saying = be self-evident/need not be mentioned

have a go = make an attempt

here we go again = the same thing is happening again

make a go of something = do something successfully

it's no go = it cannot be done

  See also: go **Dutch**; go **easy** on somebody; go **easy** on/with something; going **concern**; go to **earth**; **here** goes; **there** you go.

goat

act/play the goat = behave foolishly

get somebody's goat = (severely) annoy somebody

sort out the sheep from the goats = determine what is useful/valuable from among what is not

God

by God!/good God! = exclamation of surprise

for God's/goodness' sake! = exclamation of annoyance/surprise

God forbid/please God = I hope it is not so/I hope it may never happen

God knows/goodness knows = nobody knows

honest to God! = in all truth!

little tin god = somebody with an inflated opinion of his/her own importance

in the lap of the gods = subject to chance/fate

put the fear of God into somebody = frighten somebody

the gods = uppermost balcony in a theatre

think one is God's gift to = have a conceited belief as to one's worth

ye gods! = exclamation of surprise

See also: **act** of God; **fairy** godmother; the **mills** of God grind slowly (but they grind exceedingly small).

goes

here goes = let us see what happens

how goes it (with you)? = what is happening (with you)?/what progress has been made?

that's how/the way it goes = these are the (usually unpleasant) circumstances

going

easy-going = friendly/undemanding

get going = begin/start

going concern = thriving business

going for = priced at/sold for

going strong = flourishing/thriving

hard/heavy going = difficult/hard work

how are things going?/how's it going? = general enquiry about what has been happening/what progress has been made

to be going on with = for the time being

while the going is good = while the opportunity exists

See also: **go**; have a **lot** going for one.

gold

as good as gold = very well behaved

gold-digger = young woman who forms an association with men
  merely to obtain money from them

gold mine = very profitable (retail) business

worth one's weight in gold = highly valued as an employee/member
  of a team, etc.
  See also: **crock** of gold; have a **heart** of gold; like gold **dust**.

golden

golden boy = talented young man who is expected to become
  successful

golden days = pleasant/prosperous time in the past

golden handshake = (large) payment made to an employee who leaves
  a job prematurely

golden opportunity = very favourable chance

golden rule = basic principle (which should always be adhered to)

golf

golf widow = wife who is often left alone while her husband is
  playing golf

gone

dead and gone = dead for some time

far gone = drugged/drunk (of somebody), or old/worn out (of
  something)

gone on somebody/something = very attracted to
  somebody/something
  See also: **go**.

good

a good job = fortunate

all in good time = eventually

all well and good = acceptable (but with nagging doubts)

as good as = equivalent to/very nearly

be so good as to = kindly/please

do somebody (a power of) good = improve somebody's
  behaviour/manner/health etc.

do somebody a good turn = be helpful to somebody

for good (and all) = for ever
for good measure = as an extra
good and ready = completely ready
good for nothing = worthless
good for you! = congratulation!
good gracious!/good grief! = exclamation of surprise
good Samaritan = somebody who takes much trouble to help others
good turn = favour
good while = long time
give as good as one gets = to be as effective as the other person in a contest
have a good time = enjoy oneself
in good time = with time to spare
in somebody's good books = favoured by somebody/well thought of
make good = repair damage, or succeed
make good time = do something in less time than expected
not good enough = not acceptable
on good terms = friendly
on to a good thing = in a favourable situation
put in a good word for = recommend
take in good part = accept cheerfully
that's a good one! = I do not believe you!
to the good = to an advantage/profit
up to no good = committing a crime/making mischief
  See also: as good as **gold**; good **egg**; good old **days**; in good **hands**; it's a good **thing**; my good **man**.

goodness
  See: for **God's**/goodness' sake; **God**/goodness knows

goods
deliver the goods = do something effectively/as promised
have the goods on somebody = know something incriminating about somebody
  See also: **black** goods/services.

goose
goose flesh/pimples = bumpy skin caused by cold or fear

kill the goose that lays the golden egg = destroy/spoil one's chief source of profit
say "boo" to a goose = frighten somebody
what is sauce for the goose is sauce for the gander = something that applies to one person should also apply to any other person
See also: **cook** somebody's goose; wild goose **chase**.

gooseberry
play gooseberry = be an unwanted third person with an (established) couple

gospel
take as gospel = believe to be absolutely true (without question)

got
have got to = must

grab
how does that grab you? = what do you think of that?
up for grabs = available to anyone

grace
day's grace = extra day (in which to pay a bill etc.)
fall from grace = lose favour
get into somebody's good graces = wheedle oneself into favour
grace and favour = describing something bestowed (free) by the monarch
grace note = in music, a short note that embellishes a note of a melody (usually played immediately before it)
grace with one's presence = attend (formal, or sarcastic)
saving grace = good quality among bad ones
with bad/good grace = unwillingly/willingly
See also: **airs** and graces.

gracious
See: **good** gracious!

grade
make the grade = attain a required standard

grain
See: **go** against the grain

grandmother
teach one's grandmother to suck eggs = inform somebody who is
  more knowledgeable than oneself

granted
take somebody for granted = assume somebody is content without
  asking him/her
take something for granted = assume something is true

grape
sour grapes = bitter feeling resulting from disappointment
through the grape-vine = a rumour

grasp
grasp the nettle = tackle a difficult/unpleasant task with
  determination

grass
grass on somebody = inform on somebody to the police/authorities
grass roots = ordinary but influential members of a
  group/organization
grass widow/widower = woman/man whose husband is away
let the grass grow under one's feet = procrastinate/waste time
put/send out to grass = make somebody retire (from work)
  See also: be (as) **green** as grass; not let the grass grow under one's
  feet; **snake** in the grass.

grate
  See: grate on the **ear**.

grave
dig one's own grave = be in difficulty because of one's own
  (misjudged) actions
goose/somebody walking over one's grave = feeling of uneasiness
  that causes one to shiver
make somebody turn in his/her grave = bad enough to anger
  somebody who is dead if he/she were still alive
  See also: have one **foot** in the grave; **silent** as the grave.

gravy
get on/join the gravy train = become wealthy

See also: **share** of the gravy.

grease
grease somebody's palm = bribe/tip somebody
grease the wheels = make things run smoothly
like greased lightning = very quickly
smell of the grease-paint = performing in a circus/theatre
  See also: **elbow** grease.

great
no great shakes = not much good
that's great! = that is excellent!
the great I am = person who thinks he/she is very important
  See also: go great **guns**; great **minds** think alike.

Greek
all Greek to me = too difficult to understand/unknown

green
be (as) green as grass = naive/inexperienced
green about the gills = looking as if one is about to vomit (because of
  excess drink, motion sickness, shock, etc.)
green-eyed monster = jealousy
green fingers = talent at gardening
green light = approval/permission to start, a go-ahead
not to be as green as one is cabbage-looking = not to be as stupid as
  one appears
  See also: green with **envy**.

grey
grey area = something that is imprecisely defined/known
grey-beard = elderly man
grey matter = brain/intellect

grief
come to grief = be damaged/destroyed, have an accident
  See also: **good** grief!

grievance
air a grievance = make known that one feels unfairly treated

nurse a grievance = retain a feeling of bitterness because of (supposed) unfair treatment

grill
grill somebody = interrogate somebody

grim
cling/hold on like grim death = hold something tenaciously

grin
grin and bear it = suffer without making a complaint
  See also: **wipe** the grin/smile off somebody's face.

grind
grind somebody down = oppress somebody
grind to a halt = gradually stop
keep one's nose to the grindstone = work long and hard
the daily grind = daily work
  See also: have an **axe** to grind; the **mills** of God grind slowly (but they grind exceeding small).

grip
come/get to grips with = deal with
get a grip on oneself = get oneself under control
in the grip of = in the control/power of
lose one's grip = lose control

grist
all grist to the mill = everything has some value

groove
be/get into/run in a groove = be in a routine/unchanging job or way of life

ground
break new ground = do/find something new
common ground = area of mutual experience/interest
cover a lot of/the ground = deal with a wide range of topics
down to the ground = appropriate/suitable for somebody
gain ground = advance/progress
get off the ground = initiate/put into action
give ground = (be forced to) retreat/yield

go to ground = hide (to evade pursuers/searchers)

ground-swell of opinion = views of the majority (of ordinary people)

hold/stand one's ground = be firm/unyielding

let somebody in at/on the ground floor = allow somebody to join a company on the same terms as its founders

on one's home ground = where one has the advantage of local knowledge/personal experience

rooted to the ground = immobile/fixed in one spot

run somebody to ground = find somebody (who has been evasive)

shift one's ground = change one's opinion/viewpoint

stamping ground = somebody's favourite haunt

suit somebody down to the ground = totally meet somebody's needs/requirements

thick/thin on the ground = common/uncommon

See also: cut the ground from under somebody's **feet**; get in on the ground **floor**; ground **rules**; have one's **ear** to the ground; have one's **feet** on the ground; **lose** ground.

grow

growing pains = difficulties that occur during the initial stages of a development

grown-up = adult

grow on one = become slowly acceptable/likeable

grow out of = become too large/mature for

grow up = behave like an adult

See also: **money** doesn't grow on trees.

growth

cancerous growth = something bad which spreads out of control

grudge

bear a grudge = retain feelings of bitterness (because of unfair treatment)

guard

catch somebody off his/her guard = take somebody by surprise (unprepared to meet an attack)

drop/keep up one's guard = be unprepared/prepared to meet an attack

guard against = beware of

off/on one's guard = unprepared/prepared to defend oneself
  See also: **old** guard.

guardian
  See: guardian **angel**.

guess
guessing game = situation of (very) uncertain outcome
guess what = here is a surprise
your guess is as good as mine = I know as little about it as you do
wild guess = haphazard guess
  See also: **anybody's** guess; **educated** guess.

guest
be my guest = (feel free to) do as you please

gum
up a gum tree = in a difficult/untenable position
  See also: gum up the **works**.

gun
big guns = important/powerful people
give something the gun = test something to its maximum potential
go down with all guns blazing/firing = lose while still fighting
go great guns = be successful/do well
gun for somebody = seek somebody in order to do him/her
  harm/mischief
spike somebody's guns = anticipate and counter criticism
stick to one's guns = hold fast to one's principles
  See also: **jump** the gun; **son** of a gun.

guts
hate somebody's guts = have a strong dislike for somebody
have the guts to = have the courage to
  See also: **slog** one's guts out.

gutter
gutter press = lower (sensation-seeking) forms of journalism
out of the gutter = from a deprived/very humble background

guy
fall guy = a dupe, somebody who is left to take the
  blame/punishment for somebody else's misdeeds
wise guy = somebody who thinks he/she knows everything

H

habit
break/get out of the habit = break/change a routine
creature of habit = somebody who always follows the same
  predictable pattern of behaviour
deep-rooted habit = long-standing pattern of behaviour
fall into a /the habit = acquire the habit
from force of habit = because of (a need to conform to) a long-
  standing pattern of behaviour
make a habit of = adopt as routine behaviour

hackles
make one's hackles rise = make one (angrily) defensive

hail
hail-fellow-well-met = (over)friendly
hail from = be born at/come from

hair
don't lose your hair over it/keep your hair on = do not overreact/do
  not worry needlessly
get in somebody's hair = annoy somebody (by getting in his/her way)
get/have somebody by the short hairs = have somebody at a total
  disadvantage
hair-raising = frightening/terrifying
hair's breadth = very small distance
harm a hair of somebody's head = harm somebody even slightly
let one's hair down = relax and enjoy oneself
make one's hair curl/stand on end = cause deep fear/revulsion
not turn a hair = remain calm
put hairs on somebody's chest = make somebody manly/virile
split hairs = be (over)fastidious/argue over trifles
tear one's hair out = be very frustrated/worried
wear a hair shirt = be penitent
without turning/not turning a hair = be calm/unaffected

See also: hair of the **dog** (that bit you); **keep** one's hair/shirt on; neither **hide** nor hair of.

half

at half mast = falling down (of trousers, etc.)
by half = by too much
by halves = incompletely
go halves = share (equally)
half a loaf is better than none/no bread (at all) = be grateful for what one has, even if it is not everything that one wants
half a moment/tick = a very short time
half-and-half = equal(ly)
half-baked = ill-conceived/incomplete (of a thing), or feeble-minded (of a person)
half-hearted = unenthusiastic
half seas over = fairly drunk
half-way house = mid-point
half-witted = stupid/mentally unsound
have half a chance = a small chance/opportunity
have half a mind = inclination
how the other half lives = how people less/more fortunate than oneself live
meet somebody half-way = (agree to a) compromise
no half-measures = no compromise
not half = very definitely
one's better/other half = one's husband/wife
something and a half = good/large example of something
the half of it = (only) part
See also: go off at half **cock**; half the **battle**; see with (only) half an **eye**.

hallmark

have the hallmark of = be characteristic of/have the (outward) signs of

halt

See: **call** a halt; **grind** to a halt; halt/pause/stop in **midstream**.

ham

ham-fisted/-handed = clumsy

Hamlet
like Hamlet without the Prince of Denmark = without the chief
  participant

hammer
give somebody a hammering = beat somebody soundly
hammer away/out = keep working until a result is reached
hammer something home = get somebody to realize/understand
  something through persistent/vigorous reasoning
like hammer and tongs = very enthusiastically/vigorously
under the hammer = put up for sale at auction

hand
accept with both hands = accept eagerly/enthusiastically
all hands to the pumps = everybody must help
at/on hand = readily available
at second hand = indirectly
at/in the hands of = the responsibility of
big hand = enthusiastic applause
bite the hand that feeds one = return kindness with
  hostility/ingratitude
bound/tied hand and foot = totally helpless/restricted
by hand = manually, or personally
clean hands = blameless
close at/to hand = nearby
cool hand = somebody who remains calm
dirty/soil one's hands = be involved with something dishonest
do a hand's turn = work
(at) first hand = from somebody with personal knowledge
from hand to hand = from one person to another
from hand to mouth = in poverty
gain/have the upper hand = gain the advantage/lead
gain/have the whip hand = be in a position of control/domination
give one's hand to = accept an offer of marriage (very formal)
give somebody the glad hand = welcome warmly
great hand (at something) = adept/expert (at doing something)
hand down = bequeath/pass on as an inheritance
hand in hand = associated/united (with), or holding hands
hand it to someone = give (due) credit

hand on heart = honestly/sincerely

hand over = concede/pass on/surrender

hand over fist = quickly, or in quantity

hand over hand = (climbing etc.) using first one hand and then the other

hands off = leave alone, or remote(ly)

have a hand in = be involved in/with

have one's hands full = be very busy/fully occupied

have one's hands tied = be restricted (by regulations/rules)

have only one pair of hands = have too much work to do

have something on one's hands = be in possession of something

heavy hand = authoritarianism/severity

high-handed = arrogantly/selfishly

hold somebody's hand = accompany somebody

in good hands = well cared for

(well) in hand = being done, or under control

in the hands of = in the possession of

keep in hand = retain a stock/store of

lay hands on = find

left hand doesn't know what the right hand is doing = lack of communication between two parts of the same group/organization

lend a hand = help

lift/raise one's hand against = threaten

off hand = casual, or unprepared/without notice

off one's hands = no longer one's concern/responsibility

old hand/stager = somebody who is experienced

on all hands/on every hand = in every direction/surrounding

on one's hands = in one's possession

on one's hands and knees = in a begging manner

(on the one hand) ... (and) on the other hand = alternatively

open hand = generosity

out of hand = out of control

out of one's hands = out of one's possession/responsibility

overplay one's hand = be overconfident to the point that puts one at a disadvantage

play into somebody's hands = do exactly what somebody else wants one to do

put one's hand in one's pocket = pay

reveal/show one's hand = reveal one's intentions

right-hand man = principal assistant

second-hand = not new (in the possession of the second owner)

shake hands on it = make an agreement

sit on one's hands = be idle/unoccupied, or (deliberately) take no action

sleight of hand = deviousness/trickery

stay one's hand = hold back/take no action

strong hand = firmness/resolution

take a hand in = be involved in/take part in

take in hand = take charge of

take something off somebody's hands = relieve somebody of possession/responsibility

throw in one's hand = give up/resign

try one's hand at = make an attempt to

turn one's hand to = (be able to) adapt one's skills to

wait on somebody hand and foot = satisfy somebody's every need (in a servile manner)

wash one's hands of = dissociate oneself from

win hands down = defeat effortlessly

work hand in hand with = co-operate, work closely with

See also: at **first** hand; be a **dab** hand at; **bird** in the hand; **bite** the hand that feeds one; **blood** on one's hands; **catch** somebody with his/her hands in the till; **change** hands; **empty-handed**; extend the hand of **fellowship**; **force** somebody's hand; **free** hand; go **cap** in hand; hand in **glove** with somebody; get one's **eye**/hand in; have somebody **eat** out of one's hand; have the **whip** hand; hold/play one's cards/hand close to one's **chest**; iron hand/fist in a velvet **glove**; **keep** one's hand in; **live** from hand to mouth; many hands make light **work**; **near** at hand; **raise** one's hand against; **ready** to hand; **rub** one's hands; **show** of hands; with one hand tied behind one's **back**; with one's **bare** hands.

handle

give/put a handle to = give a name to

handle to one's name = a title

too hot to handle = too risky to possess

See also: **fly** off the handle.

handshake
See: **golden** handshake.

hang
get/lose the hang of = become familiar/unfamiliar with
hang about/around = wait a moment, or loiter
hang back = hesitate
hang by a thread = be in a precarious position
hang heavy = pass slowly (of time)
hang in = persevere
hanging matter/offence = (action that is regarded as a) serious
    misdemeanour
hang in the balance = be in a state of indecision (regarding a situation
    that could get better or worse)
hang it = mild expletive
hang (up)on = depend (up)on
hang one's head = be ashamed
hang on somebody's lips/words = listen attentively
hang out = to frequent
hang together = be complete/consistent, or share the responsibility
hang up = terminate a telephone call
have something hanging over one's head = be under a threat (of
    unpleasantness)
hung up on = obsessed with
I'll be hanged = expression of disbelief/surprise, or of resoluteness
let it all hang out = do as you like
thereby hangs a tale = there is more to this matter, but it is best left
    unsaid
    See also: have a hangdog **air**; hang **fire**; hang/put the **flags** out; hang
    up one's **hat**; one might as well be hung for a **sheep** as a lamb.

happen
happen one's way = become available to one (by chance)
happen what may = whatever happens
it's all happening = there is much activity
    See also: worse things happen at **sea**.

happy
go to the happy hunting-ground = die

happy as a dog with two tails/lark/sandboy/Larry = very happy
happy-go-lucky = carefree
happy hunting-ground = place where one finds pleasurable/
  profitable pursuits
happy landings! = (goodbye and) good luck!
happy medium = sensible compromise (between two extremes)
trigger-happy = too ready to employ violence
  See also: as happy as the **day** is long; happy **event**; many happy
  returns.

hard
be hard on somebody = be overcritical/unfair to somebody
be hard put to do something = have difficulty/trouble in doing
  something
go hard with somebody = be to somebody's disadvantage
hard and fast = firm/immovable
hard at it = working busily
hard-bitten = inflexible/tough
hard-boiled = unemotional/tough
hard by = close/very near
hard cash = money (coin and banknotes only)
hard done by = receiving bad/poor treatment
hard drinker = somebody who drinks (spirits) habitually
hard-earned = gained through much effort
harden one's heart = feel little emotion/sympathy
hard-faced/hard-featured/hard-nosed = grim/tough, unsympathetic
hard-headed = practical/sensible, unemotional
hard-hit = adversely affected
hard-hitting = of great impact
hard/tough nut to crack = difficult problem/person
hard of hearing = partially deaf
hard on the heels of = close behind
hard put to it = find it difficult to do something
hard stuff = spirit drink (as opposed to beer or wine)
hard times = difficult/worrying situation
hard up = without much money
hard words = critical/scolding comments

play hard to get = try to make oneself more attractive/wanted by being difficult to contact
take a hard line = be firm/uncompromising
take something hard = be upset by something
  See also: **die**-hard; drive a hard **bargain**; hard as **nails**; hard **case**; hard **cheese**; hard **core**; hard **facts**; hard **lines**/luck; hard-luck **story**; (hard) **pressed** for; **hold** hard; no hard **feelings**.

hare
hare-brained = foolish/irresponsible
mad as a March hare = silly/mentally unstable
run with the hare and hunt with the hounds = simultaneously support both sides in a dispute

hark
hark back = refer back

harm
out of harm's way = in safety
  See also: harm a **hair** of somebody's head.

harness
in double harness = working as a pair
in harness = at work
  See also: **die** in harness/with one's boots on.

harp
harp on = keep talking about (to the point of boredom)

Harry
  See: any/every **Tom**, Dick and Harry.

harvest
reap a barren/rich harvest = get no/much reward

hash
make a hash of = do something badly
settle somebody's hash = neutralize a trouble-maker

haste
more haste, less speed = a quick approach to a task often results in carelessness/mistakes

hat

at the drop of a hat = at once/without hesitation

brass hat = high-ranking (army) officer

eat one's hat = admit one is wrong

(perform the) hat trick = succeed in scoring/winning three times in succession

hang one's hat up (in a house) = make oneself at home

hang on to one's hat = cling/hold on, or be ready for something unusual

keep something under one's hat = keep a confidence/secret

old hat = out-of-date/old-fashioned

pass/send/take the hat round = collect money

raise/take off one's hat to = admire/express approval for

talk out of/through (the top of) one's hat/head = talk nonsense

throw one's hat into the ring = issue a challenge

tip one's hat to somebody = (respectfully) acknowledge somebody's ability/superiority

wear two different hats = do two different jobs at once

See also: bad egg/hat/lot; **knock** into a cocked hat; put the (tin) **lid/hat on.**

hatch

batten down the hatches = anticipate/prepare for trouble

down the hatch! = cheers! (said to somebody taking a drink)

hatches, matches and dispatches = (announcements of) births, marriages and deaths (in a newspaper)

See also: don't count one's **chickens** (before they're hatched).

hatchet

bury the hatchet/one's differences = agree to forget a former disagreement

do a hatchet job on = attack/discredit

hatchet man = somebody who is employed to perform an unpleasant task (relating to others)

hate

blinded by hatred = letting hatred interfere with one's better judgement

---

hate somebody's guts = have an absolute dislike of somebody
pet hate = a particular annoyance

hatter
as mad as a hatter = quite mad (= anything from mildly
  eccentric/silly to mentally deranged)

haul
long haul = protracted/tiring task
  See also: haul over the **coals.**

have
have a go = make an attempt/try, or attack (verbally or physically)
have a head like a sieve = be (habitually) forgetful
have an ear to the ground = remain alert for new information/news
have anything or something to do with = be concerned with/involved
  in
have a way with = have a natural flair for
have been around = to be experienced
have done (with) = be finished (with)
have enough/a lot on one's plate = undertake sufficient/much to do
have had it = have died/failed/lost/missed an opportunity
have it away/off = have sexual intercourse
have it/what's coming to one = to deserve what happens to one
have it in for somebody = intend to cause somebody harm/trouble
have it in one = have the ability/skill
have it out = settle an argument/dispute
have no time for = dislike/not tolerate
have somebody on = trick somebody
have (somebody) up = prosecute somebody
have something on = be occupied, be wearing something
have it taped = have control of a situation/solution to a problem
have/want nothing to do with = dissociate oneself from
have (got) to = must
have to do with = affect, concern/be relevant to
have/keep up one's sleeve = keep concealed until needed
have what it takes = possess what is needed to successfully do
  something
have wind of = hear a rumour of

let somebody have it = attack somebody (physically or verbally)
what have you = and so on/anything else
  See also: have a screw **loose**; have/keep an **eye** on; have it **both** ways;
have one's **eye** on; have no/not a **clue**; have not an **earthly**; have
one's **hand**s full; have one's **head** screwed on; have one's **work** cut
out; have the **advantage** of; have the **edge** on.

havoc
play havoc with = cause damage to/disrupt

hawk
hawk-eyed = with very keen eyesight
  See also: **watch** somebody like a hawk.

hay
go haywire = go out of control
hit the hay = go to bed/sleep
make hay while the sun shines = make the best of an opportunity

haystack
look/search for a needle in a haystack = try to find something (small)
  that is lost among many other things

head
above/over one's head = beyond one's level of understanding
bang/knock one's head against a brick wall = do something to no
  avail
bang/knock somebody's heads together = threat to put an end to a
  dispute
bite/snap somebody's head off = answer angrily/curtly
bring/come to a head = bring to a point where action is needed
by a short head = by a (very) small margin
come/enter into one's head = occur to one
come to/reach a head = reach a critical stage
count heads = count the people present
get one's head down = go to bed (and sleep)
get something into one's head = grasp an idea, or learn/memorize
give/let somebody have somebody his/her head = allow somebody
  freedom to act as he/she wishes
go off one's head = go mad/lose control of one's reason

go to one's head = make one arrogant/conceited, or make one
  (slightly) drunk
go over somebody's head = contact somebody's superior
have a good head on one's shoulders = be clever/sensible
have a head for = have the ability/flair for
have a (good) head for heights = be untroubled by heights
have a swollen head = be conceited
have one's head in the clouds = be daydreaming
have one's head screwed on (the right way) = be capable/shrewd
head and shoulders above = very much better than
head off = divert/intercept
head of the family = senior member of a family
head on = in direct confrontation
head-over-ears/heels = completely/totally
heads I win, tails you lose = I win, no matter what the outcome
heads or tails? = which side of a coin will show after it has been
  tossed?
head start = initial advantage (over competitors)
heads will roll = somebody will be in grave trouble
hold a pistol to somebody's head = threaten somebody
hold one's head high/up = be proud/unashamed
keep a level head/keep one's head = remain calm
keep one's head above water = remain out of debt
keep one's head down = remain inconspicuous, or keep working
  (busily)
make neither head nor tail of something = not understand
  something
make one's head spin = confuse one
need one's head examined = be foolish/slightly mad
not know whether one is on one's head or one's heels = be completely
  confused
off/out of one's head = very foolish/mad
off the top of one's head = without thinking
old head on young shoulders = (uncharacteristic) wisdom in youth
on one's (own) head = one's (own) responsibility
on your own head be it = you will be responsible (for any trouble)
put something into somebody's head = suggest something
put one's head in(to) a noose/on the block = court disaster

put one's head in the lion's mouth = take a grave risk (by putting oneself at the mercy of somebody else)

put one's heads together = discuss something between/among oneselves

put something out of one's head = deliberately forget

raise/rear its ugly head = (re)appear (of something unpleasant)

soft/weak in the head = foolish/slightly mad

standing on one's head = effortlessly/with ease

swollen-headed = conceited

take something into one's head = (foolishly) decide to do something

talk somebody's head off = talk so much that one makes somebody bored/weary

turn somebody's head/brain = make somebody conceited

two heads are better than one = two people co-operating have a better chance of solving a problem than one person by himself/herself
See also: **bury** one's head in the sand; **eat** one's head off; **empty**-headed; **enter** somebody's head; hard-**headed**; **hang** one's head; have a **roof** over one's head; have a **tongue** in one's head; have **eyes** in the back of one's head; hit the **nail** on the head; **lose** one's head; need something like a **hole** in the head; **price** on somebody's head; put one's head on the **block**; **right** in the head; **scratch** one's head; **shake** one's head; **short** head; **shout** one's head off; **snap** one's head off; **talk** out of/through (the top of) one's hat/head

headache
be a headache = cause difficulty/problems

headlines
hit the headlines = make news

headway
make headway = make progress

heap
See: **strike** somebody all of a heap.

hear
fair hearing = impartial assessment
hear from = receive a communication from
hear! hear! = exclamation of agreement

hearing things = hearing something that is not there/was not said
hear of = be informed of
I've heard that one before! = I do not believe you
I've never heard of such a thing = how extraordinary/unusual
lose one's hearing = become deaf
out of hearing = beyond audible range
unheard of = extraordinary/unique
will not hear of = refuse to accept/allow
  See also: **hard** of hearing; never hear the **end** of something.

heart
after one's (own) heart = of the kind one likes
allow one's heart to rule one's head = let one's emotions override
  common sense
at heart = mainly/really
break one's heart = cause one (great) sorrow
change of heart = change of attitude/viewpoint
close/near to one's heart = among things that most affect/concern
  one
do one's heart good = make one glad/happy
find it in one's heart = convince/persuade oneself
from the bottom of one's heart = most sincerely
give one/have heart failure = be greatly shocked
have a heart! = be reasonable!
have a heart of gold = be very considerate/kind
have a heart of oak = be loyal/trustworthy
have a heart of stone = be totally unfeeling
have no heart = be insensitive/unsympathetic
have no heart for/not have the heart for = be unenthusiastic
have one's heart (sink into)/in one's boots = be in a state of despair
have one's heart in one's mouth = be very apprehensive
have one's heart in the right place = be kind/sincere (despite
  appearances to the contrary)
heart and soul = totally/with maximum effort
heart goes out to = feel sympathy for
heart of the matter = the fundamental/main point
heart-rending = distressing
heart-to-heart talk = frank discussion

in good heart = cheerful/happy

in one's heart of hearts = in all honesty

know/learn (off) by heart = know from memory/memorize

not have the heart to = be unwilling to

not have one's heart in it = be unenthusiastic

one's heart aches/bleeds for somebody = one feels great sympathy for somebody (usually meant sarcastically)

one's heart goes out to somebody = one feels great sympathy for somebody (usually meant sincerely)

one's heart stands still = one is (very) afraid

pour one's heart out = confide one's troubles (to a sympathetic hearer)

pull/tug one's heart-strings = stimulate feelings of pathos/sympathy

put (fresh) heart into = encourage/stimulate

set one's heart upon = desire intensely

sick at heart = thoroughly dejected/dispirited

steel one's heart against = suppress one's natural emotions

take heart = receive encouragement/moral support

take somebody to one's heart = accept somebody lovingly

take something to heart = take seriously, or be upset/offended by

wear one's heart on one's sleeve = display one's feelings openly

win the heart of = gain the admiration/love of

with a heavy/sinking heart = with a feeling of sadness

with a light heart = with a feeling of happiness

with all one's heart (and soul) = most enthusiastically/sincerely

See also: **down**-hearted; **eat** one's heart out; **harden** one's heart; have heart **failure**; **lose** heart; **lose** one's heart; **open** one's heart; **steal** somebody's heart; to one's heart's **content**; warm the **cockles** of one's heart; **young** at/in heart.

heat

at fever heat/pitch = at maximum activity/enthusiasm

in the heat of the moment = while excited/emotionally aroused

turn on the heat = (cruelly) put pressure on somebody

See also: **dead** heat.

heave

give somebody/something the (old) heave-ho = get rid of somebody/something

heave in/into sight = come into view
make one heave = make one disgusted

heaven
for heaven's sake = exclamation of mild annoyance
good heavens/heavens above = exclamation of surprise
heaven forbid = may it not be so
heaven only knows = I do not know/nobody knows
in heaven's name = exclamation of annoyance/surprise (in a
  question)
like heaven on earth = idyllic/perfect
manna from heaven = sudden source of comfort/relief
move heaven and earth = do everything in one's power
seventh heaven = state of extreme happiness
smell/stink to high heaven = have an offensive smell
thank heavens = expression of gratitude/relief
the heavens opened = it poured with rain

heavy
lie heavy on = be a burden/worry to
make heavy weather of = have (unnecessary) difficulty with
time hangs heavy = time passes slowly
  See also: hard/heavy **going**; heavy **hand**; with a heavy **heart**.

hedge
  See: hedge one's **bets**.

heel
Achilles' heel = weak/vulnerable point
bring somebody to heel/make somebody come to heel = make
  somebody comply obediently
(hard) on the heels of = be immediately behind
set somebody by the heels = imprison somebody
set somebody (back) on his/her heels = shock/surprise somebody
take to one's heels = run away
tread on somebody's heels = compete with somebody (for his/her
  job/position)
turn on one's heel = turn (and walk) away
well-heeled = wealthy

See also: **cool** one's heels; **dig** one's feet/heels/toes in; **down**-at-heel; **head** over heels; **kick** one's heels; show a **clean** pair of heels.

hell
all hell breaks loose = a state of chaos ensues
come hell or high water = whatever happens/at whatever cost
for the hell of it = (just) for fun
frighten/scare the hell out of = terrify
give somebody hell = make life very unpleasant for/punish somebody
go to hell = go away
hellbent on = determined
hell for leather = recklessly fast
hell to pay = serious consequences/trouble
like (merry) hell = enthusiastically/vigorously, or emphatically not
not have a hope in hell = have no hope at all
play (merry) hell with = make worse, or severely damage/disrupt
raise hell = create a great fuss/noise
to hell with = I do not care at all
until hell freezes over = for ever
what the hell = it does not matter, or whatever
when the hell = whenever
where the hell = wherever
who the hell = whoever
See also: cat's/snowball's **chance** in hell; like a **bat** out of hell.

helm
at the helm = in charge/control
take the helm = take charge/control

help
help oneself to = freely take
not if I can help it = only without my agreement

hem
hem in = confine/trap

hen
hen-party = all-female gathering
hen-pecked = dominated by one's girlfriend/wife

like a hen with one (only) chicken = over-protective of an only child
mother hen = woman who constantly fusses (over her children)

here
be up to here = have more than one can do/tolerate
here and now = at this present time
here and there = in various places
here goes = said before doing something difficult/risky/unpleasant
here's to... = toast to success
here, there and everywhere = everywhere
here today and gone tomorrow = (only) temporary
neither here nor there = irrelevant/trivial
  See also: here we **go** again.

hero
hero's welcome = enthusiastic welcome

herring
red herring = deliberately misleading factor

hide
neither hide nor hair of = no trace of
on a hiding to nothing = situation in which one must lose
tan somebody's hide = beat/smack somebody
  See also: hide one's **light** under a bushel.

high
all-time high = (world) record achievement
blow something sky high = prove something to be wrong
for the high jump = about to be disciplined/punished (for a misdeed)
high and dry = stranded/in a very difficult situation
high and mighty = arrogant/self-opinionated
high as a kite = intoxicated (with drink or drugs)
high days and holidays = special occasions
high-falutin(g) = pompous/pretentious
high-flown = extravagant
high-flyer = somebody who is ambitious
high life = luxurious (way of) life
highly-strung = very nervous/tense
high-minded = (very) moral/strict

high places = superior/upper levels of a group
high-sounding = pompous/pretentious
high spot = main attraction/feature
high table = raised table (at dinner) for important/senior people
hightail it = run away
high tea = small meal eaten in late afternoon/early evening
high time = enjoyable time, or time to do something that is late/overdue
hunt/search high and low = make a thorough search
in high dudgeon = feeling offended
run high = be intense
  See also: high-**handed**; live high off the **hog**; on one's high **horse**; **riding** high; **search** high and low.

highway
highway robbery = exorbitant charge/price
Queen's highway = public road

hill
old as the hills = very old
over the hill = past its/one's best
up hill and down dale = everywhere

hilt
up to the hilt = to the maximum

hindmost
  See: **devil** take the hindmost.

hinge
hinge upon = depend on

hint
broad hint = obvious clue
drop/give/throw a hint = give a (casual) clue

hip
shoot from the hip = react quickly

history
ancient history = familiar story/stale news

go down in history = be remembered
make history = do something that will be long remembered

hit
hit-and-run = fail to stop after causing injury when driving
hit back = retaliate/defend oneself
hit below the belt = use unfair tactics
hit hard/hard hit = harmed by misfortune
hit it off = become friends
hit-or-miss = lacking in organization/careless
hit somebody when he/she is down = take advantage of somebody
  who is in trouble
hit the deck = (deliberately) fall to the floor/ground
hit the headlines = become public knowledge/make news
hit the nail on the head = make a (very) accurate description/guess
hit the road/trail = begin a journey
hit the roof = (suddenly) lose one's temper
hit upon = make an (unexpected) discovery
make a hit = meet with approval/friendliness
smash hit = big success
  See also: hit **man**; hit the **hay**; hit the **jackpot**; hit the **sack**.

hive
hive off = pass on to somebody else

hobby
hobby horse = favourite subject
rich man's hobby = expensive (self-)indulgence
ride a hobby horse (to death) = constantly refer to a favourite subject

Hobson
  See: Hobson's **choice**

hog
go the whole hog = do something completely
live high off the hog = have a luxurious lifestyle
  See also: **road** hog.

hoist
hoist with one's own petard = caught in one's own trap

hold

get hold of = obtain (something), or contact (somebody)

have a hold over somebody = have somebody in one's power

hold all the aces = be in control

hold back = delay/restrain

hold cheap = consider worthless/of low esteem

hold dear = value highly

hold forth = speak at length (publicly)

hold good = remain valid

hold hard = delay/stop

hold (oneself) in = restrain oneself

hold it! = stop!

hold it against somebody = blame/have a low opinion of
  somebody

hold off = fail to arrive

hold on = wait

hold one's own = maintain one's advantage/position, compete
  successfully

hold one's peace/tongue = keep silent

hold out = retain one's position/survive, or extend

hold over = postpone/retain for later

hold somebody to something = make somebody keep a
  promise/follow a set of rules

hold sway = have superiority

hold the floor = speak at/dominate a meeting etc.

hold together = remain firm/united, or be complete/consistent

hold up = delay, or raise, or support

hold water = be correct/withstand investigation

hold with = agree

no holds barred = total freedom of choice/method (without
  conforming to established rules)

there's no holding somebody = it is difficult/impossible to restrain
  somebody

See also: cannot/not fit to hold a **candle** to; hold a **pistol** to
  somebody's head; hold **court**; hold/keep at **bay**; hold **everything!**;
  hold/keep in **check**; hold/stand one's **ground**;
  hold on like **grim** death; hold somebody to **ransom**; hold the **fort**;
  hold your **horses**; keep/hold at **arm**'s length.

hole
be in a hole = be in difficulties
like the Black Hole of Calcutta = very crowded and hot
make a hole in = use the largest part of
need something like a hole in the head = not need something at all
nineteenth hole = bar (in the club house of a golf course)
pick holes in = criticize/find fault with
square peg in a round hole = somebody who is unsuited to his/her
job/position
  See also: **ace** in the hole; **burn** a hole in one's pocket; **glory**
  hole; hole-and-corner **affair**.

holiday
  See: **busman**'s holiday.

hollow
have a hollow ring = appear insincere/untrue
hollow laugh = unamused laughter
hollow promise = promise that will not be kept
  See also: **beat** hollow.

holy
holy of holies = most revered/special place (within a building)
holy terror = child who is badly behaved
  See also: holier-than-thou **attitude**; holier-than-thou **expression**.

homage
do/pay homage to = acknowledge the superiority of/revere

home
at-home = occasion on which one receives any guests/visitors to one's
home
bring something home to somebody = make somebody aware of (an
unpleasant truth)
close to home = uncomfortably near the truth
come home to roost = return of unpleasantness as a result of a
previous (antisocial) action
drive/hammer something home = try to get somebody to
accept/understand something (using forceful/repeated argument)
feel at home = feel comfortable/relaxed

get something home to = make something clear/obvious to

home and dry = safe/successful

home from home = place where one feels as comfortable/relaxed as in one's own home

home in on = aim for/be drawn to

home is where the heart is = wherever one's family/partner lives is equivalent to home

last home = final resting place/tomb

make oneself at home = be as comfortable/relaxed as if one were in one's own home

nothing to write home about = unremarkable

romp/waltz home = win easily

See also: bring home the **bacon**; **broken** home; **charity** begins at home; **eat** somebody out of house and home; home **truth**; **romp** home; **strike** home; till the **cows** come home.

homework
do one's homework = make adequate preparation

honest
earn an honest penny = make money honestly

See also: honest **broker**; make an honest **woman** (out) of.

honey
be as sweet as honey = be very pleasant (in order to gain an advantage)

honeymoon
the honeymoon is over = end of a peaceful period at the beginning of a new venture

honour
debt of honour = debt that has no legal obligation

do the honours = act as host/hostess

honour bound = having a moral obligation

honours are even = each side has achieved equal success

in honour of = as a sign of esteem/respect

point of honour = matter of (moral) principle

there's no honour among thieves = dishonest people cannot trust each other

hook

by hook or by crook = by any means (fair or foul)
be hooked on = be addicted to
hook, line and sinker = completely
let somebody off the hook = allow somebody to escape from a
  difficulty/problem
sling one's hook = go away

hoop

be put/go through the hoop = have to suffer unpleasantness
  See also: be **cock**-a-hoop.

hoot

not to care two hoots = not to care at all

hop

hop it = go away
hopping mad = very angry
  See also: **catch** somebody bending/napping/on the hop.

hope

fond hope = a genuine wish for something that is unlikely to happen
I hope you feel proud of yourself! = I hope you are pleased (although
  I think you should not be)
hope against hope = keep hoping (but with little chance of fulfilment)
pin one's hopes on = (optimistically) rely on
raise somebody's hopes = increase somebody's expectations that
  something will happen
some hopes! = there is no point in being hopeful (because what you
  desire is very unlikely)
(great) white hope = somebody/something on whom/which a group
  depends for success
  See also: **dash** somebody's hopes.

horizon

on the horizon = within view

hornet

bring a hornet's nest about one's ears = do something to precipitate
  trouble
stir up a hornet's nest = create trouble

horns

draw/pull in one's horns = act with more restraint

lock horns with somebody = argue/fight with somebody

  See also: on the horns of a **dilemma**; take the **bull** by the horns.

horse

back the wrong horse = put one's faith/trust in somebody who later loses, or something which fails

(straight) from the horse's mouth = direct from a (reliable) source

hold your horses! = wait a minute!/slow down!

horses for courses = everybody has his/her own special attributes

horse laugh = loud/raucous laugh

horse of a different/another colour = somebody/something of a different type

horse sense = common sense

horse-trading = hard bargaining

old war horse = veteran fighter/soldier

stalking horse = somebody who is employed to stimulate action in others

swap/change horses in midstream = change allegiance/tactics in the middle of a project

you can take a horse to water (but you cannot make it drink) = you can encourage somebody to do something, but you cannot force him/her

Trojan horse = apparent asset that turns out to favour a competitor

white horses = white-topped waves at sea

wild horses wouldn't (make one do something) = nothing would (make one do something)

willing horse = somebody who is (always) willing to help

  See also: a **nod** is as good as a wink to a blind horse; **dark** horse; **eat** like a horse; **flog** a dead horse; **high** horse; lock the stable **door** after the horse has bolted; **look** a gift horse in the mouth; one horse **race**; put the **cart** before the horse; ride a **hobby** horse (to death); **work** like a horse/Trojan.

hot

be hot on = be keen on, or be very knowledgeable about

feel/look not too hot = feel/look unwell

hot and bothered = flustered

hot-blooded = emotionally volatile
hot favourite = the one most likely to succeed
hot-headed = likely to act irrationally/in anger
hot line = direct communication link (for emergencies)
hot stuff = somebody with great ability
in hot water = in trouble
in the hot seat = in a difficult/responsible position
make it hot for somebody = put somebody in a difficult situation
piping hot = very hot
  See also: **blow** hot and cold; go like hot **cakes**; hot **air**; hot **potato**;
  hot **seat**; hot under the **collar**.

hour

after hours = after the time that a public house/shop usually closes
(till/until) all hours = very late (at night)
hour of need = when one is in great need of help
keep regular hours = sleep/work to a regular routine
rush hour = peak period of commuting traffic
(wee) small hours = very early in the morning
witching hour = midnight
zero hour = time at which something is due to happen/start
  See also: **eleventh** hour.

house

(all) around/round the houses = in a roundabout manner
bring the house down = cause much applause/laughter
empty house = very poorly attended cinema/theatre
free house = public house that is not tied to one particular brewery
full house = cinema/theatre that is full, or a hand at poker that
  contains three cards of the same rank and two other cards of the
  same rank
half-way house = something that is intermediate between two
  extremes
house of cards = impractical scheme (which is sure to fail)
house of ill-fame/ill-repute = brothel
house-to-house = calling at every house
house-warming = party to celebrate moving into a new home
in the best houses = among high-born/wealthy people
keep open house = always make casual visitors welcome

like the side of a house = very large
on the house = free (of drinks/food provided by the host)
put/set one's house in order = arrange one's affairs in an orderly way
rough house = brawl/fight
safe as houses = very safe/secure
shout the house down = shout very loudly
the House of God = a church/place of worship
  See also: **disorderly** house; **drink** on the house; **eat** somebody out of
  house and home; (in the) **dog**-house; like a house on **fire**; (under)
  house **arrest**.

household
head of the household = senior member of the family
household name = somebody who is very well known
household word = word that is very well known

how
and how! = emphatically yes
any old how = in a careless manner
how about? = would you consider/think about?
how come? = why?
how do you do? = formal greeting made when one is introduced to
  somebody (and not requiring an answer)
how come? = why is it so?
how on earth...? = however...?
how's that for...? = what do you think of that as an example of...?
  See also: how **goes** it (with you)?; how's **tricks**?

hue
hue and cry = great/loud commotion, public outcry

huff
huff and puff = appear confused (pompously)
in a huff = having taken offence/grumpy

hum
hum and haw = dither/hesitate
make things hum = make things happen (effortlessly and quickly)

humble
  See: **eat** humble pie.

humour
dry humour = subtle (and often sarcastic) sense of fun
out of humour = ill-tempered/irritable
sick humour = joke that is in bad taste

hump
over the hump = past a critical/maximum point

hundred
a hundred and one = very many
not a hundred miles away = very close

hungry
hungry as a hunter = very hungry

hunt
hunt down = continue searching until one finds somebody/something
hunt high and low = make a thorough search
hunt up = look/search for
pot-hunter = somebody who enters competitions merely for the prize
  money and not for entertainment
run with the fox/hare and hunt with the hounds = try to be on both
  sides of a contest at the same time

hunting-ground
  See: **happy** hunting-ground

hurdle
first hurdle = initial obstacle

hush
hush-hush = secret
hush money = money paid to somebody to ensure his/her silence
  (about a misdeed/potential scandal)
hush up = conceal/suppress, or be quiet

I

i
dot the i's and cross the t's = take care of the (minor) details

ice
black ice = thin, invisible film of ice
break the ice = lessen shyness (by initiating a conversation) when
  meeting somebody for the first time
cut no ice = fail to have an effect
put on ice = postpone
skate/tread on thin ice = take an (unnecessary) risk
  See also: **icing** on the cake

iceberg
tip of the iceberg = relatively minor factor that represents something
  much larger

icing
icing on the cake = decorative (but unnecessary) addition

idea
half-baked idea = impractical/incomplete plan
moth-eaten idea = old-fashioned/outmoded plan
not have an/the foggiest idea = have no knowledge at all
not one's idea of = opposite to what one believes/thinks
put an idea into somebody's head = suggest something to somebody
run away with an idea = assume
that's the idea! = you are nearly correct
the very idea! = I do not agree with you
toy with an idea = consider a plan/proposal
what's the big idea? = What do you think you are doing?

idle
  See: **bone** idle.

ilk
of that ilk = of the same name

ill
diplomatic illness = feigned illness as an excuse not to do something
go ill with somebody = end in trouble for somebody
ill-at-ease = uncomfortable (because of the circumstances/ situation
  one is in)
ill-gotten gains = money obtained dishonestly
it's an ill wind = an apparently unfavourable situation has its good
  aspects
speak ill of = slander/ say uncomplimentary things about

illusion
be under no illusion = be fully aware of the truth

image
the (spitting) image of = very like/similar to

imagine
by no stretch of the imagination = it is extremely unlikely that
(just) imagine that! = expression of surprised disbelief
  See also: **figment** of one's imagination.

immemorial
from time immemorial = from before anybody can remember

impression
be under the impression that = to believe/think that
create/give a false impression = mislead
create/make a good impression = appear at one's best/be regarded
  favourably

impulse
  See: **blind** impulse.

in
fall in = realize/understand
have it in for somebody = be waiting for a chance to harm somebody
in and out of = continually in a certain place
in for = about to happen
in for it = about to be in trouble
in keeping with = appropriate/corresponding to, matching
in (right) lumber = in trouble

in on = be a party to/informed about
ins and outs = details
(well) in with = be friendly/in association with
nothing/not much in it = (very) little difference, no/little truth in the case in point
See also: in double **harness**; in **harness**.

inch
every inch a = a complete
give somebody an inch and they'll take a mile = make somebody a concession and he/she will take advantage and seek even more
within an inch of = very close to
within an inch of one's life = to be dangerously close to death

incline
be inclined to = be slightly in favour of doing something

incumbent
incumbent upon one = my duty/responsibility to

industry
key industry = industrial activity that is important/significant in national terms
See also: **captain** of industry; **cottage** industry.

inference
draw an/the inference = conclude

influence
under the influence = drunk

information
fish for information = try to find out about something (in a subtle/surreptitious manner)

iniquity
den/sink of iniquity = place where wrong-doers gather

initiative
on one's own initiative = without authorization/ prompting
take the initiative = adopt the role of leader/decision-maker

innings
have a good innings = live for a comparatively long time

inroad
  See: **make** inroads into.

inside
know something inside out = know everything about something

insolence
dumb insolence = refusal to comply with regulations/rules etc., but
  without saying anything at all

instance
in the first instance = initially/at first

insult
add insult to injury = add offensive/unkind behaviour to the harm
  that one has already done to somebody

intent
to all intents and purposes = as far as is important/significant

interest
in an interesting/certain condition = pregnant
in the interest of = for/in order to have
pay back with interest = make the punishment exceed the harm that
  invoked it

interim
in the interim = meanwhile

into
be into something = be enthusiastic/knowledgeable about

iota
one iota = the smallest part

iron
iron fist/hand in a velvet glove = ruthlessness that is disguised by an
  outward appearance of gentleness
iron out = resolve/remove
have several irons in the fire = be involved in several activities at once

strike while the iron is hot = take an opportunity while it presents
 itself
with an iron hand = ruthlessly
 See also: iron **curtain; man** of iron/steel; **rule** with a rod of iron.

issue
at issue = under dispute
confuse the issue = introduce irrelevances/divert attention from the
 main point
force an issue = bring a dispute to a decision point
side issue = something of secondary importance
take/join issue with somebody = disagree with somebody

it
this is it = this is what you have been expecting, or this is the critical
 point/stage

itch
have an itching palm = want/be greedy to obtain money

ivory
ivory tower = protected/unrealistic way of life

J

Jack
before you can say Jack Robinson = very quickly
cheap-jack = inexpensive but poorly made/shoddy
every Jack has his Jill = for every man there is a woman partner
  somewhere
I'm all right, Jack/pull up the ladder, Jack = I am in a
  happy/satisfactory position (and I do not care about anybody else)
jack-in-office = pompous/self-important person in a position of
  authority/power
jack in (something) = give up/stop doing (something)
jack-in-the-box = somebody who fidgets/does not sit still
Jack is as good as his master = a labourer/servant is as worthy as the
  person who employs him/her
jack of all trades = somebody who can do various kinds of jobs (but
  does none exclusively)
Jack Tar = sailor (in the Royal Navy)
jack up = increase
  See also: **every man jack (of them).**

jackpot
hit the jackpot = gain/win a lot of money/success

jail
jail-bird = somebody who has been in prison (habitually)
  See also: jail **bait.**

jam
in a jam = in difficulty
jam on it = extra benefit in an already favourable situation
money for jam/old rope = money obtained very easily

Jane
plain Jane = woman who is not particularly attractive

jaw
jaw away = talk incessantly

jaws of death = place/point at which one is in danger of dying
set one's jaw = adopt an attitude of grim determination
sock on the jaw = sudden setback/shock
take it on the jaw = accept a setback/punishment without complaint
  See also: **glass** jaw

jay
jay-walker = pedestrian who wanders into the road in front of
  moving traffic

Jekyll
Jekyll and Hyde personality = character that has two opposite sides
  to it

jib
cut of somebody's jib = somebody's overall appearance
jib at = baulk at/be unwilling to do something

jinks
high jinks = boisterous fun

Joan
  See: **Darby** and Joan.

Job
Job's comforter = somebody who does not comfort at all
try the patience of Job = test even somebody with unlimited patience

job
a good job (that) = fortunate/just as well (that)
axe a job = stop the work on a job/task
bad job = (very) unfortunate event
boot somebody out of a job = dismiss somebody
dead-end job = job with no prospects of promotion
do a job = commit a crime (usually robbery)
give something up as a bad job = stop doing something that looks as
  though it will end in failure
hatchet job = ruthless action
have a job to = have difficulty in

inside job = crime that involves an employee of the organization affected

job lot = miscellaneous collection

jobs for the boys = situation in which contracts/jobs are obtained by people who are associated with those who make the decision to place the work

land a plum job = obtain a good contract/job

make a good job of = do something well

make the best of a bad job = compromise/get some benefit from an unfavourable situation

on the job = at work/while working, or having sexual intercourse

put-up job = contrived scheme (designed to deceive)

the devil's own job = great difficulty

See also: **just** the job/thing/ticket.

jockey

jockey for position = manoeuvre into a position (of advantage)

jog

jog along = proceed gently/unhurriedly

jog a person's memory = remind somebody

joint

See: put somebody's **nose** out of joint.

joke

beyond a joke = no longer funny

corny joke = well-known joke

crack a joke = tell a joke/funny story

it's no joke = it is serious

joking apart = seriously

practical joke = prank that makes fun at somebody else's expense

sick joke = remark intended to be funny but made in (very) bad taste

standing joke = something that is always humorous even when repeated often

take a joke = accept in good humour a joke/trick played on one

that's a joke!/you must be joking! = I do not believe what you say

Jones
keep up with the Joneses = ensure that one's social standing is equal
to that of one's neighbours
See also: **Davy Jones' locker**

jot
jot down = make a note of
jot or tittle = smallest amount/quantity
not to care a jot = not to care at all

jowl
cheek by jowl = (very) close

joy
full of the joys of spring = very happy
get no joy = fail to obtain what one seeks
wish somebody joy = hope that somebody will enjoy doing something
(while being glad that one does not have to do it oneself)
See also: **pride** and joy.

judge
See: **sober** as a judge.

judgement
against one's better judgement = regretfully (= now I regret it)
sit in judgement = adopt the role of arbiter/critic (often without the
right or necessary ability)
snap judgement = quick decision

jugular
go for the jugular = take aggressive action

juice
stew in one's own juice = suffer because of one's own foolishness

jump
be one jump ahead = anticipate what is likely to happen (and be
ready for it)
for the high jump = about to be punished/reprimanded
go take a running jump (at yourself)! = go away!
jump at = eagerly seize an opportunity
jump bail = forfeit bail by failing to appear for trial

jump down somebody's throat = talk to somebody in an
  abrupt/angry way
jumping-off place = point of departure
jump out of one's skin = be frightened
jump the gun = be too eager/hasty
jump the queue = fail to wait one's turn (and move ahead of others
  who are waiting)
jump to it = act quickly
  See also: climb/jump onto the **bandwagon**; jump to a **conclusion**.

jumper
shove it up one's jumper = do whatever one likes with it

jungle
law of the jungle = rules (or lack of them) that apply to a fierce
  contest which is outside civilized control

just
just about = almost/nearly
just a minute/moment/second/tick = please wait for a very short
  while
just as well = fortunate/for the best
just in case = to allow for the event that
just so = neat and tidy, or precisely
just the job/thing/ticket = exactly what is required

justice
do justice to = treat fairly/reveal the merit of
do somebody/something justice = present somebody/something
  fairly/to best advantage
poetic justice = accidental but appropriate reward for goodness or
  retribution for wrongdoing
rough justice = overharsh punishment

K

kangaroo
kangaroo court = body which (without formal/judicial power) passes judgement

keel
keel over = suddenly fall over
on an even keel = balanced/calm

keen
  See: keen as **mustard**; sharp/keen as a **razor**.

keep
for keeps = for ever/permanent(ly)
in keeping with = (as is) appropriate/suited to
keep abreast of = keep up with/maintain one's position)in a competitive situation)
keep aloof = deliberately remain remote (from everyday/practical things)
keep an/one's eye on = watch carefully
keep a stiff upper lip = remain calm and unemotional (in adversity)
keep a straight face = deliberately fail to laugh, even though one is amused
keep at it = persevere
keep at arm's length = remain remote from
keep back = retain, or restrain
keep company with = associate with (often referring to a sexual relationship/courtship between a man and a woman)
keep cool/keep one's head = remain calm
keep going = continue (to function)
keep in touch = remain in communication
keep in with somebody = maintain an association/friendship (for one's own advantage)
keep it dark = preserve a confidence/secret
keep it to yourself = do not tell anyone
keep it up = carry on (doing something)

keep off = avoid
keep on (at somebody) = nag
keep one's (own) counsel = keep a confidence/secret
keep one's distance = not get too close/friendly
keep one's end up = maintain one's contribution/share (in an activity)
keep one's eyes peeled/skinned = be alert/on the watch
keep one's feet = maintain one's balance/upright posture
keep one's fingers crossed = wish for success
keep one's hair/shirt on = remain calm/not lose one's temper
keep one's hand in = practice (to maintain one's skill at something)
keep one's head above water = remain financially solvent
keep one's nose clean = stay out of trouble
keep one's word = keep a promise
keep out = exclude
keep out of the way = stay away
keep something back = fail to be completely frank
keep something from somebody = be secretive/fail to tell somebody something
keep the ball rolling = maintain the momentum/progress (of an activity)
keep the peace = maintain tranquillity/prevent fighting
keep (oneself) to oneself = be retiring/inclined to introversion
keep to the straight and narrow (path) = obey the law
keep/lose track of = follow/fail to follow
keep up with = maintain the same rate of progress/ position as
worth its/one's keep = worth the cost of maintenance
you can keep it! = I don't want it!
See also: have/keep something up one's **sleeve**; keep a low **profile**; keep a tight **rein** on; keep on an even **keel**; keep one's **eye** on the ball; keep one's **options** open; keep **pace** with; keep/set/start the **ball** rolling; keep something under **wraps**; keep **tabs** on; keep up with the **Joneses**.

ken
See: **beyond** one's ken.

kettle
a different kettle of fish = something that is very different

fine/pretty kettle of fish = confused situation/mess/muddle
  See also: **pot** calling the kettle black.

key

get/have the key to the door = reach the age of majority (currently
  eighteen in Britain, formerly twenty-one)
(all) keyed up = agitated/anxious/excited
key position = important/principal job/position
key to a problem = aspect of a problem that, if dealt with, leads to a
  solution
low key = quiet/without emphasis
skeleton key = composite key that will open many different locks

kick

for a kick off = first/to start with
for kicks = for fun/thrills
kick-back = commission/reward for a favour paid out of the receipts
  that result from that favour
kick off = begin(ning)/start
kick one's heels = be kept waiting
kick over the traces = behave unconventionally/break the rules
kick somebody in the teeth = cause somebody great
  discouragement/disappointment
kick somebody upstairs = promote somebody in order to render
  his/her job vacant
kick somebody when he/she is down = add to the misfortunes of
  somebody who is already in an unfortunate situation
kick up a fuss = create a disturbance
kick up one's heels = depart
  See also: **alive** and kicking; kick the **bucket**.

kid

kid's stuff = very easy/simple
with kid gloves = (very) gently
you're kidding! = I don't believe you!
  See also: **whizz** kid.

kill

dressed to kill = dressed in one's best/to impress
in at the kill = present at the end

(could) kill oneself = greatly regret something
kill oneself laughing = be very amused
kill time = occupy oneself while waiting
kill two birds with one stone = (take the opportunity to) do two
  things simultaneously
kill with kindness = be overkind
make a killing = make a large profit
  See also: kill or **cure**; kill the fatted **calf**; kill the **goose** that lays the
  golden egg.

kin
kith and kin = family/relations
next of kin = nearest relative/person who have a legal claim to an
  inheritance (in the absence of a will to the contrary)

kind
in kind = in the same way, or in goods rather than in cash
two of a kind = two people/things that are very similar
  See also: **cruel** to be kind; **nothing** of the kind/sort.

kindly
not take kindly to = be annoyed by/not like

kindred
kindred spirits = people with the same attitudes/points of view

king
a cat may laugh/look at a king = a humble/ordinary person has every
  right to look at an important person
fit for a king = luxurious/of the best quality
king of the castle = (the) most important person
king's ransom = very high price

kingdom
send to kingdom come = destroy/kill
until kingdom come = for a very long time/for ever

kiss
kiss of death = something that brings about ruin
kiss of life = mouth-to-mouth resuscitation
kiss somebody/something goodbye = never expect to see again

kitchen

If you don't like the heat get out of the kitchen = if you cannot stand the pace/pressure required to do something, then you should stop doing it
See also: **everything** but the kitchen sink.

kite

fly a kite = make a suggestion merely in order to gauge people's reaction to it
See also: **high** as a kite.

kitten

have kittens = be very anxious/nervous
See also: **nervous** as a kitten; **weak** as a kitten.

knee

bring somebody to his/her knees = make somebody feel defeated/humble
on (one's) bended knees = humbly/like a beggar
See also: **weak**-kneed.

knickers

get one's knickers in a twist = become excited/panic

knife

have/get one's knife into somebody = bear a grudge against/be persistently hostile to somebody
on a knife-edge = finely balanced
put the knife in = add to somebody's sufferings
under the knife = undergoing surgery
you could cut the air with a knife = you could detect an emotionally-charged atmosphere
See also: **accent** you could cut with a knife.

knight

knight in shining armour = benefactor/somebody who helps one when in trouble

knit

knit one's brows = frown/think hard

knob
with knobs on = (that is) even better/more

knock
knock-about = boisterous/informal
knock about with = associate with
knock back = drink quickly
knock-down price = cheap, bargain price
knocking shop = brothel
knock into a cocked hat = beat/be better than
knock it off! = stop it!
knock off = cease work, or steal
knock over = complete (quickly)
knock something down = offer/sell something cheaply, at a bargain price
knock something on the head = cancel/stop doing something
knock the bottom out of = reduce/undermine the worth of
knock spots off/the living daylights out of/the stuffing out of somebody = soundly beat/thrash somebody
knock together/up = improvise/make hurriedly
take a knock = suffer (a setback)
See also: knock somebody for **six**; knock somebody into the middle of next **week**.

knot
at a rate of knots = very quickly
tie somebody (up) in knots = confuse somebody
tie the knot = get married
See also: **cut** the (Gordian) knot.

know
for all I know = I do not know (and do not care) but
have known better days = not to be as good/wealthy as formerly
I don't know about you = I don't care what you think/want
I knew it = I was certain (that something would happen)
know a thing or two (about) = have a good knowledge (of), or show good common sense
know all the answers/a thing or two = be well informed
know somebody by sight = recognize somebody but not know his/her name

know something backwards/inside out = know something very well
know the ropes = be experienced
know the score = be aware of the true situation
in the know = in possession of information/knowledge
not know one is born = not to have encountered any trouble in life
not know the first thing about = know nothing about
not know when one is well off = not realize how fortunate one is
not that I know of = not as far as I am aware
you know = remember
you never know = perhaps/possibly
  See also: don't know somebody from **Adam**; know one's **place**;
  know one's **stuff**; know something **straight** off; know what one is
  talking about; not know one **end** of something from the other.

knowledge
come to one's knowledge = be told about/find out

knuckle
knuckle down to something = begin working in earnest at something
knuckle sandwich = a punch (to the face) with a closed fist
knuckle under = give in/submit
near the knuckle = bordering on the indecent
rap somebody on the knuckles = reprimand/scold somebody

L

labour
black-leg labour = people employed (by the management) when the regular workers are on strike
labour a point = make a point (of discussion) (too) frequently
labour in vain = work but with no result
labour of love = task done for no reward, just one's own satisfaction
labour under a delusion = be under a misapprehension

lace
lace a drink = add a spirit (brandy, rum etc.) to a non-alcoholic beverage (coffee, tea etc.)
See also: **strait**-laced.

lad
See: **bit** of a lad.

ladder
top (rung) of the ladder = highest position in a career
See also: **pull** up the ladder, Jack.

lady
ladies' man = man who likes (and seeks) the company of women
Lady Bountiful = rich/generous woman (usually pejorative)
lady in waiting = woman who is pregnant
lady-killer = man popular with women
lady of the town = prostitute
one's good lady = one's wife
the old lady of Threadneedle Street = the Bank of England

laid
get laid = have sexual intercourse
laid back = (very) relaxed
laid up = out of commission (through disrepair or illness)

lamb
go like a lamb (to the slaughter) = do something meekly/without resistance

one might as well be hung for a sheep as a lamb = if punishment is due, one might as well do something really bad and enjoy it while one can

mutton dressed up as lamb = describing an older woman who dresses and behaves as if she were much younger

See also: in two **shakes** (of a lamb's tail).

lame
See: lame **duck**; lame **excuse**.

land
be landed with = end up with
in the land of Nod = asleep
in the land of the living = active/alert
land of milk and honey = fertile region
land of the midnight sun = northern Norway and other places north of the Arctic Circle where the sun never sets (even at night) during summer months
land on one's feet = be fortunate/lucky
land somebody with something = pass a difficult/unpleasant task to somebody else
land up = finish at
lie of the land = situation as it applies (before doing something)
no man's land = neutral ground between opposing forces
see how the land lies = analyse the situation (before doing something)
See also: **happy** landing; live off the **fat** of the land; **spy** out the land.

landscape
See: **blot** on the landscape.

landslide
landslide victory = overwhelming win

lane
go down memory lane = indulge in nostalgic memories

language
daughter language = language derived from another (earlier) one
dead language = language that is no longer spoken in everyday use
murder a language = speak a language very badly

pick up a language = acquire the ability to speak a language (without formal tuition)
second language = language (that is spoken/understood) other than one's mother tongue
speak/talk the same language as somebody = share the same views as somebody
  See also: (using) **bad**/strong language.

lap
drop/land in one's lap = achieve without effort
in the lap of the gods = dependent on chance
lap of luxury = luxurious situation

large
at large = free
larger than life = with an exaggerated character

lark
happy as a lark = very happy
lark about/have a lark = fool about/play the fool
rise/get up with the lark = rise very early in the morning

lash
lash out = hit out, or spend lavishly

last
at (long) last = in the end
at/with one's last gasp = with one's last (dying) breath
last but not least = said of the best item on a list that is deliberately left until last
last out = endure/last
last straw (that breaks the camel's back) = final factor that, in addition to others, makes a situation impossible
on one's last legs = near to breakdown/collapse
stick to one's last = not depart from what one is best at
the last = the least likely/wanted
the last word = very up-to-date
  See also: **see** the last of somebody.

latch
latch on to = grasp (an idea/object), or join
  See also: latch-key **child**.

late

at the latest = by a certain time (and preferably sooner)

better late than never = a late occurrence is preferable to one that doesn't happen at all

(a bit) late in the day = too late

of late = recently

sooner or later = eventually

lather

in a lather = agitated/upset

Latin

See: **dog** Latin.

laugh

don't make me laugh! = I don't believe you!/that is ridiculous!

have the last laugh = be finally proved right

have the laugh on somebody = be able to make fun of somebody

laughing-stock = object of ridicule

laugh like a drain/laugh one's head off = laugh very loudly/for a long time

laugh in somebody's face = regard somebody with total scorn

laugh on the other side of one's face = have apparent happiness/success turned to disappointment/failure

laugh something away/off = regard difficulties as being unimportant

laugh something out of court = scornfully dismiss/disregard something without even considering it

laugh up one's sleeve = laugh in secret, or laugh inwardly without showing amusement

no laughing matter = serious matter

you're laughing = you will have nothing to worry about

See also: **die** laughing; **hollow** laugh; **horse** laugh; **kill** oneself laughing; laughed out of **court**; laughter is the best **medicine**; **raise** a laugh.

launch

launch out = begin (something expansive/grand)

laurels

look to one's laurels = make sure one continues to perform as well as in the past *rest on one's laurels* = rely on one's past reputation to maintain one's position (without making any further effort)

law

beyond the law = outside the jurisdiction of the courts
call in the law = call the police
have the law on somebody = ensure that the police/courts take legal action against somebody
in the eye(s) of the law = from a strictly legal point of view
law-abiding = honest/upholding the law
law unto himself = describing somebody who rejects convention or the usual rules
lay down the law = state something forcefully and without heed of any objections
Murphy's/sod's law = adage which states that if anything can go wrong it will
Parkinson's law = adage which states that a task tends to expand to take up the time available for it
take the law into one's own hands = obtain what one regards as justice without using the legal process
unwritten law = accepted, but not formal, rule/code of behaviour
See also: long **arm** of the law; law of the **jungle**.

lawyer

barrack-room lawyer = somebody who is always quoting the rules

lay

lay a bet = make a wager
lay about one = strike out in all directions
lay about/into somebody = belabour/berate somebody
lay aside = postpone/put to one side
lay bare = expose
lay emphasis/stress/weight on = emphasize
lay hold of/one's hand on = obtain
lay in/up = put in store
lay it on thick/with a trowel = exaggerate/flatter
lay low = flatten, or make ill
lay off somebody = stop annoying/harming somebody
lay on = provide

lay oneself open (to) = be vulnerable to
lay open = expose/uncover
lay out = arrange a corpse after death
lay somebody off = (temporarily) end somebody's employment
lay somebody to rest = bury somebody (after death)
lay waste = completely destroy (over an area)
   See also: lay at somebody's **door**; lay down the **law**; lay one's **cards** on the table.

lead
give a lead = give an indication for others to follow
lead a double life = have two different lifestyles simultaneously
leading light = somebody who is highly regarded/influential
leading question = question whose phrasing anticipates/provokes the required answer
lead nowhere = fail/make no progress
lead off = speak angrily (and at length)
lead somebody astray = tempt somebody into wrongdoing
lead somebody by the nose = force somebody to submit to what one wants
lead up to = gradually prepare for
swinging the lead = avoiding work/ malingering
take the lead = play the leading part
   See also: lead a **dog**'s life; lead somebody a (merry) **dance**; lead the **way**; (lead somebody) up the **garden** path; put lead in one's **pencil**.

leaf
leaf through = quickly turn the pages (of a book)
shake like a leaf = tremble, be very cold/frightened
take a leaf out of somebody's book = follow somebody's example
turn over a new leaf = start behaving in a better way
   See also: **loose**-leaf(ed).

league
bottom/top of the league = worst/best
in league with = allied/associated with (often for no good purpose)
not in the same league as = not as good as

leak
leak out = be known/revealed

lean

lean on somebody = depend on somebody, or persuade somebody using slight pressure
  See also: bend/lean over **backwards**; lean/thin **time**.

leap

by leaps and bounds = very quickly
leap in the dark = action of uncertain outcome

learn

learn something by heart = memorize something (so that it can be instantly recalled)
learn a lesson = learn how to/not to do something (often after a mishap/mistake)
learn something the hard way = learn something through one's own (bitter) experience
learn the ropes = learn the details/procedure of a craft/undertaking
you live and learn = one learns through experience

lease

new lease of life = opportunity for an extra period of active/useful life

leash

straining at the leash = eager/impatient

least

in the least = at all
least of all = particularly not
least said, soonest mended/the least said the better = saying as little as possible is the best policy in a difficult situation
not least = particularly
to say the least = without overstatement

leather

hell for leather = as fast as possible

leave

beg one's leave of somebody = ask somebody if one might leave
leave a lot/much to be desired = be undesirable/unsatisfactory

leave a nasty taste in one's mouth = leave one with feelings of
  bitterness/regret
leave in the lurch = abandon
leave it at that = say no more (about something)
leave it out! = don't do/say that!
leave no stone unturned = make a (very) thorough search
leave of absence = permission not to attend/be present
leave off = stop
leave one cold = not affect/impress one
leave oneself wide open = be vulnerable/have no defence
leave out = omit
leave over = stop, or postpone
leave somebody at the post = leave somebody way behind
leave somebody to it = let somebody continue on his/her own
leave standing = be superior to
leave well alone = avoid/make no change
leave word = leave a message
take it or leave it = please yourself; you can have it only under these
  conditions
take leave of one's senses = go (slightly) mad
without so much as a by your leave = without comment/permission
  See also: leave somebody to his/her own **devices**; leave the **door**
  open; left holding the **baby**; left on the **shelf**; take **French** leave.

leech
cling/stick like a leech = remain adhered/very close to

leeway
make up leeway = regain lost distance/time

left
have two left feet = move clumsily
left, right and centre = in large quantities and in all directions

leg
find/get one's sea legs = become accustomed to travelling on a
  boat/ship
give a leg up = help somebody to reach a higher level
have no/not enough legs = not be going fast enough (to reach a
  particular place)

leg it = run away/fast
leg-pull = prank/joke
not have a leg to stand on = have no excuse/justification for one's
    actions/views
pull somebody's leg = jokingly try to lie to somebody
shake a leg! = hurry up!
show a leg! = wake up!
stretch one's legs = go for a walk (after a time of inactivity)
walk somebody off his/her legs = make somebody walk farther than
    he/she can go without becoming (very) tired
    See also: **cost** an arm and a leg; on one's **last** legs; talk the hind leg
    off a **donkey**; with one's **tail** between one's legs.

leisure
at one's leisure = when one has time

lemon
    See: the **answer**'s a lemon.

lend
lend itself to = be usable on
lend one's name to = allow one's name to be associated with
    something
    See also: give/lend a (helping) **hand**; lend an **ear**.

length
at (great) length = for a long time/in detail
go to any lengths = do anything (regardless of the consequences)
    See also: keep/hold at **arm**'s length.

leopard
a leopard never changes its spots = somebody's basic nature cannot
    be changed

lesson
let that be a lesson (to you) = learn from your (recent) mistake
object lesson = classic/clear example
teach somebody a lesson = reprimand/punish somebody in order to
    discourage bad behaviour

let
let alone = not including
let blood = injure/wound
let-down = disappointment
let drop/fall/slip = (accidentally) reveal
let fly = speak out angrily
let off = (allow to) explode
let off steam = give vent to pent-up feelings (in angry words/vigorous
  activity)
let on = disclose (a secret)
let oneself go = take no trouble about one's appearance, or behave
  without restraint
let out = allow somebody/something to escape/leave
let somebody down = disappoint somebody/fail to keep an
  appointment/promise
let somebody have it = make a vigorous attack on somebody
let somebody in = allow somebody to enter
let somebody in for something = cause somebody to become involved
  in difficulty/unpleasantness
let somebody in on something = share something (a
  secret/undertaking) with somebody
let somebody loose on = allow somebody a free hand (to do as he/she
  wishes)
let somebody off = waive a punishment
let something (well) alone = avoid changing something
let something pass = allow something to be said/occur without
  comment
let something slide = allow something to become late/worse
let up = diminish
  See also: **blood**-letting; let **bygones** be bygones; let one's **hair** down;
  let sleeping **dogs** lie; let that be a **lesson** (to you); let the **cat** out of
  the bag; not let the **grass** grow under one's feet; let something **rip**.

letter
French letter = condom, contraceptive sheath
to the letter = exactly
within the letter of the law = exactly in accordance with written
  instructions/regulations (if not necessarily the spirit of them)

See also: red-letter **day**; **man** of letters.

level
find its own level = settle at its natural position/rank
level pegging = having equal ability/score
keep a level head = remain calm/sensible
on the level = fair/honest
   See also: do one's (level) **best**.

liberty
take liberties = behave with a lack of respect
take the liberty = do something without permission

licence
licence to print money = very profitable venture

lick
lick and a promise = quick (cursory) wash
lick one's wounds = comfort oneself (immediately) after suffering
 discomfort/pain
lick something into shape = make something better/more perfect
   See also: lick somebody's **boots**/shoes; lick/smack one's **lips**.

lid
blow/lift/take the lid off = disclose
flip one's lid = go mad (with anger)
put the (tin) lid/hat on = bring something to an end (in an unpleasant
 way)

lie
give the lie to = expose/prove wrong
lie at one's door = one is responsible/to blame
lie doggo/low = remain hidden/quiet
lie in/through one's teeth = lie blatantly
lie in wait = ambush/wait in order to make an attack
lie of the land = particulars of a given situation
lie up = hide
live a lie = pursue a dishonest/false way of life
take something lying down = accept something without
 argument/protest
thumping/whacking/whopping great lie = big lie

white lie = lie told for convenience/to avoid hurting somebody's feelings

See also: **bare**-faced lie; let sleeping **dogs** lie; make one's **bed** and (must) lie in it; **pack** of lies.

life

as large as life = present in person

breath of life = something that enlivens/invigorates

breathe life into = enliven/invigorate

come to life = come alive (of something non-living), or come awake (of somebody sleeping/unconscious)

depart this life = die

for dear life = very quickly (in desperation)

for the life of one = emphasizes one's inability to do something (even if one's life depended on it)

have/lead a charmed life = have continuing good luck

have the time of one's life = have a very enjoyable time

high life = luxurious lifestyle

larger than life = exaggerated

lay down one's life = sacrifice one's life (for the sake of others)

life and soul = with total commitment

life and soul of the party = somebody who is (ostentatiously) amusing/jolly

life of Reilly/Riley = life without trouble/worry

low life = criminal/disreputable people

matter of life and/or death = something that is critical/very urgent

new lease of life = opportunity for a better/longer life

not on your life! = definitely not!

prime of (one's) life = age of maximum ability/fitness

risk life and limb = endanger oneself (physically)

run for one's life = run as fast as possible

see life = experience how other people live

take one's life in one's hands = take a (grave) risk

take one's own life = commit suicide

that's life! = that is the way things generally occur!

there's life in the old dog yet = I/he may be elderly, but I'm/he's still active and alert

throw a lifeline to somebody = help somebody in (financial) difficulty

time of one's life = very enjoyable time
to save one's life = even if one's life depended on it
to the life = exactly resembling
true to life = real/closely resembling actuality
walk of life = occupation/social background
where there's life there's hope = while it is even remotely possible
  there will be an improvement in a difficult situation, do not despair
you (can) bet your life = certainly/surely
  See also: **autumn** of one's life; **facts** of life; lead a **cat** and dog's life;
  lead a **charmed** life; lead a **dog's** life; **lead** a double life; **seamy** side
  of life; **staff** of life; **variety** is the spice of life.

lift
lift one's hand against = threaten (to hit somebody)
lift one's spirits = make one cheerful
thumb a lift = signal passing vehicles for a free ride
  See also: blow/lift/take the **lid** off; lift/stir a **finger**; lift/bend the
  elbow.

light
according to one's lights = according to one's point of view
bright lights = show business and its attractions
bring to light = discover/reveal
cold light of day = time when something is considered
  calmly/unemotionally
come to light = emerge/be revealed
give the green light to = formally authorize
go out like a light = suddenly fall asleep/unconscious
hide one's light under a bushel = fail to reveal one's ability/skill
in a bad/good light = unfavourably/favourably
in its/one's true light = as it/one actually is
in the cold light of dawn/day = when considered calmly/practically
in the light of = considering (information available)
light as a feather = very light
lighter side = less serious aspect
light-fingered = with a tendency to steal
light-footed = agile/nimble
light of one's life = person whom one most admires/loves
light upon = discover

make light of = regard/treat as unimportant
make light work of = do/fulfil something with ease
red light district = part of a town that caters for sexual pleasures
see the light (of day) = happen, or accept/realize (the merit of something)
see the light at the end of the tunnel = have the end of an undertaking in sight
see the red light = anticipate approaching danger
shed/throw light on = explain/make clear
shoot the (traffic) lights = drive past traffic lights when they are red
strike a light! = exclamation of surprise
  See also: all **sweetness** and light; many **hands** make light work.

lightning
lightning strike = sudden bold attack
like greased/a streak of lightning = very quickly

like
I'd like to see (somebody do something) = I would be surprised if
if you like = if it pleases/suits you
I like that! = exclamation of anger/surprise
like anything/billy-o/blazes/crazy/mad/the clappers = very fiercely/quickly
likely enough = probably
like it's going out of fashion = without restraint
like-minded = of the same inclination/opinion
nothing like = bear no resemblance to
not likely! = definitely not!
that's more like it = that's better
the like = similar things
the likes of = such people as
  See also: like **father**, like son.

likelihood
in all likelihood = probably

lily
lily-livered = cowardly
lily-white = pure white
  See also: **gild** the lily.

limb
out on a limb = exposed to danger/risk (on one's own)

limbo
in limbo = in a state of neglect/uncertainty

limelight
in the limelight = at the focus of (public) attention

limit
within limits = somewhat/to a certain extent (but not to excess)
the limit = as much as can be borne (and more than which is
  intolerable)
  See also: the **sky**'s the limit.

limpet
  See: **cling** (on) like a limpet/grim death.

line
all along the line = at every stage (in a sequence), completely
bring something into line = make something correspond (with others)
come/fall into line = agree/correspond (with others)
draw the line (at) = set a limit (beyond which one/somebody must not
  go)
end of the line = point at which something finishes
fall out of line = disagree with/move away from
hard lines = bad luck
in line ahead = (of ships) one behind the other
in line for = have a (good) chance of obtaining (something)
in line with = in agreement with
in somebody's line = within somebody's competence/experience
in the firing line/line of fire = vulnerable (to attack)
in the line of duty = within one's obligations/responsibilities
lay something on the line = to risk losing something, or say something
  with (frank) emphasis
line one's pockets = make money/profit (at somebody else's expense)
line up = place/stand in line, queue
marriage lines = marriage certificate
on the lines of = resembling
read between the lines = extract a meaning that is not explicitly stated

stand in line = queue, wait one's turn

shoot a line = give an exaggerated account (about oneself)

step out of line = fail to behave in the accepted/required way

take the line of least resistance = adopt a course of action that causes the least difficulty/trouble

toe the line = conform/obey the rules
   See also: **drop** a line; **end** of the line/road; in one's line of **country**; **off**/on line; **sign** on the dotted line; **story** line.

linen

wash one's dirty linen in public = have an open disagreement/discussion about private difficulties

lion

as brave as a lion = very brave

beard the lion in his den = face up to somebody in authority/power in his/her own environment

lion-hunter = somebody who seeks the friendship of famous people

lion's share = biggest part

put one's head in the lion's mouth = adopt a position that is dangerous/risky

throw somebody to the lions = endanger somebody (to save oneself)

twist the lion's tail = defy Britain or its policies
   See also: lion's **den**.

lip

curl one's lip = make a scornful facial expression

give somebody lip = be cheeky

lick/smack one's lips = look forward to something eagerly

my lips are sealed = I will not tell anybody

pay lip service to = pretend to agree to something with no intention of doing it
   See also: **bite** one's lip; **keep** a stiff upper lip.

list

black list = list of companies/people who are (regarded as) dishonest/untrustworthy

enter the lists = take part in a contest

short list = list of (comparatively) few items/people, selected from a longer list, from which a final choice is made

litter

litter-bug = somebody who drops litter (in a public place)

little

little by little = gradually
think little of = have a poor opinion of
  See also: a little **bird** told me; little things please little **mind**s.

live

live and learn = learn by (bitter) experience
live and let live = be unconcerned what other people do, as long as
  they tolerate what one does oneself
live by one's wits = survive using cunning/one's mental ability (rather
  than, for example, by hard work)
live from hand to mouth = to have only sufficient for one's
  immediate needs, with nothing for the future
live in sin = live together as man and wife without being married
live it up = enjoy oneself (through excessive spending/indulgence)
live on one's reputation = succeed because of former achievements
  (without making new efforts)
live rough = live in difficult conditions (with few/no amenities)
live something down = lead a normal life until a misdeed is forgotten
live to tell the tale = survive
live up to = equal a (good) example set by somebody else
live wire = somebody who is energetic/enthusiastic
live with = endure (something unpleasant)
within/in living memory = within the lifetime of people still alive
  See also: do something/live in **style**; live beyond/within one's **means**;
  live like a **lord**; live like fighting **cocks**; live off the **fat** of the land.

lively

  See: chirpy/lively as a **cricket**

lo

lo and behold = exclamation of surprise (when somebody/something
  suddenly appears)

loaf

use one's loaf = use one's common sense
  See also: **half** a loaf is better than none/no bread (at all).

load
a load off one's mind = relief from a worry
get a load of = pay (particular) attention to
loaded question = question inviting an answer that discredits the
  speaker
what a load of cobblers/rubbish! = what nonsense!
  See also: the **dice** are loaded.

local
local colour = detailed information that indicates an intimate
  knowledge of a place
local pub = one's nearest/regular public house
  See also: local **rag**.

lock
behind locked doors = in secret
lock, stock and barrel = completely
under lock and key = in a locked building/container/room
  See also: lock **horns** with somebody; lock the stable **door** after the
  horse has bolted.

locker
  See: Davy Jones' locker.

locusts
swarm like locusts = crowd round greedily

log
  See: as easy as **falling** off a log; **sleep** like a log/top.

loggerheads
be at loggerheads = disagree

logic
stand logic on its head = be illogical

loins
  See: **gird** up one's loins

lollipop
lollipop lady/man/woman = somebody who is employed to control
  traffic where children cross the road (to and from school)

lone
lone wolf = somebody who shuns the company of others

long
go a long way towards = be nearly enough for/to
have/pull a long face = look in a disapproving/unhappy manner
in the long run = eventually
long-drawn-out = extended (in time)
long in the tooth = old
long odds = a remote chance
long shot = a guess
long-standing = existing for a long time
long-suffering = very tolerant
long-term = lasting for a long time
long-winded = boringly long (of a speaker/speech)
not long for this world = on the point of death
the long and (the) short of it = an abbreviated account
   See also: as **broad** as it's long; by a long **chalk**; the long **arm** of
   coincidence; the long **arm** of the law.

look
by the look(s) of/from the look of things = judging by appearances
look about (one) = look in all directions
look after somebody/something = take care of/tend
   somebody/something
look a gift horse in the mouth = find fault with something given free
look askance at = look at disapprovingly/suspiciously
look at = examine
look back on = remember/reminisce
look bad (for somebody) = appear to indicate trouble
look before you leap = be cautious/take care before acting
look blue = appear to be depressed/unhappy
look down (up)on = regard as inferior
look down one's nose at = regard with contempt
look for = search
look forward to = anticipate (with pleasure)
look good = look appealing/attractive
look in on = pay a brief (uninvited) visit
look into = investigate

look here! = exclamation of protest
look like = appear probable (that)
look lively/sharp = hurry up/be quick
look out! = beware!/take care!
look out for = be aware/careful of, or try to find
look over = look at (something large)
look sheepish = look guilty
look small = appear to be foolish/insignificant
look the other way = deliberately ignore
look to somebody = expect/rely on somebody (to do something)
look up = visit somebody, find an entry in a (reference) book
look up to somebody = respect somebody
not get/have a look in = be excluded/ignored
not like the look of something = be suspicious of something
not much to look at = unattractive
now look what you've done! = expression of rebuke
one's own look-out = something that is one's sole responsibility
  See also: ask/look for **trouble**; **black** look/stare; **dirty** look; look
  at/see/view things through **rose**-tinted spectacles; look **daggers** at;
  look/spoil for a **fight**; look for a **needle** in a haystack; look on the
  bright side; look/show one's **age**; look snappy; look the **part**; not as
  green as one is cabbage looking.

loom
loom large = approach (of something important/significant)

loophole
loophole in the law = flaw in legislation (that allows somebody to
  avoid being charged with breaking the law)

loose
at a loose end = idle/unoccupied
cut loose = break away (from convention), or release
have a screw/slate/tile loose = be (slightly) mad
keep a loose/tight rein on = allow plenty of/little freedom
loose-leaf(ed) = having pages that can be removed/replaced
loose-limbed = lithe/supple
loosen somebody's tongue = persuade somebody to talk
loose off = fire (bullets, words etc.)

on the loose = behave in an unrestrained manner
play fast and loose = deceive somebody (for selfish reasons)
tie up loose ends = complete the final details

lord

as drunk as a lord = very drunk
live like a lord = live in luxury
lord it over somebody = adopt a superior attitude to somebody
Lord knows = I do not know
one's lord and master = one's husband

lorry

fall off the back of a lorry = be stolen

lose

fight a losing battle = attempt to do something that must end in
   failure
lose face = lose one's reputation/respect
lose ground = retreat, lose an advantage
lose heart = become discouraged
lose one's cool/rag/wool = lose one's temper
lose one's bottle = lose one's nerve
lose oneself in = become engrossed in
lose one's head = panic/lose control (of oneself)
lose one's heart = fall in love
lose one's marbles/reason = go mad
lose one's shirt = lose all one's money (through gambling)
lose one's sight = become blind
lose one's touch = lose the ability/skill to do something
lose out = fail (because of a disadvantage)
lose sight of = forget/fail to pay attention to
lose the drift/thread = fail to understand the connection between the
   stages in an argument
   See also: keep/lose **track** of; lose **ground**; lose one's **grip**; lose one's
   hearing; lose one's **tongue**; lose one's **voice**; lose one's **way**; lose **sleep**
   over; lose one's **nerve**; lose **touch** (with); what you lose on the
   swings, you gain on the roundabouts; win/lose the **toss**.

loss

at a loss/lost for words = speechless (because one cannot think of
   anything to say)

be at a loss = be puzzled/undecided
cut one's losses = cease doing something in order to minimize one's losses
  See also: **dead** loss.

lost

get lost! = go away!
lost in admiration = very favourably impressed
lost on somebody = have no effect on somebody
  See also: get lost in the **wash**; lost **cause**; at a loss/lost for **words**.

lot

bad lot = somebody who is disreputable
cast/throw one's lot (in) with = join somebody/something and share his/her/its fortunes
fat lot = very little (used sarcastically)
have a lot going for one = have many advantages
that's your lot = that is all you are getting
whole lot = many
  See also: **cast** lots; **draw** lots; **fall** to one's lot; **leave** a lot to be desired.

loud

loud and clear = very clearly/emphatically
  See also: for **crying** out loud!

love

do something for love = do something without expecting payment
for the love of Mike/Pete = exclamation of frustration
labour of love = task done for pleasure (rather than financial reward)
love birds = (young) lovers
love in a cottage = marriage in which there is not much money
love me, love my dog = if you like somebody, you should also like his/her family/friends
I must love you and leave you = I must go
no love lost = great dislike/hatred
not for love or money = not for any reward
Platonic love = spiritual (non-sexual) love
  See also: all's **fair** in love and war; **calf**/puppy love; **cupboard** love.

low

at (a) low ebb = at a low level
be/get low on something = be nearly without (enough of) something
in low spirits = depressed
keep a low profile = (try to) remain inconspicuous
lay low = make ill (enough to have to stay in bed)
lie low = hide (and remain quiet)

luck

as luck would have it = fortunately/luckily
better luck next time = I hope you are more successful at your next
  attempt
down on one's luck = suffering from misfortune/lack of money
hard/tough luck = bad luck/misfortune
hard-luck story = account of misfortune (to the teller), often to gain
  sympathy (and usually untrue)
just one's luck = one's characteristic misfortune
luck of the devil/the Irish, or the devil's own luck = very good
  (although undeserved) luck
luck of the draw = as things happen
lucky dip = choice over which one has no control
no such luck = no (unfortunately)
push one's luck = risk a success by trying too hard to gain/profit
  even more
run of luck = succession of fortunate occurrences
strike (it) lucky = be very fortunate (in a particular instance)
take pot luck = take a chance (in a situation where there has been no
  preparation for one's involvement/participation)
thank one's lucky stars = be grateful for good fortune
try one's luck = attempt to do something (which may/may not
  succeed)/take a chance
with any luck = hopefully
worse luck = unfortunately
you'll be lucky = you will be fortunate (ironically)
you never know your luck (unless you try) = you may be fortunate
you should be so lucky! = why should you be so fortunate?
  See also: bad/lucky **break**; lucky **dog**.

lull

lull somebody into a false sense of security = mislead somebody into
  thinking that the situation is satisfactory, in order to gain a surprise
  advantage

lump

bring a lump to one's throat = cause one to feel deep
  pathos/sympathy
if you don't like it, you can lump it = you must accept the situation
  whether you like it or not
lump sum = single payment (instead of a series of smaller payments)
lump together = put several (different) things into one
  category/group

lunatic

  See: lunatic **fringe**.

lurch

leave somebody in the lurch = abandon somebody who is in difficulty

luxury

  See: in the **lap** of luxury.

lynx

lynx-eyed = with very keen eyesight

M

machine
 See: **cog** in the machine.

mackerel
 mackerel sky = thin, mottled clouds in rows
 sprat to catch a mackerel = small risk to make a large gain

mad
 drive/send mad = annoy/frustrate/irritate
 like mad = furiously/vigorously
 mad about/on = very enthusiastic about
 mad-cap = reckless/irresponsible
 method in one's madness = seemingly silly way of achieving
  something
 midsummer madness = foolish behaviour (brought on by the heat of
  summer)
  See also: **hop**ping mad; mad as a **hatter**; mad as a March **hare**; mad
  moment; (stark) **raving** mad.

madam
 little madam = precocious girl

made
 be made for somebody/something = ideally suited to
  somebody/something
 have it made = be (very) successful
 self-made man/woman = somebody who succeeds entirely through
  his/her own efforts
 what one is made of = one's ability/worth
  See also: made of **money**; made to **measure**; **make**.

magic
 wave one's magic wand = achieve something as if by magic
 work like magic = be very effective

magnitude
 See: of the **first** magnitude/order/water.

magpie
chatter like a magpie = chatter incessantly

maid
  See: **old** maid.

maiden
maiden lady = unmarried woman (middle-aged or elderly)
maiden name = surname of a woman before she marries
maiden speech = first speech (of somebody who is newly
  appointed/elected)
maiden voyage = first voyage of a plane/ship

main
in the main = generally/usually
splice the mainbrace = have a celebratory drink
with might and main = with all one's strength
  See also: eye on/to the main **chance**.

majority
attain one's majority = reach the age of legal responsibility
silent majority = (apathetic) majority of people who support the
  prevailing situation

make
be the making of somebody = bring out somebody's true
  character/potential
have the makings of = have the potential to be
in the making = in the process of becoming
make after = chase
make as if to (do something) = feign/pretend
make believe = pretend
make do (with) = make best use of what is available
make fast = secure/tie up
make for = aim at/move towards a particular place
make inroads into = make a start/have an effect on something
make it = succeed, or keep an appointment
make it up = recompense/make amends for, or settle one's
  differences
make it snappy = be quick

make of = understand
make off (with) = run away (with)
make out = cope/fare, or distinguish, or understand
make over = bequeath
make much of = make a fuss/exaggerate
make off = run away
make off with = steal
make or break = crucial test (resulting in success or failure)
makes no matter = does not matter
make so bold as = presume/take the liberty
make something (out) of it = cause an argument/fight
make something up = invent/lie
make the grade = reach a required standard
make the most of = take best advantage of a situation
make up = invent, or complete
make up for something = compensate/supply a substitute for
  something
make up to somebody = flatter/patronize somebody (for gain)
on the make = trying to make a gain/profit
that makes two of us = so am I
what do you make of something? = what is your opinion?
See also: get to/make first **base**; make a/the **break**; make a clean
  breast of; make a clean **sweep**; make a **day** of it; make **advances** to;
  make a **dead** set at; make a **dent** in; make a **fool** of somebody; make
  a **fuss**; make a **fuss** of; make a **go** of something; make a **habit** of
  something; make a **hash** of; make a **killing**; make all the **difference**;
  make a **man** of; make a **meal** (out) of something; make a **mountain**
  out of a molehill; make a **move**; make a **name** for oneself; make an
  example of somebody; make an **exhibition** of oneself; make a **night**
  of it; make a **packet**; make a **pass** at somebody; make a **play** for;
  make a **point** of doing something; make a **splash**; make a **stand**;
  make a **virtue** of necessity; make **believe**; make **demands** on; make **do**
  and mend; make (both) **ends** meet; make (sheep's) **eyes** at; make
  faces; make **free** with; make **friends** with; make **fun** of; make **good**;
  make good **time**; make **hay**; make **headway**; make **heavy** weather of;
  make **light** of; make **light** work of; make **merry**; make **money**; make
  neither **head** nor tail of something; make no **bones** about it; make
  old **bones**; make one's **blood** boil; make one's **blood** run cold; make

oneself at **home**; make oneself **scarce**; make one's **hackles** rise; make one's **hair** curl/stand on end; make one's **head** spin; make one's **mark**; make one's **peace** with somebody; make one's **point**; make one's **presence** felt; make one's **way**; make **overtures**; make **play** with; make **room** for; make short **work** of; make somebody's **day**; make somebody's **flesh** creep; make the **best** of (a bad job); make **time** for; make **tracks**; make up one's **mind**; make **water**; make **way** for; make **waves**.

maker

(go to) meet one's maker = die

male

male chauvinist pig = man with a domineering/superior attitude towards women

man

as one man/to a man = together/unanimously

be a man = act bravely/independently

dead men = empty bottles

dirty old man = somebody with a morbid interest in sex

every man for himself = each person must take care of himself/herself

every man has his price = each person is willing to agree to something as long as the inducement is sufficient

every man to his trade = each person should keep to what he/she is best at

family man = married man (with children) who spends much of his time with his family

front man = somebody employed to represent/divert approaches to those in authority

hit man = hired assassin

hit a man when he's down = add to the misfortune of somebody who is already unfortunate

I'm/he's your man = I am/he is the person you want

inner man = somebody's hunger/stomach

like a man = resembling a brave/resourceful person

make a man of = cause a youth to become mature/resourceful

man-about-town = socialite/somebody who is well known in society *man and boy* = all one's life

man in the street = average/typical person

man of breeding = somebody of high birth/aristocrat

man of his day = somebody who is famous among his/her contemporaries

man of his word = somebody who is honourable/trustworthy

man of iron/steel = somebody with great strength of character

man of letters = an author/writer

man of straw = somebody who is cowardly/weak-willed

man of the day/moment = somebody who has (short-lived) fame at a particular time

man of the old school = somebody with traditional views

man of the world = somebody with worldly experience, who has seen many aspects of life

man of the year = somebody who achieves fame/notoriety in a particular year

man to man = (honestly) on equal terms

marked man = somebody who is well known for a misdeed

may the best man win = I hope that the best person succeeds

my good man/woman = impolite form of address made by somebody who regards himself/herself as superior

sandwich man = somebody who carries advertisement boards in front and behind

sort out the men from the boys = select the best members of a group from the rest

you can't keep a good man down = a determined person will succeed

white man = somebody who is honourable/trustworthy

See also: **brotherhood** of man; **dead** man's shoes; **dead** men tell no tales; **every** man Jack (of them); **family** man; girl/man **Friday**; **hatchet** man; **lady**'s man; **lollipop** lady/man/woman; man in the **Moon**; man/somebody of few **words**; man of many **parts**; man of the **cloth**; **no** man's land; **odd** man out; **old** man; one-man **band**; one man's **meat** is another man's poison; one's **own** man; rich man's **hobby**; **right**-hand man; white man's **burden**.

manger
  See: **dog** in the manger.

manna
See: manna from **heaven**.

manner
all manner of = all kinds/types of
by no (manner of) means = in no way/absolutely not
in a manner of speaking = up to a point/in a way
(as if) to the manner born = naturally/(as if) used to something

many
a good/great many = a large number
many a long day = a long time
many hands make light work = the task will be completed quicker if
  everybody helps
many happy returns (of the day) = happy birthday
many's the time = frequently/often
  See also: **few** too many; **one** too many.

map
off the map = remote
put (a place) on the map = bring something/(somewhere) to the
  public notice

marbles
See: **lose** one's marbles/reason.

march
get one's marching orders = be dismissed
steal a march (on somebody) = gain an advantage over/get the better
  of somebody
  See also: **mad** as a March hare.

mare
See: mare's **nest**.

marines
(you can) tell that/it to the marines = I do not believe you

mark
beside/off the mark = off the point of discussion
close to/near the mark = nearly correct
easy mark = somebody of whom it is easy to take advantage

full marks = high praise
get off the/one's mark = begin doing something (quickly)
make one's mark = distinguish oneself/leave an impression
mark (something) down/up = decrease/increase the price of
  something
mark/put down to experience = be stoic about the difficulties of life
mark my words = be warned/remember what I say
mark time = wait/(deliberately) take no action
mark you = note what I say
near the mark = risqué/nearly obscene
off/wide of the mark = inaccurate/wrong
overshoot the mark = exceed what is required/go too far
overstep the mark = go beyond accepted limits of behaviour/protocol
quick/slow off the mark = quick/slow to begin/react
up to the mark = up the the required standard/healthy
  See also: marked **man**.

market
be in the market for = have an interest in buying
drug on the market = something that is difficult to sell
on the market = up for sale
  See also: **corner** the market.

marrow
chilled/frozen to the marrow = very cold

martyr
be a martyr to = suffer because of

mass
in the mass = as a whole
masses of = plenty
mass murder = unlawful killing of many people, genocide
mass survey = statistical analysis that involves questioning a large
  number of people
the masses = people in general/the population as a whole

mast
before the mast = at sea (as a member of the crew)
  See also: at **half** mast; **nail** one's colours to the mast.

master
master mind = instigator/organizer
master-mind = control/organize
master of oneself = have oneself under complete control
master-stroke = outstanding (and timely) action
  See also: **old** master; one's **lord** and master; **past** master.

mat
  See: on the **carpet**/mat.

match
be a match for someone = be equal to somebody in ability
match point = point that, if gained, wins the whole match for a
  competitor
meet one's match = deal with somebody who is as able/capable as
  oneself
more than a match for = better than
(whole) shooting match = everything
  See also: **needle** match.

material
  See: material **witness; raw** material.

matter
a matter of life or death = critical/urgent
a matter of opinion = something about which people hold different
  views
as a matter of course = naturally/routinely
as a matter of fact = in truth (used to emphasize a statement)
be a matter of = be a question of what is necessary
be a matter of time = will happen sooner or later
be the matter (with) = be the difficulty/problem
for that matter = concerning that
matter in question = point being considered/discussed
matter of course = something that happens naturally/routinely
matter of fact = the truth
matter-of-fact = practical/prosaic
no matter = never mind/it is unimportant
not to mince matters = to be frank

what's the matter? = what is the problem/what is wrong?
  See also: **grey** matter; **heart** of the matter; no **laugh**ing matter.

may
be that as it may = (even) having taken that into account

maybe
and I don't mean maybe = I mean what I say
that's as maybe = that may be so

meal
make a meal (out) of something = take excessive time/trouble in
  doing something
meal ticket = provider who does not expect to be paid
mealy-mouthed = hypocritical
square meal = satisfying/wholesome meal

mean
do you mean to say? = are you telling me?
do you see what I mean? = do you understand what I say?
I see what you mean = I understand
mean well = be good intentioned (even if offence results)
what do you mean by? = what is your motive/reason for?
  See also: and I don't mean **maybe**; mean **business**.

means
by all means = of course
by no means/not by any means = emphatically not, or not entirely
by what means? = how?
live beyond/within one's means = spend more/less than one earns
means to an end = method used to achieve a desired result
  See also: all **manner** of means; by **fair** means or foul.

meantime/meanwhile
in the meantime/meanwhile = while something is happening

measure
for good measure = as an addition
get/have somebody's measure/have the measure of somebody =
  judge the character of somebody
in some measure = partly

made to measure = manufactured to suit a particular requirement
measure one's length = fall full length on the ground
measure up to somebody/something = reach somebody else's/a
  specified standard
short measure = less than the required amount
take measures to = do something to ensure that
take somebody's measure = assess somebody's character
measure up somebody/something = study/get information about
  See also: for **good** measure.

meat
be meat and drink to (somebody) = be essential/important to
  (somebody)
one man's meat is another man's poison = something beneficial
  to/liked by one person may be the exact opposite to somebody else
  See also: **easy** meat/touch.

medicine
dose/taste of one's own medicine = unpleasantness suffered by
  somebody who usually does unpleasant things to others
laughter is the best medicine = cheerfulness makes one forget
  troubles/worry
medicine man = magician, wise man in primitive society
take one's medicine = tolerate unpleasantness (of one's own making)

medium
  See: **happy** medium.

meet
be met with = receive
meet one's match/Waterloo = finally suffer defeat
meet the case = suffice
  See also: make (both) **ends** meet; meet a **deadline**; (go to) meet one's
  maker; meet one's **match**; meet somebody **half** way; meet
  somebody's **eyes**; more than meets the **eye**.

melt
be in the melting-pot = be changing (into something new)
melt away/into = disappear/merge with one's surroundings

melt down = melt (a metal article), or melting and fire in the core of a
  nuclear reactor

memory
burden one's memory = be remembered with difficulty
commit to memory = memorize
down memory lane = in the (enjoyable) past
if my memory serves me correct/right = if I am remembering
  accurately
  See also: memory like an **elephant**; within/in **living** memory.

mend
make do and mend = improvise (using what is available)
mend one's ways = reform one's (bad) behaviour
on the mend = getting better/healing
  See also: **least** said, soonest mended.

mental
  See: mental **block**.

mention
don't mention it = you need not refer to it/it does not matter (said in
  declining thanks)
honourable mention = non-prizewinning award (in a competition)
I hate to mention it, but... = may I remind you that...
not to mention = in addition to (introducing something important, or
  something trivial)

mercy
angel of mercy = somebody who arrives to help just when he/she is
  needed, a nurse
at the mercy of (somebody or something) = in the power of
be thankful for small mercies = when in difficulty, be grateful for any
  help (no matter how small)
leave (somebody) to the tender mercies of = leave somebody to be
  dealt with by a cruel/unsympathetic person

merry
make merry = rejoice/enjoy oneself
make merry at somebody's expense = make fun of somebody

merry-go-round = frustrating/worthless activity (involving a lot of work)
the more the merrier = the more people there are, the better
 See also: lead somebody a (merry/pretty) **dance**; play (merry) **hell** with.

mess
make a mess of/mess up = do something incorrectly/spoil something
mess about = misbehave, or cause a nuisance (usually through inefficiency), or do something/work to no apparent purpose
mess of pottage = something cheap/of little value

message
get the message = understand (take a hint/heed a warning)

method
 See: there's method in his/her/their **madness**.

mettle
put somebody on his/her mettle = test somebody's ability

Methuselah
as old as Methuselah = very old

mice
 See: **mouse**.

mickey
take the mickey out of somebody = make fun of somebody

Midas
the Midas touch = the ability to succeed (financially) whatever one does

middle
be in the middle of (doing something) = in the act of (doing something)
knock somebody into the middle of next week = hit somebody very hard
middle-of-the-road = average/moderate
 See also: **pig**(gie)-in-the-middle.

midnight
  See: **burn** the midnight oil.

midstream
halt/pause/stop in midstream = (temporarily) stop while in the act of
  doing something
  See also: swap/change **horses** in midstream.

midsummer
  See: midsummer **madness**.

might
  See: **high** and mighty; with might and **main**.

Mike
  See: for the **love** of Mike/Pete.

milch
  See: milch **cow**.

mildly
put something mildly = deliberately understate something

mile
be miles away = be inattentive/day-dream
mile away/off = great distance
stand/stick out a mile = be obvious
talk a mile a minute = speak continuously and rapidly
  See also: give somebody an **inch** and they'll take a mile; a **miss** is as
  good as a mile; not a **hundred** miles away; **run** a mile.

milk
milk and water = weak/without substance
milk of human kindness = sincere/sympathetic attitude towards
  others
milk somebody = deceive somebody into parting with money
mother's milk = something that one especially enjoys (naturally)
  See also: **cry** over spilt milk; **land** of milk and honey.

mill
calm as a millpond = very calm (of water)
go/be put through the mill = be forced to endure an ordeal

mill about/around = move around aimlessly

the mills of God grind slowly (but they grind exceeding small) = the punishment/reward for one's actions will eventually happen, even after a long delay

See also: all **grist** to the mill; millstone round one's **neck**; **run** of the mill.

million

See: feel/look like a million **dollars**; **one** in a million/thousand

mince

make mincemeat of = completely defeat/destroy

not mince words = speak frankly/straightforwardly

mind

apply/give one's mind to = give attention/consideration to

at the back of one's mind = (always) in one's thoughts

bear/keep in mind = remember/retain in one's thoughts

be/rest easy in one's mind = be calm/unworried

be in two minds = be undecided

be of one/the same mind = agree/think alike

bring/call to mind = recall/remember

broaden one's/the mind = provide one with new experience/knowledge

cast one's mind back = remember a past event/incident

change one's mind = reconsider/decide on a different course of action

closed mind = attitude that is not open to criticism/suggestion

come (in)to one's mind = be remembered

cross one's mind = occur to one

do you mind? = would you please (do, or emphatically not do, something)

give somebody a piece of one's mind = be openly critical of somebody/angrily scold somebody

go out of one's mind = become emotionally upset, or become forgotten, or become mad

great minds think alike = similar ideas/views are shared by clever people (said in a jocular way)

have a good/half a mind to = be inclined to

have a mind of one's own = be independent
have it in mind to = have the intention of doing
have/keep an open mind = be undecided/open to suggestion
have something in mind = have an idea about something
have something on one's mind = be preoccupied with/troubled by
something
I don't mind if I do = I would like to
I wouldn't mind = I would like
in/out of one's right mind = sane/mad
it's all in the mind = it is imaginary
keep one's mind on = concentrate on
know one's own mind = be confident in one's own opinions
leap/spring to mind = become immediately/suddenly obvious
little things please little minds = people who are small-minded are
pleased/satisfied by petty things
make one's/the mind boggle = make one amazed/confused
make up one's mind = decide
mind how you go = be careful
mind out for = be careful of
mind you = all the same/even so
mind your backs! = please get out of the way
never mind = do not worry/take no notice
never you mind = it is of no concern to you
put one in mind of = remind one of
put/set somebody's mind at rest = reassure somebody
read somebody's mind = guess what somebody is thinking
set one's mind on/to = be determined to (do something)
slip one's mind = become forgotten
speak one's mind = give one's candid opinion
stoned out of one's mind/head = very drunk or drugged
take somebody's mind off something = distract somebody
time out of mind = for a very long time
to my mind = in my opinion
  See also: **blow** someone's mind; in one's **mind's eye**; mind being a
  blank; mind one's own **business**; mind one's **p's and q's**; of **unsound**
  mind; one-**track** mind; **out** of one's mind; out of **sight**, out of mind;
  presence of mind; **peace** of mind; **prey** on one's mind; **put** one in
  mind of; **put** one's mind to; **put** out of one's mind; **small** minded.

mine
mine of information = somebody who is knowledgeable
  See also: **gold** mine.

mint
in mint condition = as new
make a mint = earn a lot of money
worth a mint = very wealthy

minute
there's one born every minute = there are many foolish people
up to the minute = up-to-date, in fashion
  See also: **talk** a mile a minute; **wait** a minute/moment.

mire
  See: **drag** somebody through the mire/mud.

mischief
do oneself/somebody a mischief = harm oneself/somebody
make mischief = cause trouble/create discord

misery
put somebody out of his/her misery = put somebody out of his/her
  suspense/satisfy somebody's curiosity
put an animal out of its misery = put an end to an animal's suffering
  (by having it humanely killed)

miss
a miss is as good as a mile = something that nearly succeeds is no
  better than something that is a total failure
give something a miss = not do something
  See also: have a **screw** loose/missing; **hit**-or-miss; miss the **boat**; **near**
  miss/thing; never miss a **trick**.

mist
Scotch mist = describes something that is present but thought
  missing/non-existent

mistake
(and) make no mistake = you can be sure
there's no mistaking it = you cannot confuse it with/mistake it for
  something else

mister
  See: Mister **Right**.

mixed
  See: have mixed **feelings** about; mixed **bag**; mixed **blessing**.

mixer
a bad/good mixer = somebody who does not/does get on well with
  others

mixture
the mixture as before = unchanged

mockers
put the mockers on = spoil/ruin

molehill
  See: make a **mountain** out of a molehill.

Molotov
  See: Molotov **cocktail**.

moment
at the moment = now
choose/pick one's moment = select the best time to act/speak
half a moment/tick = very short time
have its/one's moments = have occasions of outstanding ability/merit
in a moment = very soon
in a weak moment = a time when one easily agrees to a request
mad moment = brief period of irrational behaviour
moment of truth = crucial/testing time
on the spur of the moment = impulsively/suddenly
psychological moment = precise time to act for maximum effect on
  others
there's never a dull moment = it is always busy/interesting
unguarded moment = time when one is not paying attention/taking
  care
  See also: in the **heat** of the moment; **man** of the day/moment; **wait** a
  minute/moment.

Monday
Monday morning feeling = general apathy (on returning to work)
  after the weekend

money

be in the money/made of money = be wealthy

coin money = make a lot of money (in business)

even money = equally likely

for my money = if it were my choice/if I had to bet on it

get one's money's worth = derive maximum value from one's efforts/expense

in the money = prosperous/with (new-found) wealth

knock some money off = reduce the price of something

money doesn't grow on trees = money is hard to obtain (and must be earned)

money down the drain = wasted money

money (is) no object = regardless of cost

money talks = wealth conveys advantages/privilege

pin money = money spent on minor articles/pleasures

pocket money = relatively small amount of spending money given by parents to their children.

put one's money where one's mouth is = make a commitment

rake in the money = prosper/do well at work/business

ready money = available cash/money

rolling in money = very wealthy

spend money like water/it's going out of fashion = spend carelessly/extravagantly

throw good money after bad = waste money in an attempt to recoup previous losses

throw money at = continue to finance a loss-making venture

throw money away = waste money

you pays your money and takes your choice = it does not matter which of several equal options one chooses

  See also: **blood** money; **blue** one's money; **conscience** money; **easy** money; **hush** money; money for **jam**/old rope; not for **love** or money; see the **colour** of (somebody's) money; **time** is money.

monkey

artful/clever as a cartload/wagonload of monkeys = very crafty/sly

make a monkey (out) of somebody = make a fool of somebody

monkey business = dishonest/underhand dealings

monkey with = interfere

monkey tricks = mischievous behaviour
more trouble than a cartload of monkeys = very
  mischievous/troublesome

month
month of Sundays = an impossibly long time

mood
in a mood = bad-tempered
in the mood (for something) = receptive (to something)
  See also: **black** mood.

moon
do a moonie = expose one's buttocks
do a moonlight (flit) = move home suddenly (to avoid paying one's
  debts)
moonshine = fantasy, or illicit whisky
over the moon = very happy/ecstatic
  See also: **cry** for the moon; **once** in a blue moon.

moral
  See: moral **support**.

more
and what's more = and in addition
more or less = approximately, or nearly
the more the merrier = the more people there are, the better will be
  the result
  See also: more **fool** you; **more's** the pity.

morning
be the morning after the night before = have a hangover
  See also: **Monday** morning feeling.

mortal
  See: shuffle off this mortal **coil**.

most
at (the) most = as a maximum
make the most of = take best advantage of
  See also: for the most **part**.

mother
be mother = act as hostess (when pouring tea)
mothers' meeting = group of gossiping people
the mother and father of = the most extreme example of
   See also: mother's **boy**; mother's **darling**; mother's **milk**; mother's
   apron strings; **necessity** is the mother of invention; mother **tongue**.

motion
go through the motions = pretend to do something, or try to do
   something but with no enthusiasm
   See also: set the **wheels** in motion.

mould
be cast in the same mould as = closely resemble

mountain
make a mountain out of a molehill = make a small difficulty appear
   to be a large problem

mouse
the best-laid schemes of mice and men (gang aft agley) = anybody's
   careful plans (may fail)
   See: play **cat** and mouse with somebody; **poor** as a church mouse;
   when the **cat**'s away (mice will play); **quiet** as a mouse/the grave.

mouth
all mouth and trousers = very talkative but reluctant to take action
by word of mouth = using the spoken word (as opposed to being
   written down or printed)
have a big mouth = talk boastfully/indiscreetly/loudly
leave a nasty taste in one's mouth = leave one with a bad/bitter
   impression
make one's mouth water = be very appetizing
shoot one's mouth off = boast
shut one's mouth/face/trap = stop talking/refrain from speaking
   See also: **born** with a silver spoon in one's mouth; **butter** wouldn't
   melt in his/her mouth; **down** in the mouth/dumps; **foam** at the
   mouth; have one's **heart** in one's mouth; live from **hand** to mouth;
   look a gift **horse** in the mouth; put one's **money** where one's mouth
   is; straight from the **horse**'s mouth; take the **word**s out of
   somebody's mouth.

move
get a move on = hurry up
get something on the move = make something happen
make a move = leave
on the move = continually moving/travelling
See also: move **heaven** and earth.

much
be too much = be more than one can accept/bear
be too much for somebody = be too difficult for somebody
it's a bit much = you are expecting too much
make much of = exaggerate the significance of (boastfully), or make a fuss of
much of a muchness = similar (and usually mediocre)
not think much of = have a low opinion of
not up to much = not very good/well
so much for something = that demonstrates how bad something is
without so much as = without even

muck
make a muck of something = do something badly
muck in with = join/share with
See also: **common** as muck.

mud
here's mud in your eye! = cheers!/good health! (a toast when drinking)
throw/sling mud at = insult/vigorously discredit
See also: as **clear** as mud; **drag** somebody through the mire/mud; muddy the **waters**; somebody's **name** is mud; **stick** in the mud.

muddle
muddle through = achieve something despite carelessness/disorganization

mug
mug shot = photograph of somebody's face
no mug = somebody who is shrewd/wise
See also: mug's **game**.

mule
  See: **stubborn** as a mule.

multitude
cover/include a multitude of sins = include a wide variety of things

mum
mum's the word = do not repeat what I have just told you

murder
get away with murder = go undetected/unpunished yet do something
  bad
  See also: (scream) **blue** murder.

Murphy
  See: Murphy's/sod's **law**.

music
music to one's ears = something one is very pleased to hear
  See also: **face** the music; no **ear** for music.

mustard
keen as mustard = eager/enthusiastic

muster
pass muster = be considered to be good enough

mutton
  See: **dead** as a doornail/mutton; mutton dressed up as **lamb**.

my
Oh my = expression of annoyance/disbelief/resignation

N

n
to the nth degree = extremely/to an infinite extent

nail
fight tooth and nail = fight fiercely
hard/tough as nails = unfeeling/unsympathetic
hit the nail on the head = be accurate/correct
nail-biting = causing anxiety/nervousness
   See also: **bed** of nails/thorns; **cash** on the nail; **coffin**
   nail; nail in one's **coffin**; nail one's **colours** to the mast.

naked
   See: naked **eye**; naked **truth**.

name
call somebody names = use insulting terms for somebody
clear somebody's name = prove that somebody did not commit a
   misdeed
have a bad name = have a bad reputation
have to one's name = own
in name alone/only = only by name/title, not in reality
in the name of = on the authority/example of
make a name for oneself = earn a (good) reputation
name-dropper = somebody who habitually refers to famous people as
   if they were his/her friends
name names = announce the names of people accused/guilty of
   misdeeds
no names, no pack drill = nobody will get into trouble as long as no
   names are mentioned
one's middle name = one's best-known attribute
or my name's not... = I am definitely sure
somebody's name is mud = somebody is very badly thought of
somebody who shall be/remain nameless = somebody whom we all
   know (but not named for effect or to prevent embarrassment)

take somebody's name in vain = cite somebody's name in an
insulting/unkind manner
what's-his/her-name (what's-its-name) = somebody/something whose
name cannot be remembered
worthy of the name = deserving of its name/title
you name it... = anything you can name.../no matter what...
  See also: **answer** to the name of; **double**-barrelled name; give a **dog** a
  bad name; **household** name; **lend** one's name to; name of the **game**;
  name the **day**; name to **conjure** with; not have a **penny** to one's
  name.

nancy
  See: nancy **boy**.

nap
cat nap = brief sleep
go nap = risk everything (on a gamble)
  See also: **catch** somebody bending/napping/on the hop.

narrow
narrow escape/shave/squeak = close to, but free from, danger
narrow margin = very small (amount/distance etc.)
narrow-minded = unreceptive to others' ideas/wishes
the straight and narrow = a lawful/moral way of life

nasty
nasty piece of work = very unpleasant person
  See also: **cut** up nasty/rough.

native
go native = adopt local customs (in a foreign land)
native language = language of one's country of birth

nature
answer/obey a call of nature = go to the lavatory
in a state of nature = naked
in the nature of = approximately, or resembling
in the nature of things = normal/usual
second nature = automatic/habitual behaviour

naught
come to naught/nothing = fail

near
a near thing = a good result that was nearly a bad one
near as dammit = very nearly
near at hand = close
near miss/thing = danger/trouble that is only just avoided
nearest and dearest = close/immediate family
near miss = very nearly hitting/reaching an objective/target
near the mark = bordering on indecent/risqué, or almost correct
nowhere near = not near(ly)/well away from
See also: close/near to one's **heart; far** and near/wide; near the **bone**; near the **knuckle**.

neat
neat as a new pin = very neat/tidy

necessity
make a virtue of necessity = accept the inevitable (and try to derive an advantage from a disadvantage)
necessity is the mother of invention = inventiveness is stimulated by difficulty

neck
be breaking one's neck for = be desperate for
break one's neck for = work hard/quickly
get it in the neck = be blamed/disciplined
in something up to one's neck = closely involved in/with something
millstone round one's neck = large burden/responsibility
neck and crop = completely
neck and neck = equal/level
neck of the woods = particular location/place
neck or nothing = desperate
risk one's neck = expose oneself to danger
stick/stretch one's neck out = take a gamble/risk
See also: **breathe** down somebody's neck; **dead** from the neck up; have the **brass** neck to (do something); **noose** round somebody's neck; **pain** in the bum/neck; **talk** through the back of one's neck.

need

needs must (when the devil drives) = it is inevitable/unavoidable
need something like a hole in the head = not need something at all
that's all/the last thing I need(ed)! = that is yet another
annoyance/frustration
See also: **crying** need; **hour** of need; needs must when the **devil**
drives.

needle

get the needle = become angry/annoyed
needle match = contest in which both contestants are very eager to
win
See also: look/search for a needle in a **haystack**; on **pins** and needles;
pins and needles.

negative

in the negative = no

neither

neither here nor there = irrelevant/unimportant

Nellie

not on your Nellie! = definitely not!

nerve

bag/bundle of nerves = easily excited/frightened (person)
get on one's nerves = annoy/irritate one
have a nerve = be impudent
have nerves of steel = be very calm/brave
have the nerve = be brave/calm enough, or be impudent enough
lose one's nerve = lack courage (to continue doing something)
nerve oneself to do something = summon up the courage to do
something
touch a nerve = refer to something that angers/distresses somebody
what (a) nerve = what impudence
See also: **war** of nerves.

nervous

nervous as a kitten = very nervous

nest
foul one's (own) nest = discredit/harm oneself (through actions/behaviour near at home)
mare's nest = something non-existent that is claimed as a discovery
  See also: bring a **hornet**'s nest around one's ears; **cuckoo** in the nest; **feather** one's nest; nest **egg**; stir up a **hornet**'s nest.

nettle
  See: **grasp** the nettle.

never
(well) I never did! = exclamation of disbelief/surprise
never hear the end of something = be constantly reminded of something
never in a month of Sundays/never in the world = never
never-never land = imaginary ideal place
on the never-never = on credit/hire purchase
well I never! = exclamation of surprise
  See also: better **late** than never; never miss a **trick**; never say **die**; **now** or never.

new
brand new = absolutely new
new blood = new member of a group (intended to invigorate it)
New World = the Americas
  See also: new **broom**; new **one** on somebody.

Newcastle
  See: carry **coals** to Newcastle.

news
have news for somebody = have information that will surprise somebody
news to somebody = fact previously unknown to somebody
break the news = inform somebody about a happening
no news is good news = lack of information indicates that everything is well

next
in(to) the next world = to death/heaven
next door to = very nearly

next to nothing = very little
next to no time = very quickly
the next man = anybody else
what(ever) next? = exclamation of surprise
  See also: next **door** to; next of **kin**.

nick
in good nick = healthy/in good condition
in the nick of time = just in time

night
have a good night = have an enjoyable evening's entertainment, or sleep well
make a night of it = spend all night enjoying oneself
night after night/night in, night out = continuously for several nights
night and day/day and night = all the time/continuously
night owl = somebody who regularly stays up late
stay the night = remain overnight
  See also: **call** it a night; **dead** of night; **fly**-by-night (operator); **morning** after the night before; one-night **stand**; **ships** that pass in the night.

nine
dressed up to the nines = wearing one's best clothes
nine days' wonder = short-lived interesting/sensational event
nine times out of ten = more often than not/usually
nine to five = normal working hours
right as ninepence = fit/healthy
  See also: on **cloud** nine; **possession** is nine points of the law.

nineteen
talk nineteen to the dozen = talk rapidly (and at length)

nip
nip and tuck = equal/level
  See also: nip in the **bud**.

nit
nitty gritty = basic/fine details
nit-pick = find/look for unimportant flaws in something

no
by no means = not (at all)
no go = absence of agreement/success
no such thing = not at all, or a different thing
no thanks to somebody = despite somebody (or his/her actions)
no time (at all) = very quickly
not take no for an answer = emphasize that one wants a positive reply
  to a request
no way = definitely not
  See also: it's no **go**; it's no **joke**; no **dice**; no **end** of; no **holds** barred;
  no **man's land**; no **news** is good news; no **wonder**.

nobody
  See: like nobody's **business**; nobody's **fool**.

nod
a nod is as good as a wink to a blind horse = a hint is sufficient
in the land of Nod = asleep
nod off = fall asleep
on the nod = by (informal) agreement
  See also: have a nodding **acquaintance** with.

noise
noise something abroad = make something widely known
  See also: big **fish/noise/shot**.

none
have/want none of = not accept
none other than = the same as
none the wiser = knowing no more than previously
none the worse for = not harmed by
none too = not very
second to none = the best
  See also: **bar** none; none so **blind**.

nonsense
  See: **stuff** and nonsense.

nook
in every nook and cranny = everywhere

noose

noose round somebody's neck = heavy responsibility
  See also: put one's **head** in(to) a noose/on the block.

nose

bloody somebody's nose = hurt somebody (not necessarily physically)
cut off one's nose to spite one's face = suffer harm while trying to
  harm somebody else
get up somebody's nose = annoy somebody
have a nose for = be good at finding
here's skin off your nose! = good health! (a toast)
keep one's nose clean = stay out of trouble
no skin off one's nose = not harmful to one
on the nose = precisely on time
put somebody's nose out of joint = displace somebody in somebody
  else's affections/esteem
rub somebody's nose in it = repeatedly remind somebody of his/her
  misdeeds
thumb one's nose at = be defiant/show contempt
turn up one's nose at something = regard something with
  contempt/disdain
under somebody's nose = within somebody's sight
with one's nose in the air = in a disdainful way
  See also: **follow** one's nose; keep one's nose to the **grindstone**; **lead**
  somebody by the nose; **look** down one's nose at; nosey **Parker**; not
  look beyond the **end** of one's nose; not see beyond the **end** of one's
  nose; **pay** through the nose; **plain** as the nose on one's face; **poke**
  one's nose into; **rub** somebody's nose in the dirt.

not

  See: as **often** as not; not a **bit** (of it); not at **all**; not **half**; not **least**;
  not to **mention**; not to **worry**.

note

somebody/something of note = famous/significant
strike the right/wrong note = be entirely appropriate/inappropriate
  See also: **compare** notes (with).

nothing

all for nothing = with no result

be nothing to do with somebody = not be of somebody's concern

count for nothing = have no effect/influence

for nothing = free

good for nothing = worthless

have nothing on = be naked, or be not as good as

have nothing to do with somebody = avoid somebody

in one's nothings = naked

it is/was nothing = no thanks are needed

make nothing of = not fuss about, or fail to comprehend

mere nothing = trifle/unimportant thing

nothing doing = nothing happening/with no result

nothing for it but = only possible course of action

nothing if not = very

nothing for it = no choice

nothing of the kind/sort = not the thing expected/mentioned

nothing short of = the same as/similar to

nothing to choose between = little difference between

nothing ventured, nothing gained = risks must be taken to achieve
  something

stop at/short of nothing = do anything (however risky)

sweet nothings = trivial (whispered) conversation between lovers

there's nothing for it = there is no alternative

there's nothing in it = the competitors are evenly matched, or there is
  no truth in it

there's nothing to it = it is easy/simple

think nothing of doing something = consider doing something as easy

think nothing of it = it is unimportant

to say nothing of = in addition to

  See also: **come** to naught/nothing; like nothing on **earth**; **next** to
  nothing; nothing of the **kind**; nothing **succeeds** like success; nothing
  to write **home** about.

notice

(at) short notice = with little warning

give in one's notice = resign

give notice = announce/warn (in advance)

sit up and take notice = suddenly pay attention
till further notice = until some time in the future (yet to be decided)

now
(every) now and again/then = occasionally
just now = in the recent past, or in the near future
now, now = expression of sympathy or rebuke
now or never = this is the time to do something
  See also: **here** and now; now you're **talking**.

nowhere
get nowhere = get no result/make no progress
  See also: nowhere **near**.

null
null and void = cancelled/ineffective

number
get somebody's number = discover somebody's character
one's number comes up = one has good fortune
one's number is up = one is going to be in grave trouble/die
one's number two = one's assistant/deputy
there's safety in numbers = a large group of people is less likely to
  come to harm than is an individual person
  See also: **back** number; in **penny** numbers; number **one**; one's **days**
  are numbered; **opposite** number.

nut
be nuts about somebody/something = enthuse about
  somebody/something
do one's nut = be very angry/agitated/worried
in a nutshell = concisely
nuts and bolts = fundamental (significant) details
nutty as a fruit cake = silly/mad
off one's nut = mad
use a sledgehammer to crack a nut = use too much force/resources to
  bring about a small change

O

oar
put/stick one's oar in = interfere/interrupt
rest on one's oars = take a rest (during hard work)

oats
get/have one's oats = have sexual intercourse
off one's oats = unwell (and with a poor appetite)
sow one's wild oats = live a carefree existence (when young and before settling down)

object
no object = no restriction
See also: object of the **exercise**; object **lesson**.

obvious
See: **state** the obvious.

obligation
under an obligation = forced

occasion
have occasion to = have the need/reason to
on occasion = sometimes
rise to the occasion = show ability in an emergency/unusual situation
take the occasion to = take the opportunity to

occur
it occurs to me = I have just thought

ocean
See: **drop** in the bucket/ocean.

odd
against all/the odds = despite difficulties
be at odds with = disagree with
give/lay odds = bet/guess confidently
make no odds = not matter
odd in the head = eccentric/slightly mad

odd man out = somebody who is left over when a group has been organized, or somebody who is different in some way

odds and ends/sods = various small objects

odds on = likely

over the odds = more than necessary/normal

shout the odds = protest loudly

the odds are that = the likelihood is that

what's the odds? = it is not significant

odour

in bad/good odour with = thought badly/well of by

odour of sanctity = (exaggerated) feeling of one's holiness/piety

of

what of it? = what does it matter?

off

a bit off = an unsatisfactory situation

badly off = poor

be off with you! = go away!

fall off = decline/diminish

get off with you = I do not believe you

go off = turn bad, or begin to dislike

have it off = have sexual intercourse with

in the offing = soon to happen

off and on/on and off = sometimes/spasmodically

off limits = forbidden/out of bounds

off/on line = not connected/connected, or not working/working

off season = non-holiday period

off/on the boil = inactive/active

off the rails = irrational/not sensible

off the record = not for publication/unofficially

on the off-chance = just in case (something happens)

well off = wealthy

See also: fall off the back of a **lorry**; let somebody off the **hook**; off **hand**; off **colour**; off one's **food**; off one's **hands**; off/on one's **guard**; off the beaten **track**; off the **cuff**; off the **map**; off the **peg**; **put** off; **put** somebody off.

office

in/out of office = holding/not holding an official position
necessary offices = toilet facilities
through the (good) offices of = with the assistance of
  See also: **fill** an office; **jack**-in-office.

often

as often as not = about half the number of times
every so often = occasionally
more often than not = frequently/usually
once too often = one time too many, resulting in failure

oil

no oil painting = unattractive
oil the wheels = make something easier
strike oil = be lucky/succeed
well-oiled = drunk
  See also: **burn** the midnight oil; **pour** oil on troubled waters.

ointment

  See: **fly** in the ointment.

old

any old how = anyhow (carelessly)
a ripe old age = very old
know somebody of old = know somebody for a long time
old boy/girl = former pupil/student
old guard/school = older/traditional members of a
  group/organization
old maid = unmarried woman
old man = father, or husband, or senior person
old master = famous painter/painting
Old Nick = the devil
old school tie = symbol of class distinction/privilege
old-timer = elderly person (with lengthy experience in a particular
  area)
old wives' tales = superstition
old woman = somebody who is fussy/indecisive, or wife, or mother
  See also: **money** for old rope; old as the **hills**; old **boy** network; old
  flame; old **hand/stager**; old **hat**; old **thing**; old sweat.

olive
See: offer/hold out an olive **branch**.

on
be on to a good thing = have something advantageous/profitable
be on to somebody = discover somebody's secret
be on to something = discover something (that was concealed)
dream on = entertain your wish but it will never happen
have something on somebody = know something incriminating about
  somebody
it's (just) not on = it cannot be done
on and on = continuously
on the wagon = not drinking alcohol
you're on! = I accept/agree!
  See also: **fall** on/upon; **odds** on; **off** and on/on and off; off/on **line**;
  off/on the **boil**; on **edge**; on **end**; on the **loose**; on the receiving **end**;
  on the **shelf**.

once
all at once = suddenly
at once = at the same time, or immediately
for once = for one time (and very unusually)
give somebody/something the once-over = quickly examine
  somebody/something
just this once = on this occasion only
once and for all = finally
once in a while = occasionally
once upon a time = at some time in the (remote) past
  See also: once **bitten**, twice shy; once in a blue **moon**; once or **twice**.

one
be all one to somebody = not matter to somebody
be at one with = be in agreement/harmony with
become/be made one = be united (in marriage)
be one up on somebody = have an advantage/lead over somebody
give somebody a fourpenny one = hit somebody with one's fist
go one better = improve on something done by somebody else
new one on somebody = thing of which somebody was formerly
  unaware

not be/feel oneself = feel different from normal (because of
   emotional upset/illness)
number one = oneself (to the exclusion of all others)
one and all = everybody
one and only = (the) only one, or unique
one and the same = identical
one by one = one at a time (in a series)
one (more) for the road = a last drink before leaving
one-horse race = contest whose winner is known, even before it takes
   place
one-horse town = place with few amenities
one in a million/thousand = great rarity
one-man show = event at which only one person appears to do/does
   everything
one-night stand = (sexual) relationship that lasts for only one
   evening/night
one-off = something that is unique
(just) one of those things = something (unavoidable) that just
   happens
one or two = a few
one over the eight = too much to drink
one too many = too much alcohol
one-track mind = thoughts dominated by one subject/an obsession
one way or another = somehow
with one voice = unanimously
you are a one! = you are amusing/cheeky/outrageous etc.
   See also: a **hundred** and one; go back to **square** one; one of the **boys**;
   one of these (fine) **days**; one in the **eye** for; one-man **band**; **quick**
   one.

oneself
by oneself = unaided, or alone
   See also: **beside** oneself; make oneself **scarce**.

onion
know one's onions = be skilled/well informed

only
if only = I wish that ... so
only too = very

open
blow something wide open = reveal a secret
bring something (out) into the open = make everybody aware of
  something
come out into the open = reveal one's position/views
in the open (air) = outside
have/keep an open mind = be receptive to new ideas
lay oneself open = put oneself in a vulnerable position
open and shut case = problem whose solution is
  incontrovertible/obvious
open door policy = national policy of trading with any country
open-ended = with no planned finish or termination
open fire = begin firing/start something
open letter = letter published (in a newspaper) for general readership
  but addressed to a particular person
open one's eyes to = make one aware/conscious of
open one's heart to = confess/confide in
open secret = known fact(s) that is/are supposed to be secret
open the door to = cause to happen/encourage
open the flood-gates = remove all restrictions
open up = confess/reveal a secret
open verdict = judgement of a court that acknowledges a crime may
  have been committed but does not apportion guilt
  See also: keep one's **option**s open; keep open **house**; open as the **day**;
  open **book**; opening **gambit**; open one's **eyes** to; open **question**; open
  to **discussion**; with one's **eyes** open; with open **arms**.

opera
  See: **soap** opera.

opinion
be of the opinion = believe
matter of opinion = debatable/disputable
pass an opinion = express a viewpoint

opportunity
take the opportunity = use a particular moment/time

opposite
somebody's opposite number = somebody who holds a similar
  position elsewhere

option
have no option but to = be forced to
keep one's options open = deliberately remain undecided
soft option = easy method of doing something

oracle
work the oracle = be very persuasive (and get somebody to accept a
  proposition)

order
be given one's marching orders = be told to leave
in good order = healthy/working well
in running/working order = working satisfactorily
in short order = quickly
make something to order = make something on request (to specific
  directions)
on order = ordered (of goods)
order of the day = what is expected at a particular time
order somebody about = be domineering
out of order = not working, or not acceptable
take holy orders = become a (Christian) priest, monk or nun
take orders from = obey commands given by
tall order = very difficult request
  See also: **apple**-pie order; of the **first** order/water; order of the **boot**;
  pecking order; put/set one's **house** in order; (just) what the **doctor**
  ordered.

ordinary
out of the ordinary = unusual

other
a bit of the other = sexual intercourse
every other = alternate items in a series
this, that and the other = things in general

See also: all/other things being **equal**; in other **words**; **look** the other way; (on the one hand) ... (and) on the other **hand**; the other **day**.

out
be out of something = to lack something
be well out of something = be fortunate not to be involved in/with something
far out = very unusual
go all out = make an extreme effort
have it out with somebody = vigorously contest something with somebody
murder will out = a bad deed will always be revealed
not far out = close
on the way out = becoming obsolete/unfashionable
out and about = sufficiently well (after an illness) to go out
out and away = by far
out and out = absolute/total
out for something = wanting (to obtain) something
out of all reason = totally unreasonable
out of it/things = excluded/not part of a group
out of one's mind/tree = mad
out in the cold = excluded
out in the wilds = remote from a town or city
out to (do something) = determined to (do something)
out with it = say what you know/want to say
take it out on somebody = be angry with somebody (not necessarily with good reason)
See also: **down** and out; **edge** somebody out; **make** out; not out of the **way**; odd **man** out; out at the **elbows**; out for the **count**; out of all **proportion**; out of/beyond one's **depth**; out of one's **element**; out of **commission**; out of **date**; out of **hand**; out of **harm**'s way; out of **order**; out of **pocket**; out of **sight**; out of **sorts**; out of the **blue**; out of the **question**; out of the **ordinary**; out-of-the-**way**; out of **touch**; out of **turn**; out of/within **bounds**; out of **work**; out on a **limb**; **sit** something out; **truth** will out.

outset
from the outset = from the beginning

outside
at the outside = at most

outstay
  See: outstay one's **welcome**.

over
all over = ended, or in every part
be all over somebody = be overfriendly with somebody
over and above = additional to
over and done with = totally finished
over and over (again) = repeatedly
over the top = excessive
  See also: **fall** over backwards; **fall** over oneself; half **seas** over; **make**
  over; over my **dead** body; over the **counter**; over the **hill**; over the
  hump; over the **odds**; **think** something over.

overboard
go overboard = be over-enthusiastic

overture
make overtures = initiate an approach (to somebody)

one
owe it to oneself = feel it one's right to have

own
be one's own man = be (totally) independent
come into one's own = have the opportunity to be seen at one's best
do one's own thing = do what one pleases
get/have one's own way = (be allowed to) do what one wants
hold one's own = maintain one's position (against
  competition/illness)
in one's own right = through one's own ability
own somebody body and soul = control somebody completely
own up = admit/confess
  See also: by one's own **account**; get one's own **back**; **hold** one's own;
  in one's own **good** time; in one's own **time**; off one's (own) **bat**; **on**
  one's own; the **devil** looks after/takes care of his own.

oyster
  See: **world** is his/her oyster.

P

p
mind one's p's and q's = be careful (not to annoy somebody)

pace
keep pace with = maintain position with
pace out = measure a distance in terms of its length in paces (each
  approximating to one metre, or yard)
put somebody/something through his/her/its paces = require
  somebody/something to demonstrate his/her/its ability
set/make the pace = determine/establish the speed that everyone else
  has to follow
show one's paces = demonstrate what one can do
snail's pace = very slowly
stand/stay the pace = continue as long as/keep up with everyone else

pack
no names, no pack drill = no fuss/trouble will result as long as
  nobody is named
package deal = purchase/settlement involving various factors that
  must be accepted in their entirety
package holiday/tour = organized holiday which includes the cost of
  travel, accommmodation and meals
packed out = totally full of people
pack it in/up = stop it
pack off = send away
pack of lies = many lies (at one time)
pack up = stop doing something
pack up one's troubles = leave a difficult situation and move
  elsewhere
send somebody packing = tell somebody to go away
  See also: pack one's **bags**.

packet
cost a packet = cost a great deal of money
make a packet = earn much money
stop a packet = sustain a severe injury

paddle
See: paddle one's own **canoe**; up the **creek** (without a paddle)..

pain
be at pains/take pains = take much trouble
for one's pains = as (inadequate) compensation for what one has done
on/under pain of (death) = at the risk of (severe) punishment
pain in the bum/neck = somebody who is (always) a nuisance

paint
like watching paint dry = very boring
paint the town red = celebrate (by going out and enjoying oneself)
See also: no **oil** painting; not so **black** as one is painted.

pair
pair off = accompany somebody else to make a twosome
See also: have only one pair of **hands**; pair of **spectacles**; show a **clean** pair of heels.

pal
See: old pal's **act**.

pale
See: **beyond** the pale; pale as **death**.

palm
cross somebody's palm with silver = pay somebody (in advance for information/services)
have somebody in the palm of one's hand = have (total) control over somebody
palm something off on somebody = (fraudulently) get somebody to take something he/she does not want
See also: **grease** somebody's palm; have an **itching** palm.

pan
pan out = happen
See also: **flash** in the pan; **jump** out of the frying pan into the fire.

pancake
See: **flat** as a flounder/pancake.

pants
have ants in one's pants = fidget/be impatient
scare the pants off = frighten
 See also: **bore** stiff/the pants off/to tears; **catch** somebody with his
 pants down.

paper
commit to paper = write down (as a matter of record)
couldn't punch his way out of a paper bag = is very feeble/weak
not worth the paper it's written on = worthless
on paper = theoretically
 See also: paper over the **cracks**; paper **tiger**; put **pen** to paper.

par
above/below par = (of stock) sold/valued at more/less than the
 original price
on a par with = as good as
par for the course = as expected
up to par = at the expected/required standard (of health, quality etc.)
 See also: **below** par.

paradise
 See: **fool**'s paradise.

parallel
draw a parallel between = compare with (to demonstrate
 resemblances)

parcel
parcel out = split into portions and share among a group
 See also: **part** and parcel.

pardon
I beg your pardon = I am sorry, or I did not hear what you said, or I
 disagree with you
 See also: pardon my **French**.

Parker
nosey Parker = somebody who pries into other people's business

parlour
parlour tricks = mischief

parrot

parrot fashion = pointless repetition
  See: **sick** as a parrot.

part

for my part = from my point of view
for the most part = mostly
look the part = have the appearance of whom one intends to be
man of many parts = somebody who is versatile
on somebody's part = by/from somebody
part and parcel = inevitable/usual part
part company = end an association/partnership
parting of the ways = decision/departure point
parting shot = (defiant) comment made on leaving
part with = give up/surrender
take part in = have a share/role in
take somebody's part = side with/stand up for somebody
take something in good part = take no offence at something
  See also: **act** a part; **discretion** is the better part of valour; part
  company; part of the **furniture**; **play** a part.

party

party line = shared telephone line, or official policy as advocated by
  the leaders of a group/organization
party piece = somebody's favourite accomplishment
  See also: **stag** party; **throw** a party.

pass

come to a fine/pretty pass = result in a difficult/unacceptable
  situation
in passing = do/say something casually, when the main issue concerns
  something else
let something pass = deliberately ignore something (rather than
  question/make a fuss about it)
make a pass at somebody = try to make friends with somebody (with
  sexual overtones)
pass away/over = die
pass for = be thought of as/closely resemble
pass off = falsify/misrepresent

pass out = graduate from an educational establishment, or faint
pass over = ignore/overlook
pass the time of day = have a casual conversation
pass up = decline to accept
pass water = urinate
See also: **come** to pass; pass by on the other **side**; pass **muster**; **ships** that pass in the night.

passage
work one's passage = work to earn one's fare

past
past it/past its best = too old to be effective
past master = somebody with acknowledged skill
I wouldn't put it past him/her = he/she is quite capable of doing something (usually bad)

pat
See: pat on the **back**.

patch
go through a bad/good patch = have an unsuccessful/successful period
not a patch on = nowhere near as good as
patch up = re-establish a relationship (after a quarrel)
See also: **bad** patch.

path
cross somebody's path = encounter somebody
See also: **beat** a path to somebody's door; lead somebody up the **garden** path.

patience
enough to try the patience of a saint = very annoying/trying
See also: try the patience of **Job**.

patter
good line of patter = convincing/persuasive talk

pause
give somebody pause = make somebody hesitate

pave
pave the way for something = make something easier/possible

pay
in somebody's pay = given money by somebody (for a favour)
not if you paid me = not in any circumstances
pay off = prove to be a successful decision/investment, or settle an outstanding debt
pay off an old score = get revenge/settle an account
pay one's respects = visit somebody out of courtesy
pay one's way = pay (in full) for what one has/needs
pay on the nail = pay immediately
pay through the nose = pay an excessive price
put paid to something = destroy/prevent something
the devil/hell to pay = (serious) trouble
See also: pay **attention** (to); pay-**court** to; pay-**dirt**; pay **lip** service to; pay the **earth** for; **rob** Peter to pay Paul.

pea
as alike as (two) peas in a pod = exactly the same

peace
hold one's peace = refrain from talking
keep the peace = stop people from arguing/fighting
make one's peace with somebody = re-establish a friendship after a disagreement
peace and quiet = calm silence
peace of mind = contentedness/freedom from worry
See also: **dove** of peace.

peacock
proud as a peacock = very proud

pearl
pearls of wisdom = shrewd/wise advice

peck
keep one's pecker up = remain cheerful
pecking order = hierarchical order of importance/precedence within group

pedal
soft pedal = exercise restraint about

pedestal
put somebody on a pedestal = admire somebody (for being better than he/she really is)

peel
 See: keep one's **eyes** open/peeled/skinned.

peg
bring/take somebody down a peg (or two) = humble somebody
off the peg = ready to wear (of clothes)
peg away = work steadily
peg down = confine to a particular level/restrain
peg on which to hang something = minor topic used as an excuse for introducing a major one
peg out = die
 See also: **level** pegging; **square** peg in a round hole.

pelt
at full pelt = as quickly as possible

pen
put pen to paper = start writing
 See also: **slip** of the pen.

penalty
pay the penalty = take the consequences (for one's actions)

pencil
put lead in one's pencil = improve one's sexual prowess
 See also: **blue** pencil.

penny
bad penny = somebody of bad character
have one's (three)pennyworth = have one's (minor) say in a discussion
in for a penny, in for a pound = having made a decision, commitment to it wholeheartedly
in penny numbers = a few at a time
not cost a penny = entirely free/at no cost at all

not have a penny to one's name = have no money
pennies from heaven = unexpected money
the penny dropped = somebody (finally) understood
penny for your thoughts = what are you thinking?
pretty penny = much money
spend a penny = go to the toilet
tuppeny-ha'penny (twopenny-halfpenny) = cheap/trivial
ten/two a penny = very cheap/common
turn an honest penny/shilling = earn money in an honest way
turn up like a bad penny = (constantly) reappear
  See also: **cut** off without a penny/shilling.

peril
at one's peril = at one's own risk

perish
perish the thought = I hope it (something unfortunate/unpleasant)
  does not happen

person
as bad etc. as the next person = as bad etc. as anybody else
I'd be the first/last person to... = I am very willing/most unwilling
  to do something
in person = personally

perspective
in perspective = from a balanced/sensible point of view

pet
  See: pet **aversion**; pet **hate**.

petard
  See: **hoist** with one's own petard.

Pete
for Pete's/pity's sake! = exclamation of annoyance/surprise

Peter
  See: **rob** Peter to pay Paul.

phrase
turn of phrase = manner of saying/writing things

See also: **coin** a phrase.

pick
pick and choose = choose carefully
pick at (one's food) = eat very little of a meal
pick-me-up = reviving drink/medicine
pick off = destroy one at a time
pick of the bunch = the best (in a group)
pick one's way = step carefully (between obstructions/hazards)
pick one's words = speak carefully (after due thought)
pick on somebody = bully/speak angrily to somebody, or (unfairly)
  select somebody for an unpleasant task
pick out = choose/select, or separate from background/ surroundings
pick somebody to pieces = be very critical of somebody
pick up = get better/improve in health, or get better/increase in
  volume (of business), or get to know somebody/something, or collect
pick up the pieces = restore things to normal after disruption
  See also: **bone** to pick (with somebody); pick a **quarrel**; pick **holes** in;
  pick **sides**; pick somebody's **brains**; pick up the **tab**.

picnic
no picnic = difficult situation

picture
get the picture = understand (a situation)
keep/put somebody in the picture = inform somebody (about a
  situation)
  See also: **pretty** as a picture.

pie
have a finger in the pie = have an interest/share in an undertaking
pie in the sky = unattainable hope
  See also: **easy** as pie; **eat** humble pie.

piece
all of a piece with = all the same as
give somebody a piece of one's mind = angrily complain to/scold
  somebody
fall to pieces = become broken (mentally or physically)
go to pieces = lose control of one's emotions

nasty piece of work = somebody who is very unpleasant
pull to pieces = find fault with
say one's piece = say what one intends to say
  See also: **conversation** piece; **pick** somebody to pieces; **pick** up the
  pieces; piece of **cake**; piece of **skirt**; piece of the **action**.

pig

buy a pig in a poke = buy something unseen (and thus not know its
  worth)
live like a pig in clover = live in luxury
make a pig of oneself = over-eat (greedily)
make a pig's ear of something = do something badly/messily
pig(gie)-in-the-middle = somebody who is (involuntarily) between two
  opposing people/groups
pigs might fly = it is very unlikely to happen
  See also: **sweat** like a pig.

pigeon

not one's pigeon = not one's affair/business
stool pigeon = informer (to the police)
  See also: put the **cat** among the pigeons.

pikestaff

plain as a pikestaff = very obvious

pile

pile it on (thick) = exaggerate
  See also: pile on the **agony**.

pill

sugar the pill = make something that is unpleasant as pleasant as
  possible
  See also: **bitter** pill.

pillar

from pillar to post = from one place to another
pillar of society = upright/worthy member of the community
  See also: pillar/tower of **strength**.

pin

for two pins = for the slightest reason

not care/give two pins = not care at all
on pins and needles = anxious/nervous
pin back one's ears = listen carefully
pin one's hopes on = rely on
pins and needles = tingling in one's extremities
pin somebody down = force somebody to comit himself/herself
pin something on somebody = incriminate somebody
you can hear a pin drop = it is very quiet
   See also: pin **money**; pin one's **faith** on/put one's faith in.

pinch
at a pinch = if (absolutely) necessary/in an emergency
feel the pinch = be short of money
pinch and scrape = live in a frugal way/in poverty
take something with a pinch of salt = doubt the (complete) truth of
   something

pink
be tickled pink = be very amused/pleased
in the pink = in good health
pink of perfection = best of condition
strike me pink! = I am surprised!
   See also: pink **elephants**.

pip
give somebody the pip = anger/annoy somebody
pipped at the post = just beaten at the end of a contest

pipe
in the pipeline = being prepared
pipe down = stop talking
pipe dream = unattainable ambition/desire
pipe up = start speaking
piping hot = very hot
put that in your pipe and smoke it! = see how you like that!

pistol
   See: put a pistol to somebody's **head**.

pit
pit one's wits against = compete, using one's intellect

pitch
black as pitch/pitch black/pitch darkness = very dark
pitch in = join in/share (enthusiastically)
pitch into somebody = attack/fight somebody
pitch one's tent = settle somewhere (temporarily)
  See also: at fever pitch; queer somebody's pitch.

pity
more's the pity = unfortunately
  See also: for **Pete**'s/pity's sake.

place
all over the place = everywhere
be somebody's place = be somebody's duty/responsibility
fall into place = take up its proper position
give place to = be superseded by/yield
go places = succeed
in high places = in a position of authority/power
in (out of) place = where something does/does not belong
in the first place = from the beginning, or the first reason is . . .
  (often not followed by in the second place etc.)
know one's place = behave in a way that is appropriate to one's
  position
pride of place = best/most prominent place
put somebody in his/her place = (angrily) remind somebody of
  his/her position
put oneself in somebody's place = imagine being in somebody else's
  position
take somebody's place = replace somebody
take the place of something = act as a substitute for something
  See also: have one's **heart** in the right place.

plague
avoid somebody/something like the plague = make every effort to
  keep away from somebody/something

plain
plain as the nose on one's face = very obvious
plain sailing = easy progress

plain speaking = honest/open talk
See also: plain as a **pikestaff**; plain **English**.

plan
go according to plan = have the intended result

plank
See: **thick** as two short planks.

plant
plant something on somebody = put something in somebody's
possession to incriminate him/her

plate
have something handed to one on a plate = receive something without
making any effort
on one's plate = be one's responsibility (to get done)

play
bring/call/come into play = make use of
fair play = even-handedness/fairness in a competitive activity
foul play = crime (particularly murder)
make a play for = attempt to get
make play with = emphasize
play a part in = contribute to
play along with = agree to co-operate with (dishonestly/only
temporarily)
play at = do something without (total) commitment
play cat and mouse with somebody = tease somebody (by keeping
him/her uninformed)
play dead/possum = remain motionless and pretend to be dead
play down = minimize the importance of
played out = exhausted
play fair = be honest/straightforward, obey the rules
play false = deceive
play for time = delay in the hope of gaining an advantage
play hard to get = put difficulties in the way of somebody who wants
to meet/talk to one
play it cool = remain calm/nonchalant
play/take no part in = do not participate in

play on words = a pun, a joke that relies on a double meaning
play out = exhaust/finish
play (it) safe = take no risks
play somebody off against somebody else = gain an advantage by
  making two other people compete
play something down = reduce something in importance
play the field = distribute one's attentions among several
  people/things
play up = be a nuisance
play upon = take advantage of (somebody's fears/weakness)
play up to somebody = flatter somebody (for gain)
the state of play = prevailing situation
  See also: beat/play somebody at his own **game**; **child**'s play; play a
  waiting **game**; play **ball** with somebody; play by **ear**; play **fast** and
  loose; play **gooseberry**; play **havoc** with; play (merry) **hell** with; play
  into somebody's **hands**; play it by **ear**; play one's **ace**; play one's
  cards close to one's chest; play one's **cards** right/well; play second
  fiddle; play/act the **fool**; play the **game**; play to the **gallery**; play with
  fire; **two** can play at that game.

please
if you please = if you would believe it (a surprising fact)
pleased as Punch = very pleased
please oneself = do whatever one wants

pleasure
have the pleasure = meet somebody
it's a pleasure = I am pleased (to help)
take pleasure in = enjoy
with pleasure = certainly

pledge
sign the pledge = promise formally not to drink alcohol

plot
the plot thickens = the situation is getting more
  complicated/interesting

plough
plough back = reinvest

pluck
pluck at one's heartstrings = make one feel sympathy
  See also: muster/pluck/screw/summon up **courage**.

plum
have a plum in one's mouth = talk in an upper-class way
  See also: land a plum **job**.

plumb
  See: plumb the **depth**s.

plunge
take the plunge = take a risk

pocket
be in somebody's pocket = be under somebody's control (because
  he/she pays one)
in pocket/out of pocket = having made/failed to make a profit
live in somebody's pocket = live very closely with somebody
pocket/swallow one's pride = be forced to behave in a humble
  manner
  See also: **burn** a hole in one's pocket; **dip** into one's pocket; **line**
  one's pockets; put one's **hand** in one's pocket.

point
beside the point = irrelevant/unimportant
come/get to the point = reach the most significant part of a
  conversation/discussion
in point of fact = actually/truthfully
make a point of doing something = make an effort to do/take care in
  doing something
make one's point = state one's views persuasively
off the point = irrelevant
on the point of doing something = about to do something
point blank = directly
point of no return = position/stage after which it is impossible to go
  back
point of view = standpoint/way of looking at something
point taken = I agree with you
sore point = sensitive subject

stretch a point = disregard the rules (to be helpful)
strong point = best feature of somebody/something
take somebody's point = accept somebody's proposal/suggestion
to the point = relevant
up to a point = so far but no farther
that's the (whole) point = that is what I am trying to get you to
   accept/understand
that's not the point = that is irrelevant
you have a point there = I agree with what you suggest
   See also: **case** in point; cut-off **point**; **match** point; not to put too
   fine a point on it; point of **honour**; point the **finger** at; **up** to a point.

poison
name/what's your poison? = what would you like to drink?

poke
poke fun at = derive unkind amusement from/mock
poke one's nose in(to) = meddle in somebody else's affairs
   See also: **pig** in a poke.

poker
stiff as a poker/ramrod = rigid/very stiff
   See also: poker/straight **face**.

pole
poles apart = widely different
up the pole = mad, or in trouble

polish
polish off = finish (quickly)
polish up = improve/revise
spit and polish = elaborate (over)cleaning

pond
   See: big **fish** in a small pond.

pony
by/on shanks's pony = on foot/walking

poor
poor as a church mouse = very poor

See also: poor **relation**.

pop
pop something on = put something on quickly/temporarily
pop up = appear/occur
top of the pops = favourite
See also: pop the **question**.

port
any port in a storm = any opportunity (even if not the preferred one)

pose
strike a pose = behave in an ostentatious way (to draw attention to/emphasize something)

possess
like a man possessed = very energetically
possession is nine points of the law = the person who actually holds something is in the best position to claim its ownership
what(ever) possessed one? = what made one do something?

post
beaten/pipped at the post = defeated at the last moment
keep somebody posted = keep somebody informed
See also: **deaf** as a post; **pillar** to post; **pip**ped at the post.

pot
all to pot = confused/spoiled
a watched pot never boils = an activity seems to take even longer when one is impatient for it to finish
go to pot = deteriorate/become very bad
in the melting pot = in a state of flux/transition
pot boiler = work of art/literature created just to make money
pot calling the kettle black = unfair criticism from somebody who is guilty of the same fault
pot shot = casual attempt/unaimed shot
See also: pot **hunter**; take pot **luck**.

potato
hot potato = somebody/something that it is risky to be involved with

pound
  See: have/get one's pound of **flesh**; in for a **penny**, in for a pound.

pour
it never rains but it pours = when one thing goes wrong, other things go wrong at the same time
pour oil on troubled waters = have a calming/soothing effect
pour money down the drain = spend a lot of/waste money

powder
keep one's powder dry = be prepared for immediate action
take a powder = disappear/run away

power
do a power of good = do much good
do a power of harm = do much harm
power behind the throne = actual, but unrecognized, person in charge
powers that be = people in charge
  See also: **exercise** one's power; more power to his **elbow**.

practice
in practice = actually (as opposed to theoretically)
make a practice of = do as a matter of habit/routine
out of practice = stale through lack of recent practice
put something into practice = actually do something (that was previously only planned/thought about)

practise
practise what one preaches = do what one tells others they should do

praise
praise to the skies = give very high praise
sing somebody's praises = enthusiastically praise somebody
  See also: **damn** with faint praise.

preach
  See: **practise** what one preaches; preach to the **converted**.

precious
precious few/little = not many/much

premium
be at a premium = be in short supply because of scarcity/rarity
put a premium on something = value something highly

prepare
be prepared to = be willing to

presence
have presence = possess an imposing bearing/impressive appearance
make one's presence felt = act/behave in a way that makes one noticeable
presence of mind = common sense in an emergency

present
at present = now
for the present = for now
there's no time like the present = if something must be done, it might as well be done now
See also: present **company** excepted.

press
press ahead/on = make an effort to continue
(hard) pressed for = lacking/short of
pressgang somebody into doing something = force somebody to do something
press something into service = improvise/make use of something when the correct item/object is unavailable
press something on somebody = force somebody to accept something

pressure
bring pressure to bear on somebody = attempt to compel somebody to do something
pressure group = group of people who attempt to influence those in authority

pretence
See: **false** pretences.

pretty
pretty as a picture = very pretty
pretty much = more or less

pretty well = nearly
sitting pretty = in a favourable situation
  See also: come to a fine/pretty **pass**; lead somebody a (merry/pretty) **dance**; pretty kettle of fish; pretty **penny**.

prey
be prey to = suffer from
prey on one's mind = trouble one's mind

price
at a price = at high cost
at any price = under any conditions
beyond price = priceless
fancy price = over-expensive charge
price on somebody's head = reward for capturing/killing somebody
price oneself out of the market = charge so much that nobody will pay the price
what price...? = what chance is there for...?
  See also: **asking** price; every **man** has his price.

prick
  See: prick up one's **ears**.

pride
pride and joy = object of somebody's pride
pride oneself on = take pride in
swallow one's pride = humble oneself
take pride in = feel proud about
  See also: pride of **place**.

prime
cut off in one's prime = destroyed at one's peak of ability/performance
prime mover = initiator/instigator
  See also: prime of (one's) **life**.

principle
in principle = in theory
on principle = because of one's integrity/moral values
the principle of the thing = underlying moral consideration

print
in/out of print = available/no longer available as a new volume for sale (of books or magazines)
small print = fine details/conditions (of a contract etc.)

private
  See: private **eye**.

pro
pros and cons = arguments for and against

probability
in all probability = very probably

problem
no problem! = that will be easy!

profile
  See: keep a **low** profile.

promise
and that's a promise! = and I really mean it!
I promise you = I guarantee
  See also: **break**/keep a promise; **lick** and a promise.

proof
proof positive = definite proof
  See also: the proof of the pudding is in the **eating**.

prop
  See: prop up the **bar**.

prophet
prophet of doom = pessimist/somebody who always expects the worst

proportion
out of all proportion = very exaggerated
sense of proportion = balanced view

proud
do somebody proud = treat somebody (very) well
proud as a peacock = very proud
stand proud = project (farther than required)

public
  See: in the public **eye**.

pudding
  the proof of the pudding is in the eating = success is gauged by the
  final result
  See also: in the (pudding) **club**.

pull
  have pull = have authority/influence
  pull a face = grimace
  pull in/up = halt/stop
  pull oneself together = regain control of one's emotions
  pull one's socks up = improve one's performance
  pull one's weight = do one's share of work
  pull out = withdraw
  pull out all the stops = do something as enthusiastically/ vigorously
  as possible
  pull round/through = survive
  pull something off = succeed
  pull strings = influence people in authority
  pull the birds/girls/women = attract women (sexually)
  pull the other one (it's got bells on) = I don't believe you
  pull together = co-operate
  pull over = move/steer (a vehicle) to one side
  See also: pull a **fast** one; pull a **rabbit** out of a hat; pull one's
  punches; pull **rank**; pull somebody's **leg**; pull the **rug** from under
  somebody('s feet); pull the **wool** over somebody's eyes; pull up
  roots/stakes.

pulse
  See: keep one's **fingers** on the pulse

pump
  pump somebody = obtain information from somebody (by clever
  questioning)
  See: all **hands** to the pumps.

punch
  beat somebody to the punch = do something before somebody else

pull one's punches = fail to press home an attack
punch-drunk = confused/dazed
  See also: couldn't punch his way out of a **paper** bag; **pleased** as Punch.

punishment
  See: **glutton** for punishment.

pup
sell a pup = cheat/sell something that is worthless
  See also: calf/puppy **love**.

pure
pure and simple = and nothing but
pure as the driven snow = totally pure/untainted

purple
purple patches = florid prose

purpose
be/talk at cross purposes = misunderstand each other's meaning
put to (a) good purpose = make good use of
serve a/the purpose = have a use (even if improvised)
to no (good) purpose = with no useful outcome
  See also: **accidentally** on purpose; to all **intents** and purposes.

purse
  See: **hold** the purse strings; make a **silk** purse out of a sow's ear.

push
at a push = only with difficulty
be pushed for = be lacking in/short of
give somebody the push = dismiss somebody from his/her job
if/when it comes to the push = if/when absolutely necessary
pushing a particular age = nearly a particular age
push off = go away
push on = proceed with determination
push-over = very easy task, or opponent who is very easy to beat
  See also: push one's **luck**; push the **boat** out.

put
put by = save
put forward = propose

put in = install
put in for = apply for
put it mildly = without exaggeration/over-emphasis
put off = postpone, or distract, or deter
put one in mind of = remind one
put oneself in somebody's place = imagine what it would be like to be somebody else
put one's shoulder to the wheel = make a determined effort
put one's mind to = make a conscious effort to
put out = extinguish
put out of one's mind = (deliberately) forget
put somebody down as = regard somebody as
put somebody in the picture = keep somebody informed
put somebody off = discourage somebody, or disgust somebody
put somebody on = to deceive somebody (as a joke)
put somebody out = inconvenience somebody
put/set somebody right = correct a false impression somebody has
put somebody's nose out of joint = make somebody jealous
put somebody up to something = entice/encourage somebody to do something (wrong)
put something about = spread (a rumour)
put something across = communicate/explain something
put something down to = attribute something to
put something on = wear something, or falsify/feign something
put something right = correct a flaw/mistake
put two and two together = draw a conclusion/make a deduction
put-up job = something that is contrived/falsified
put up = provide/use accommodation, or offer
put upon somebody = take advantage of somebody
put up with something = tolerate something
stay put = remain
See also: get/put something **across**; put a brave/bold/good **face** (up)on it; put an **end**/stop to; put a **sock** in it; put a **spurt** on; put on an **act**; put one's **finger** on; put one's **money** where one's mouth is; put one's **shirt** on; put/set somebody at his/her **ease**; put somebody in his/her **place**; put somebody off his/her **stride**; put somebody's **mind** at rest; put something into **practice**; put that in your **pipe** and smoke it!; put the **cat** among the pigeons.

Q

quantity
unknown quantity = unpredictable person/thing

quarrel
pick a quarrel = deliberately provoke an argument
patch up a quarrel = resume friendly relations after a dispute

quart
try to get/fit/put a quart into a pint pot = try to achieve the impossible (because there is insufficient space)

quarter
at close quarters = (very) near
from/in all quarters, or from/in every quarter = from all directions, or everywhere
give no quarter = make no concession/show no mercy

queen
Queen Anne's dead = expression to indicate that a statement is old news/common knowledge
queen it = to dominate/take control (said of a woman)

queer
come over all queer = suddenly feel faint/giddy
in Queer Street = in (financial) difficulty
queer as a nine-bob/three-pound note = gay/homosexual
queer in the head = behaving strangely/(slightly) mad
queer somebody's pitch = ruin somebody's chances
    See also: queer/rum **customer**; queer **fish**.

question
ask a silly question (and you get a silly answer) = do not ask a question to which the answer is obvious
beyond/without question = unquestionable/without argument
fire off questions/fire questions at = ask questions in quick succession
in question = referred to/stated

it's a question of = concerning/relevant to
open question = arguable/debatable
out of the question = impossible
pop the question = ask somebody to marry one
quite so = I agree
quite something = remarkable/worthy of attention
when you're quite ready/when you've quite finished = when you have
 stopped (doing something)

quote
  See: quote **chapter** and verse.

R

three Rs = basics of education (reading, writing and arithmetic)

rabbit
breed like rabbits = produce large numbers of offspring
pull/produce a rabbit out of the hat = unexpectedly find a solution to
 a difficult problem
 See also: let the **dog** see the rabbit.

race
 See: one-**horse** race; **rat** race.

rack
go to rack and ruin = be neglected (and so fall into decay)
on the rack = very distressed/worried
 See also: rack one's **brains**.

rag
chew the rag = talk over complaints/misgivings
from rags to riches = from poverty to wealth
local rag = local newspaper
 See: **glad** rags; like a red rag to a **bull**; **lose** one's cool/rag/wool.

rage
all the rage = very fashionable/popular

rail
go off the rails = behave in a foolish/not law-abiding manner
what a way to run a railway! = what an illogical/silly way to organize
 things!

rain
as right as rain = fit/all right
come rain or shine = whatever happens
it never rains but it pours = one misfortune is usually followed by
 others
put something by/save something for a rainy day = retain something
 until it is needed

rain cats and dogs = pour with (heavy) rain
(come) rain or shine = no matter what the weather
  See also: rain (in) **buckets**.

rainbow
chase after rainbows = desire the unobtainable

raise
raise a laugh = create amusement
raise a stink = make a fuss
raise one's glass to = toast (somebody's health)
raise one's hand against = physically threaten
raise one's sights = be (more) ambitious
raise one's voice = shout
raise the ante = increase the amount of money needed to do
  something
  See also: raise **Cain**; raise **hell**; raise/rear its ugly **head**; raise one's
  eyebrows; raise/take off one's **hat** to; raise somebody's **hopes**; raise
  the **roof**.

rake
thin as a rake = very thin
rake over the ashes = re-examine past unpleasantness
rake something up = discover something (usually to somebody's
  disadvantage)

rally
rally round = form a group (to help/support somebody)

ram
ram something down somebody's throat = argue a case very
  forcefully
ram something home = express something forcibly

rampage
be/go on the rampage = roam about using violence (and causing
  damage)

ramrod
  See: **stiff** as a poker/ramrod.

random
at random = in an unsystematic way

rank
come up through/rise from the ranks = be promoted to a commissioned rank (in the services) from a non-commissioned rank, and extended to a successful person in other professions
pull rank = use one's authority/position (to gain an unfair advantage)
  See also: **break** ranks; **close** ranks; rank and **file**.

ransom
hold somebody to ransom = try to get somebody to do something by using threats
  See also: **king**'s ransom.

rant
rant and rave = talk angrily (and at length)

rap
carry/take the rap = accept the blame
not worth a rap = worthless
rap somebody on/over the knuckles = rebuke somebody sharply

rare
  See: rare **animal**; rare **bird**.

raring
raring to go = eager to begin

rat
as wet as/like a drowned rat = very wet
rat on somebody = inform on/betray
rat race = competition in business/social life
smell a rat = be suspicious

rate
at any rate = anyway, or at least/bearing in mind
at that/this rate = if that were so, or if something continues in this way
  See also: at a rate of **knots**; **second** rate.

rave

(stark) raving mad = completely mad
  See also: **rant** and rave.

raw

in the raw = in the natural/original state, or in the nude
raw material = starting material from which something can be made
  See also: raw **deal**; **touch** somebody on the raw.

razor

on the razor's edge = in a critical/dangerous position
sharp/keen as a razor = very sharp (as of a blade, or mentally)

razzle

on the razzle = out enjoying oneself (by eating and drinking)

reach

  See: reach somebody's **ears**.

read

read something into something else = extract a hidden/unintended
  meaning from
read the riot act = angrily tell somebody to stop doing something
  bad/wrong
read up on = learn by research/study
take something as read = assume something to be true
  See also: read between the **lines**; read somebody like a **book**; read
  somebody's **mind**.

ready

at the ready = prepared for action
ready to hand = readily available/within easy reach
  See also: fit/ready to **drop**; **rough** and ready.

real

for real = genuine/true
in reality = actually
not really = expression of doubt, tending to the negative
oh really? = expression of surprised interest
the real McCoy = the genuine article
well, really! = exclamation of annoyance/disapproval

rear

bring up the rear = be last
  See also: raise/rear its **ugly** head.

reason

have (good) reason to believe = have evidence/justification for
  believing
it stands to reason (that) = logical/rational thought would indicate
  (that)
listen to reason = be persuaded/acknowledge common sense
ours not to reason why = we have no right to question
see reason = adopt a more sensible attitude/be persuaded
will want to know the reason why = will be annoyed/angry
within reason = as far as common sense allows
  See also: for no **rhyme** or reason; **lose** one's marbles/reason; **out** of
  all reason.

rebound

catch somebody on the rebound = gain the love of somebody while
  he/she is still unhappy about a previous broken relationship

recall

beyond recall = irretrievable/unstoppable

receive

  See: on the receiving **end**.

reckon

be out with one's reckoning = make a mistake/miscalculation
one reckons = one thinks
reckon among = include with
reckon on = expect, or rely on
to be reckoned with = to be dealt with only with difficulty
  See also: **day** of reckoning.

record

for the record = to be formally noted
have a good track record = have experience that is to one's credit
on record = recorded (for future reference)
put/set the record straight = remedy a mistake
  See also: **break** a/the record; **off** the record; **track** record.

red
in the red = in debt
not have a red cent = have no money at all
not worth a red cent = worthless
on red alert = ready for and expecting danger
red as a beetroot = red in the face with embarrassment/shame
red-blooded = virile
redbrick university = any British university founded in about the last
  hundred years (i.e. not Cambridge or Oxford universities)
red tape = official regulations (that annoy/delay)
see red = become very angry
see the red light = be aware of approaching danger
was somebody's face red! = somebody was ashamed/embarrassed
  See also: **catch** somebody red-handed; have a red **face**; like a red red
  rag to a **bull**; **paint** the town red; (roll out the) red **carpet**; red **herring**;
  red-letter **day**; red-**light** district.

redeem
redeeming feature = compensatory aspect/factor

redress
redress the balance = re-establish equality/equilibrium

reed
  See: **broken** reed.

reel
reel off = recite something easily (and quickly)

reflect
on (due) reflection = after time to consider
reflect on = recollect/think about
reflect upon somebody = discredit somebody

refresh
refresh one's memory = remind oneself (usually by reading/being
  told)

refuse
first refusal = priority offer
  See also: refuse to/wouldn't be seen **dead**.

regards
as regards/with regard to = concerning
kindest regards = best/good wishes

region
in the region of = about/approximately

regular
regular as clockwork = very regular(ly)

rein
give (free) rein to = allow complete freedom to
keep a tight rein on = keep under strict control
take the reins = assume control

relation
poor relation = inferior member of a group

relieve
relieve oneself = urinate
relieve somebody of something = steal/take something from
  somebody

remember
something to remember one by = a beating/tirade of abuse

render
render an account = give somebody a bill (for payment)

repeat
not bear repeating = too unpleasant to repeat
repeat oneself = say something more than once

resistance
  See: take the **line** of least resistance.

resort
as a/in the last resort = as a final attempt/method

resource
leave somebody to his/her own resources = allow somebody to do
  what he/she likes or find his/her own way out of a difficulty

respect
be no respecter of persons = remain independent of the
   importance/status of others
in respect of/with respect to = concerning
with all (due) respect = expression of polite disagreement
   See also: **pay** one's respects.

rest
a change is as good as a rest = if one cannot do nothing (to take a
   rest) one should do something completely different
at rest = not moving, or dead
come to rest = cease moving
(why don't you) give it a rest! = stop doing it!
last resting-place = grave/tomb
lay to rest = bury (in a grave)
put/set somebody's mind at rest = reassure somebody
(you can) rest assured = you can be sure
rest on = depend on
rest with = be the duty/responsibility of
   See also: rest on one's **laurels**; rest on one's **oars**.

retreat
   See: **beat** a (hasty) retreat.

return
answer by return = reply to correspondence immediately
in return for = in exchange for
many happy returns = may you have many more happy birthdays
   See also: **point** of no return; return the **compliment**; return to the
   fold.

reveal
   See: reveal/show one's **hand**.

rhetorical
   See: rhetorical **question**.

rhyme
be without/have no rhyme or reason = be illogical/lacking in
   common sense
for no rhyme or reason = without cause

rib

stick to one's ribs = satisfy one's hunger
tickle somebody's ribs = amuse somebody
  See also: **Adam**'s rib; **dig** somebody in the ribs.

rich

rich as Croesus = very wealthy
strike (it) rich = obtain a lot of money
that's rich = that's ridiculous/unbelievable
  See also: richly **deserve**; rich man's **hobby**.

riddance

good riddance to = I am glad to be rid of

ride

along for the ride = for the company/to make up the numbers
  (without taking part)
give somebody/have a rough ride = submit somebody to/receive
  harsh treatment
let something ride = let something continue without interfering
ride something out = tolerate a difficulty until it is over
ride up = move up gradually (from the normal position)
ride roughshod over somebody = bully somebody
riding high = successful
take somebody for a ride = cheat somebody, or murder somebody
  See also: ride for a **fall**.

rig

rig up = make a (temporary) construction (from materials easily
  available)

right

be/get/keep on the right side of somebody = be
  on/establish//maintain friendly relations with somebody
be on the right track = acting/thinking in a way that will lead to a
  correct conclusion
by right(s) = according to the law/rules
dead to rights = with no excuse
get it/something right = correctly understand something
go right = happen correctly/successfully

in one's right mind = sensible/sane
in the right = correct (legally or morally)
Mister Right = a woman's perfect (marriage) partner
put/set somebody right = correct a mistaken idea/impression
put/set something right = correct a wrong, or repair something
right away = immediately
right-hand man = trusted deputy
right in the head = sane/sensible
right you are = certainly
see somebody right = ensure that somebody is paid/rewarded
serve somebody right = be what somebody deserves
too right!/true! = I agree totally
  See also: as right as **rain**; **bit** of all right; get/start off on the
  right/wrong **foot**; give one's right **arm** (for); have one's **heart** in the
  right place; I'm all right, Jack; in one's **own** right; (my) right **arm**;
  put/set somebody right; **see** somebody right; strike the right **note**;
  take something in the right spirit; two **wrongs** don't make a right.

ring
have a ringside seat = be a nearby witness
have a hollow ring to it = seem false/insincere
have a true ring to it = seem meritorious/worthy
make/run rings round somebody = defeat easily
ring off = deliberately end a telephone call
ring true = sound as if true
run rings round somebody = defeat easily
  See also: **dead** ringer (for somebody); ring a **bell**; ring down the
  curtain; ring the **changes**; three-ring **circus**; throw one's **hat** into the
  ring.

riot
run riot = do something in an uncontrolled way
  See also: **read** the riot act.

rip
let something rip = allow something to go as fast as possible

ripe
  See: ripe old **age**.

rise
give rise to = originate
rise above oneself = think one is better than one really is
rise and shine! = get up! (out of bed)
take a/the rise out of somebody = tease/play a joke on somebody
See also: rise from the **rank**s; rise to the **bait**; rise to the **occasion**; rise/get up with the **lark**.

risk
at one's own risk = be unable to claim for any damage/loss
run the risk of = do something involving a risk
See also: risk one's **neck**; run/take the **risk**.

river
sell somebody down the river = betray somebody

rivet
See: rivet one's **attention**.

road
get the show on the road = get something started
in/out of the road = in/out of the way
on the road to recovery = getting better (after being ill)
on the road to ruin = heading towards (financial) disaster
road hog = (dangerously) discourteous driver
take to the road = become a tramp
See also: **end** of the line/road; **middle**-of-the-road; **one** (more) for the road.

roar
do a roaring trade = do much business

rob
rob Peter to pay Paul = use money intended to pay for one thing to pay for another
rob somebody blind = deceive/cheat somebody into parting with his/her money
See also: **daylight** robbery; fair **exchange** is no robbery.

robin
round robin = petition (originally with signatures in a circle, so that nobody could be seen to have signed first)

Robinson
  See: before you can say **Jack** Robinson.

rock
go off one's rocker = become mad
on the rocks = in financial difficulty (of a person or business), or
  served with ice (of a drink), or breaking down (of a marriage)
  See also: rock **bottom**; rock the **boat**; **steady** as a rock.

rocket
give somebody a rocket = reprimand somebody
go like a rocket = go very quickly

rod
rule with a rod of iron = be very strict
spare the rod and spoil the child = strict discipline is good for
  children
  See also: make rod for one's own **back**.

rogue
rogues' gallery = collection of photographs of criminals used by the
  police for identification purposes
  See also: rogue **elephant**.

roll
have/make somebody roll in the aisles = make an audience laugh very
  much
roll in = come in large quantities
rolling in money = wealthy
roll on (the day) = may it/the day soon come
roll up = arrive, or come here, or a hand-made cigarette
roll up one's sleeves = be prepared for hard work
  See also: **head**s will roll; keep/set/start the **ball** rolling.

Rome
Rome wasn't built in a day = it takes time to complete something that
  is difficult/important
when in Rome, do as the Romans do = follow the example of people
  around one
  See also: **fiddle** while Rome burns.

romp
romp home = win easily

roof
bring the roof down/raise the roof = make a lot of noise
have a roof over one's head = have somewhere to live
shout something from the rooftops = tell something to everybody
  See also: **hit** the roof.

room
make room for = create (a) space for
  See also: **bugged** room; **elbow** room; no/not enough room to swing a
cat.

roost
come home to roost = be affected by a previous (bad) action
rule the roost = be head of a group

root
be rooted in = originate in
pull up roots/stakes = move somewhere else from a place one has
  lived in for some time
put down roots = become established/settled in a place
root and branch = totally
rooted to the spot = unmoving (although capable of doing so)
root for somebody = support somebody
root out = discover (and destroy)
take root = become established
  See also: **grass** roots.

rope
give somebody enough rope = allow somebody freedom to continue a
  foolish/wrong course of action until he/she suffers the consequences
know the ropes = be experienced/know how to do something
on the ropes = on the verge of collapse/ruin
rope somebody in = persuade somebody to (join a group to) do
  something
  See also: at the **end** of one's rope/tether; **money** for jam/old rope;
  on a **tight-rope**.

rose

a rose by any other name (would smell as sweet) = a name/title does
  not matter in itself
everything's coming up roses = everything is going well
look at/see/view things through rose-tinted spectacles = be very
  optimistic
roses all the way = free from difficulty/uncomplicated
  See also: **bed** of roses.

rotten

  See: rotton **apple** (in the barrel).

rough

be rough on somebody = treat somebody harshly, or be unfortunate
  for somebody
cut up rough = behave in an aggressive/unpleasant way
feel the rough edge of somebody's tongue = be talked to angrily
live rough/rough it = live without modern comforts/conveniences
rough and ready = usable but not finely finished
rough and tumble = horseplay/scuffle
rough something out = plan something in broad outline (but not in
  detail)
sleep rough = sleep in the open, without proper shelter
take the rough with the smooth = accept the disadvantages along with
  the advantages
  See also: dirty/rough end of the **stick**; give somebody/have a rough
  ride; **ride** roughshod over somebody; rough **diamond**.

round

daily round = routine occurrences of life
do the rounds = go from person to person/place to place
get round somebody = get one's way by flattering/persuading
  somebody
get round to = find time to
go the rounds = be passed from person to person/place to place
in the round = three-dimensional, visible from all round
round about = approximately, or near
round down = decrease an awkward number to the nearest convenient
  one

round off = to complete
round on somebody = attack somebody (verbally)
round the bend/twist = mad
round trip = return journey
round up = collect together, or increase an awkward number to the nearest convenient one
talk somebody round = persuade somebody
See also: in round **figures**; round **robin**; round the **clock**; round the **corner**; square peg in a round **hole**.

roundabout
what you lose on the swings, you gain on the roundabouts = disadvantages in one area are balanced by advantages in another

row
in a row = consecutively

rub
not have two ha'pennies/pennies to rub together = be very poor
rub along with = be friendly with
rub down = smooth (using friction)
rub off on(to) = be acquired through close contact with
rub one's hands = show pleasure
rub shoulders with = be in close company with
rub somebody up the wrong way = annoy/irritate somebody
rub somebody's nose in it/the dirt = degrade somebody
rub something in = continually remind somebody of something
there's the rub = that is the difficulty/problem
See also: rub **salt** into the wound; rub **shoulders** with; rub somebody's **nose** in it.

rubber
rubber-stamp something = agree/approve of something one has not formally considered

rude
See: rude **awakening**.

ruffle
smooth somebody's ruffled feathers = calm somebody (who is offended)

ruffle somebody's feathers = offend/upset somebody

rug
pull the rug from under somebody('s feet) = suddenly place somebody at a disadvantage
See also: **snug** as a bug in a rug; sweep something under the **carpet**/rug.

ruin
mother's ruin = strong drink (usually gin)
See also: go to **rack** and ruin; on the **road** to ruin.

rule
as a rule = usually
ground rules = basic rules
rule of the sea/road = accepted "laws" governing ships/road vehicles
rule of thumb = practical (rather than theoretical) method
rule out something/rule something out (of court) = exclude something
work to rule = pay strict attention to working regulations (and thus slow down work)
See also: **golden** rule; rule the **roost**; rule with a **rod** of iron; the **exception** proves the rule.

rumour
ugly rumour = rumour that is nasty/unpleasant

run
dry run = rehearsal
have a (good) run for one's money = get (good) value for one's expenditure
have the run of the house = be free to go anywhere in a house
in/out of the running = having/not having a chance of being successful
make the running = set the pace/standard
on the run = having escaped from custody
run across somebody = meet somebody by accident
run along = go away
run a mile = run quickly away (in panic)
run away with = win easily, or accept unthinkingly
run down = exhausted/in poor health, or in a poor condition

run for it = escape/run away

run into somebody = meet somebody accidentally

run-of-the-mill = ordinary

run on something = great demand for something

run out = be ended/expire

run out of = be used up/have no more of

run out of steam = expend all one's energy

run out on somebody = desert somebody

run somebody down = criticize somebody

run somebody in = arrest somebody

run somebody through = pierce somebody's body with a sword

run something in = run a new machine until it is working properly

run somebody/something over = knockdown/drive over with a road vehicle

run something into the ground = consume/use something until it is exhausted/no longer functioning

run/take the risk = do something involving risk

run the show = be in control

run through something = rehearse, or go through from the beginning

run to something = have (enough of) something

run up = make in a quick (but approximate) way, or allow to accumulate

run up against = encounter

run wild = behave in an undisciplined way

(go) take a running jump (at yourself) = go away

trial run = first test of something new, a rehearsal

See also: **also-ran**; **cut** and run; fall/run **foul** of; go/run to **seed**; in the long **run**; run a tight **ship**; run **counter** to; run in one's **blood**; run in the **family**; run its **course**; run/**rushed** off one's feet; run **riot**; run **short**; run somebody/something to **earth**; run somebody to **ground**; run the **gauntlet**; (run) true to **form**; run with the **hare** and hunt with the hounds; **still** waters run deep.

rush

give somebody the bum's rush = throw somebody out

See: rush **hour**; rush off one's **feet**; rush one's **fences**.

rustle
rustle up something = obtain something quickly (using improvisation)

rut
in(to) a rut = in a monotonous manner

S

sack
get the sack = be dismissed from a job
give somebody the sack = dismiss somebody from a job
hit the sack = go to bed
wear sackcloth and ashes = be contrite/penitent

sacred
swear by all that is sacred = give a solemn undertaking/vow
See also: sacred **cow**.

sacrifice
make the supreme sacrifice = give up one's life (for a cause/friend),
  or surrender one's virginity

saddle
in/out of the saddle = in/out of control
saddle somebody with something = pass on a difficulty/responsibility
  to somebody

safe
be on the safe side = do something to avoid danger/risk
better (to be) safe than sorry = caution is better than taking a risk
safe and sound = unharmed
See also: **play** (it) safe; safe as **houses**; there's safety in **numbers**.

said
after/when all is said and done = after everything has been considered
no sooner said than done = something will be done immediately
See also: **say**.

sail
plain sailing = easy
sail against the wind = take an opposite view to most people
sail close to the wind = be risqué
sail into somebody/something = tackle somebody/something with
  force/vigour

---

sail under false colours = pretend to be what one is not (to gain an advantage)

set sail = start a voyage

trim one's sails = modify one's actions/views to suit the circumstances

See also: take the **wind** out of somebody's sails.

saint

enough to make a saint swear = very annoying/frustrating

saints alive!/saints preserve us! = expression of (exasperated) surprise

See also: my giddy/sainted **aunt**; try the **patience** of a saint.

sake

(just) for old times' sake = because of pleasant memories

for the sake of = in the interests of, or without justification

(just) for the sake of argument = as a basis for discussion/ hypothetically

See also: for **God**'s/goodness' sake.

salad

See: salad **days**.

Sally

See: **Aunt** Sally.

salt

above/below the salt = in/not in a position of honour/privilege

put salt on somebody's tail = apprehend/catch somebody

salt a mine = introduce something valuable among worthless things to make all of it seem worth more than it really is

salt something away = store something for the future

take something with a grain/pinch of salt = be disinclined to believe something

worth one's salt = be conscientious in one's work (and thus be worthy of one's pay)

See also: like a **dose** of salts; **rub** salt into the wound; salt of the **earth**.

Samaritan

See: **good** Samaritan.

same
all/just the same = make no difference, or nevertheless
at the same time = nevertheless
be all the same to = (do) not matter
much the same = unchanged/very similar
not in the same street as = cannot be compared (favourably) with
same again = another dish/drink the same as the previous one
same as ever = consistent/unchanged
same here = I agree wholeheartedly
same old story = recurrent happening
(and) the same to you = I wish you the same
  See also: be of the same **mind**; by the same **token**; in the same **boat**;
  in the same **breath**; **one** and the same.

sand
build on sand = initiate something without proper foundation
happy as a sand-boy = very happy
the sands (of time) are running out = time is getting short
  See also: **bury** one's head in the sand.

sandwich
  See: **knuckle** sandwich.

sardine
packed (in) like sardines = packed together very closely/tightly

sauce
I want none of your sauce = do not be cheeky
  See also: what's sauce for the **goose** is sauce for the gander.

sausage
not a sausage = absolutely nothing

save
save somebody's skin = rescue somebody/save somebody's life
save something for a rainy day = retain something for lean times/an
  unfavourable situation
  See also: saved by the **bell**; save **face**; save somebody's **bacon**; save
  the **day**; saving **grace**; save your **breath**; **scrimp** and save; to save
  one's **life**.

say

and so say all of us = we all agree

as they say/as the saying goes = expression emphasizing that an idiom/saying has been used

as you say = I agree

don't say... = expression of annoyance/surprise

have no say (in) = have no authority/opportunity to express one's point of view

have nothing/something to say for oneself = be unable/able to account for one's actions/behaviour

have one's say = express one's point of view (forcefully)

I can't say = I do not

I couldn't say = I do not know

if I may/might say so = if you want to know my point of view

I'll say! = emphatically yes

I mean to say = expression used to draw attention to a statement already made

I'm not just saying that/this = I really mean it

I must say = I must emphasize

I say = expression of surprise, or to attract somebody's attention

I wouldn't say = I do not mean exactly

it goes without saying = you can assume it/it need not be mentioned

I wouldn't say no = I would gladly agree

I wouldn't say that = I disagree

say no more = I do not need to be persuaded

(just) say the word = say what you require

says you! = according to you!

that is to say = in other words

there's no saying = one cannot even guess

they say that = it is rumoured that

what would you say to? = would you like?

you can say that again = I agree with you

you don't say? = is that a fact/true?

(do) you mean to say? = do you really mean?

See also: I **dare** say; never say **die**; say **when**; **suffice** it to say; to say **nothing** of; to say the **least**.

scales

remove the scales from somebody's eyes = make somebody aware of the (unpalatable) truth

tip/turn the scales = be the small additional factor that precipitates an action/decision

scarce

make oneself scarce = run/stay away

scare

scare somebody out of his/her wits/scare somebody stiff = greatly frighten somebody

scare (the) hell out of/pants off somebody = greatly frighten somebody

scarlet

See: scarlet **woman**.

scatter

scatter to the four winds = spread widely

scene

arrive/come on the scene = arrive

be one's scene = be what one likes/excels at

behind the scenes = out of public view

create/make a scene = make a (noisy) fuss

set the scene = establish/talk about the background to something

scent

on the (right) scent = having a clue/information about what one seeks

put/throw somebody off the scent = divert somebody's attention or mislead somebody

schedule

according to schedule = as planned

ahead of/behind schedule = before/after the planned time

on schedule = on time

school

of the old school = belonging to an old-fashioned/traditional group

tell tales out of school = break a confidence/reveal a secret

See also: **old** school tie.

science
  See: **blind** with science.

score
know the score = be acquainted with the facts
have a score to settle with somebody = have reason to avenge oneself
on that score = for that cause/reason
score (points) off somebody = do/say something that makes
  somebody else look foolish
settle a score/old scores = avenge oneself (for past wrongs)
  See also: **know** the score.

scot
  See: scot **free**.

scrape
scrape along/by = just manage (financially)
scrape through = just succeed
  See also: scrape (the bottom of) the **barrel**; scrape up an
  acquaintance with.

scratch
be/come up to scratch = be of the required standard
do something from scratch/start from scratch = begin something
  (again or with no previous experience/preparation)
scratch one's head = think hard
scratch somebody's back = do somebody a favour
(only) scratch the surface = tackle only a small part of a problem
  See also: **start** from scratch.

screw
put the screws on somebody = apply pressure/use force to get
  somebody to do something
  See also: have a screw **loose**; muster/pluck/screw up one's **courage**.

scrimp
scrimp and save/scrape = spend as little as possible

sea
(all) at sea = bewildered/confused
stranger things happen at sea = even more unusual things can occur

worse things happen at sea = the present difficulty could be even
worse (intended as consolation)
See also: **arm** of the sea; between the **devil** and the deep blue sea;
find/get one's sea **legs**; **half** seas over; there are plenty more **fish** in
the sea.

seal

put/set one's seal on = agree/authorize
set the seal on something = ensure that something will happen
See also: my **lips** are sealed; seal somebody's **fate**.

seam

come/fall apart at the seams = collapse/become ruined
seamy side of life = nasty aspects of life

search

search high and low = look everywhere (to find
somebody/something)
search me = I do not know/do not ask me
See also: look/search for a **needle** in a haystack.

season

silly season = time (when there is little news, during late summer)
when the news media devote time/space to trivia
See also: **compliments** of the season; **off** season.

seat

have a good seat = ride (a horse) well
hot seat = difficult position/responsibility
take a/one's seat = sit down
See also: have a **ringside** seat; in the **driver's** seat; take a **back** seat.

second

get one's second wind = find new resources of energy after being
tired/exhausted
second-class citizen = underprivileged member of a group/society
second-rate = inferior
second sight = clairvoyance
second thoughts = change of mind/revised opinion
split second = very brief moment of time

See also: at second **hand**; **just** a minute/moment/second/tick; **play** second fiddle; (come off) second **best**; second **childhood**; second **hand**; second **nature**; second to **none**.

secret
See: **open** secret.

see
as far as I can see = according to my judgement/understanding
as I see it = in my opinion
do you see what I mean? = do you understand?
have seen better days = be less attractive than formerly
I'll be seeing you = goodbye
I'll see (about that) = I might
I see (what you mean) = I understand
let me see/let's see = I am trying to calculate/decide/remember
see about something = deal with something
see double = see (or think one sees) two images of the same object
see here! = exclamation of anger/annoyance
seeing is believing = only a sight of something is real proof of its existence
seeing that... = because/considering that...
seeing things = having a hallucination/observing a visual illusion
see into something = investigate something
see one through = last/persist
see over something = inspect/view something
see somebody off = beat somebody/chase somebody away, or go with somebody to where he/she starts a journey
see somebody out = outlive, or go with somebody to an exit
see somebody right = ensure that somebody is paid/rewarded for his/her work
see somebody through = help somebody overcome a difficulty
see something through = persist in doing something
see the last of = see for the very last time
see through somebody/something = realize that somebody/something intends to deceive
see to somebody/something = attend to/deal with somebody/something
see to it that = make sure that

see you later = goodbye

so I see = that is obvious

when you've seen one you've seen them all = they are so alike that
seeing any one of them is all that is needed

you see = I told you so

See also: glad to see the **back** of somebody/something; I'd like to see
(somebody do something); not see beyond the end of one's **nose**; not
see the **wood** for the trees; not to see somebody for **dust**; refuse
to/wouldn't be seen **dead** with; see **daylight**; see **eye** to eye; see how
the **land** lies; see **life**; see one's **way** (clear) to; see **red**; see **stars**; see
the colour of somebody's **money**; see the **light** (of day); see the
world; see the **writing** on the wall; see which way the **wind** blows; see
with (only) half an **eye**; **wait** and see.

seed

go to seed = become shabby through lack of care

seize

seize on something = eagerly accept something

seize up = stop functioning (because of jamming/sticking)

self

self-made man = somebody from a humble background who has
become wealthy/important entirely by his own efforts

self-possessed = confident and unflappable

self-righteous = overconfident in one's own moral
standards/superiority

self-willed = wanting to have one's own way in all things/very
uncooperative

sell

be sold on something = be convinced of something's worth

sell off = sell at a low price

sell-out = betrayal, or an organized event with a full attendance (all
tickets sold)

sell out = sell a share in a business

sell short = present as less good than in reality

sell up = sell what one owns

sold out (of) = out of stock

See also: go/sell like hot **cakes**; sell a **pup**; **sell one's soul** for something; sell somebody down the **river**.

send

send away/off for something = order something by post/mail order
send somebody down = expel somebody from university
send somebody/something up = parody somebody/something
  See also: drive/send somebody up the **wall**; pass/send/take the **hat** round; send chills/shivers up somebody's **spine**; send **flying**; send somebody about his/her **business**; send somebody **packing**; send somebody to **Coventry**.

sense

bring somebody to his/her senses = make somebody use common sense/reason
come to one's senses = regain consciousness, or realize the truth
in a sense = to some extent
in one sense = regarded from one point of view (but not another)
out of one's senses = mentally unbalanced/mad
sixth sense = extrasensory/paranormal feeling
  See also: **horse** sense; sense of **proportion**; take **leave** of one's senses.

separate

separate the men from the boys/separate the sheep from the goats = separate the better members of a group from the rest

sepulchre

painted/whited sepulchre = somebody who hides his/her misdeeds behind a pretence of goodness/piety

serious

you can't be serious = you cannot really mean it

servant

what did your last servant die of? = why don't you do it yourself?

serve

serve its turn = act as a (temporary) substitute for/suffice for a particular purpose
serve one right = be what one deserves
serve one's time = remain in a job for the full allotted period

serve time = be imprisoned
  See also: **first** come, first served; if my **memory** serves me (right);
  serve a/the **purpose**; serve somebody **right**.

service
at one's service = available for use/to help
be of service to somebody = assist/help somebody
have seen good service = have had long/satisfactory use
  See also: pay **lip** service to; **press** something into service.

sesame
  See: **open** sesame.

set
all set = prepared/ready
be set on something = keenly desire something
make a dead set at = determindly approach/attack somebody
set about somebody = attack somebody
set about something = start to do something (purposefully)
set aside = save money
set in = become established
set off = begin a journey
set somebody against somebody (else) = foment hatred between two
  people
set somebody/something on somebody = allow somebody/something
  to attack somebody
set something off to advantage = display something to show it at its
  best
set to = (begin to) do something purposefully
set up = establish
well set up = secure/well provided for
  See also: have one's **mind** set on something; keep/set/start the **ball**
  rolling; put/set somebody **right**; put/set something **right**; put/set the
  clock back; set a **thief** to catch a thief; set one's **cap** at; set one's **face**
  against; set one's **heart** upon; set one's **seal** on; set one's **sights** on;
  set one's **teeth** on edge; set somebody by the **ears**; set somebody by
  the **heels**; set somebody (back) on his/her **heels**; set/make the **pace**;
  set the **record** straight; set the **wheels** in motion; set to **work**.

341   shake

settle
settle down = establish oneself in a place, or begin to do something
settle for something = accept something reluctantly/as a compromise
settle on = choose
settle something on somebody = (formally) donate something to
  somebody
settle up with somebody = pay off a debt
  See also: an **account** to settle; settle an old **score**; settle somebody's
  hash; settle/square an **account** with somebody; when/after the **dust**
  has settled.

seven
  See: at **sixes** and sevens; seventh heaven.

sew
sewn up = completed/finalized

sex
  See: **fair** sex.

shack
shack up with somebody = live with somebody

shade
put in the shade = make seem less important/significant
shades of = reminiscent of

shadow
be afraid of one's own shadow = be timid/easily frightened
shadow of one's former self = much less energetic/healthy than
  formerly
worn to a shadow = made tired/thin through working hard

shaggy
  See: shaggy **dog** story.

shake
in two shakes (of a lamb's tail) = very soon
no great shakes = not very good/well
shake in one's shoes = tremble with fear
shake like a jelly/leaf = tremble with fear
shake off = get rid of

shake one's fist = express anger/threaten (by waving one's clenched fist)

shake one's head = indicate disagreement/sorrow

shake up = enliven

See also: shake a **leg**; shake **hands** on it; shake somebody to the **foundations**; shake the **dust** from one's feet.

shame

put somebody/something to shame = make somebody/something appear to be inferior (by being much better)

shame on you! = you ought to feel ashamed!

what a shame! = how unfortunate/unlucky!

See also: **crying** shame.

shanks

See: shanks's **pony**.

shape

get into shape = get fit

in any shape or form = at all, or no matter what form something takes

in good shape = satisfactory, or (physically) fit

in the shape of = in the form of

knock into shape = make something conform to a requirement

shape up/take shape = develop (towards a particular form)

See also: all ship-shape and **Bristol** fashion; **lick** into shape.

share

go shares with = share (usually cost/money)

share and share alike = share equally

share of the gravy = share of the proceeds/profits

See also: **lion**'s share.

sharp

have a sharp tongue = talk angrily/sarcastically

look sharp (about it)! = be quick!

sharp practice = dishonesty (in business dealings)

sharp's the word! = be quick!/hurry!

See also: keen/sharp as a **razor**.

shave
See: **close** call/shave.

shed
See: shed/throw **light** on.

sheep
count sheep = keep counting to oneself in an attempt to fall asleep
See also: **black** sheep (of the family); make (sheep's) **eyes** at; might as
well be hung for a sheep as a **lamb**; **separate** the sheep from the
goats; **wolf** in sheep's clothing.

sheet
between the sheets = in bed
sheet anchor = somebody/something that provides long-term support
three sheets to the wind = drunk
with a clean sheet/slate = with no faults/misdemeanours recorded
against one
See also: **white** as a sheet.

shelf
left on the shelf = unlikely to get married (because of age or
unattractiveness)

shell
come out of one's shell = become less shy/more confident
go into one's shell = behave in a timid/shy way
shell out = pay

shift
See: shift one's **ground**.

shilling
See also: **cut** off without a penny/shilling; **turn** an honest
penny/shilling.

shine
take a shine to somebody = form a liking for somebody
take the shine off/out of = cause to appear inferior/less important
(than formerly regarded)
See also: come **rain** or shine; make **hay** while the sun shines; **rise** and
shine!

ship
run a tight ship = maintain strict control
ships that pass in the night = people who have only one (accidental)
 meeting
spoil the ship for a ha'porth of tar = fail to complete something
 valuable by omitting an inexpensive detail/finishing touch (ha'porth
 is short for halfpennyworth)
when one's ship comes in = when one becomes wealthy
 See also: all ship-shape and **Bristol** fashion; ships that pass in the
 night.

shirt
put one's shirt on = bet all one's money on
stuffed shirt = somebody who is humourless/pompous
work in one's shirt-sleeves = work without wearing a coat/jacket
 See also: **keep** one's hair/shirt on.

shiver
give one the shivers = evoke a feeling of horror
send shivers down/up one's spine = cause a feeling of
 excitement/revulsion

shoe
be in somebody's shoes = be in somebody's place/position
on a shoestring = at minimum cost
step into somebody's shoes = succeed somebody (to a job/position)
where the shoe pinches = what causes financial problems
 See also: **dead** man's shoes; **fill** somebody's shoes; **lick** somebody's
 boots/shoes.

shoot
shoot ahead = rapidly progress/take the lead
shoot up = grow/rise rapidly
the whole bang shoot = the lot/everything
 See also: shoot a **line**; shoot down in **flames**; shoot one's **bolt**; shoot
 one's **mouth** off; (whole) shooting **match**.

shop
all over the shop/show = scattered/spread everywhere
set up shop = start a business

shop around = compare things before buying/choosing one of them

shut up shop = stop working (temporarily or permanently)

talk shop = talk about one's job

See also: **closed** shop; **cop** shop; like a **bull** in a china shop.

short

at short notice = with little warning

bring somebody up short = make somebody suddenly stop what he/she is doing

caught/taken short = have the (sudden) desire to urinate

cut a long story short = recount something briefly

for short = in abbreviated form

give somebody short shrift = devote little time to somebody (and in an abrupt manner)

go short = have too little of something

in short = stated briefly

in short supply = scarce

in the short term = over a short amount of time

little short of = nearly the same as

make short work of = complete/conclude quickly

nothing short of = (exactly) the same as

run short = not have enough

sell somebody/something short = fail to present somebody/something to best advantage

short and sweet = brief and to the point

short change somebody = give somebody insufficient change (when paying for something)

short-circuit = omit usual formalities to hasten a procedure

short for = abbreviation of

short-handed/short-staffed = with insufficient helpers/staff

short head = small amount/distance

short of = except/without going as far as, or not as far as

short of breath = breathless/panting

short on something = lacking in something

short-tempered = easily angered

short weight = less than the proper weight (as required/paid for)

stop short of = not go as far as

See also: as **thick** as two short planks; **cut** short; **fall** short; have somebody by the short and **curlies**; in short **order**; the **long** and (the) short of it; short **cut**; short **list**; short **measure**.

shot

get shot of = get rid of/dismiss
like a shot = eagerly/quickly
shot across the bows = warning
shotgun wedding = enforced marriage (usually because the bride is pregnant)
shot in the arm = fillip/stimulant
(all) shot to pieces = destroyed/spoiled, or very distressed
  See also: **big** fish/noise/shot; **call** the shots/tune; leap/shot in the **dark**; **long** shot.

shoulder

have broad shoulders = be able/willing to accept much responsibility
put one's shoulder to the wheel = start hard work
shoulder to cry on = somebody who listens to one's troubles sympathetically
shoulder to shoulder = close together (in mutual support)
shrug one's shoulders = display indecision/lack of interest
straight from the shoulder = directly/without compromise
  See also: **chip** on one's shoulder; **cold** shoulder; have a good **head** on one's shoulders; **head** and shoulders above; old **head** on young shoulders; **rub** shoulders with; shoulder the **blame**/responsibility.

shout

shout one's head off = shout loudly
shout somebody down = make so much noise that a speaker cannot be heard
  See also: all over **bar** the shouting; shout one's **mouth** off; shout something from the **rooftops**.

shove

shove off = go away
  See also: shove it up one's **jumper**.

show

for show = for appearance's sake only

give the show away = reveal a confidence/secret
good show! = well done!, or I am pleased
on show = displayed for everyone to see
show (good) cause = provide good reason
show off = display one's possessions/talents in order to impress
  somebody
show of force = demonstration of power
show of hands = vote made by people raising their hands
show somebody up = make somebody appear foolish/inept, or
  accompany somebody upstairs
show up = arrive, or reveal faults/features
steal the show = attract the most attention/praise (away from
  somebody/something else)
to show for (it) = have as recompense
  See also: **all** over the shop/show; get the show on the **road**; give the
  game/show away; hoist/show/wave the white **flag**; **look**/show one's
  age; **run** the show; show a **clean** pair of heels; show a **leg**; show **fight**;
  show one's **face**; reveal/show one's **hand**; show oneself in one's true
  colours; show one's **paces**; show one's **teeth**; show somebody the
  door; show the **flag**; show the white **feather**.

shrift
  See: give somebody/something **short** shrift.

shrink
  See: shrinking **violet**.

shrug
shrug off = dismiss/regard as trivial
  See also: shrug one's **shoulders**.

shuffle
  See: shuffle off this mortal **coil**.

shut
shut one's eyes to = deliberately ignore
shut the door on/to something = make something impossible
shut up = stop talking etc.
  See also: **open** and shut case; shut one's **eyes** to; shut one's
  mouth/face/trap; shut/slam the **door** in somebody's face; shut up
  shop; with one's **eyes** closed/shut.

shutter
put up the shutters = cease business activity

shy
have a shy at = make an attempt
 See also: **fight** shy of; once **bitten**, twice shy.

sick
fall sick = become ill
make one sick = cause one to be angry/upset
sick and tired of = very tired of
sick as a dog = very sick (vomiting)
sick as a parrot = very disappointed/envious/upset
worried sick = very worried
 See also: sick at **heart**; sick **joke**; sick of the **sight** of
 somebody/something; sick to **death** of.

side
from/on all sides = from/in all directions
let the side down = perform badly to the cost of other members of
 one's group
on every side = in all directions/everywhere
on the old (etc.) side = fairly old (etc.)
on the right/wrong side of = nearly/just more than
on the side = in addition to one's regular job
pass by on the other side = ignore somebody in trouble
pick sides = choose members of each team before a contest
put on side = pretend to be what one is not
put something on/to one side = postpone something
side by side = close beside/neighbouring
side with somebody/take somebody's side = favour/support
 somebody in a dispute
split one's sides = laugh heartily/violently
take sides = favour/support one party in a dispute
take somebody on/to one side = talk to somebody privately (away
 from others)
(on) the other side = (life after) death
to be on the safe side = as a contingency/for reassurance
 See also: **bit** on the side; **brush** aside/to one side; get on the **wrong**

side of somebody; get out of **bed** (on) the wrong side; have one's **bread** buttered on both sides; keep on the **right** side of somebody; know which side one's **bread** is buttered; **laugh** on the other side of one's face; like the side of a **house**; look on the **bright** side; on the side of the **angels**; on the wrong side of the **blanket**; on the wrong side of the **tracks**; other side of the **coin**; **seamy** side of life.

sidelines
sit on the sidelines = observe something without taking part in it

sideways
knock somebody sideways = confuse/shock somebody

sieve
See: have a **head** like a sieve.

sight
catch sight of = start seeing, or get a glimpse of
do something on sight = do something immediately/without hesitation
get out of my sight! = go away!
in one's sights = in one's range of vision, or in one's awareness (with a view to possession)
in sight of = close enough to be seen
keep/lose sight of something = remain aware/unaware of something
keep something in sight = stay within visual range of something
know somebody by sight = recognize somebody (to whom one has not been introduced)
not be able to stand the sight of somebody/something = have a strong dislike for somebody/something
out of sight = excellent
out of sight, out of mind = what one is no longer aware of can (easily) be forgotten
second sight = ability to foretell the future
set one's sights on = try to obtain
sick of the sight of somebody/something = very tired of seeing somebody/something
sight unseen = without having been seen/examined
See also: at **first** sight; **lose** one's sight; sight for sore **eyes**.

sign

sign of the times = characteristic of now (the present)

sign on the dotted line = make one's signature on a (legally binding/official) document

sign the pledge = promise/undertake not to drink alcohol

See also: sign somebody's **death** warrant.

signal

give somebody a/the signal = indicate when somebody should do something

silence

silence is golden = it can be best to say nothing (in a difficult situation)

silent

as silent as the grave = very quiet

See also: silent **majority**.

silk

make a silk purse out of a sow's ear = make something good out of bad/poor quality materials

take silk = become a Queen's Counsel

silly

play silly beggars = behave in a foolish manner, or deliberately annoy/obstruct

See also: silly **season**.

silver

See: born with a silver **spoon** in one's mouth; cross somebody's **palm** with silver; every **cloud** has a silver lining.

simple

the simple life = way of life that lacks extravagance or luxuries

See also: **pure** and simple.

sin

for one's sins = as an annoyance/punishment

See also: cover/include a **multitude** of sins; **live** in sin; **ugly** as sin.

since
  See: **ages** since.

sing
sing for one's supper = perform a favour/service in return for something one needs
  See also: sing somebody's **praises**.

sink
be sunk = be in a hopeless situation
sinking feeling = feeling of apprehension/dread
sink or swim = commit to success or total failure
sink to somebody's level = be/perform as badly as somebody else
  See also: **everything** but the kitchen sink; **hook**, line and sinker.

sit
sit back = relax
sit for = pose for an artist/photographer, or take an examination
sit in on something = be present (without taking part)
sit on = deliberately take no action, or be a member of a board/committee etc.
sit out = not take part in a dance, or stay to the end
sit something out = wait until something (usually unpleasant) is over
sit tight = be unwilling to move, or to change one's point of view
sit up (and take notice) = pay attention/take notice
sit up and beg = grovel/be subservient, or not go to bed
sit up for = wait for somebody to come home
  See: sit at somebody's **feet**; sit in **judgement**; sitting **duck**; sitting **pretty**; sitting **target**; sit on one's **hands**; sit on the **fence**.

six
(all) at sixes and sevens = confused/disorganized
knock/hit somebody for six = defeat somebody completely, or surprise somebody
six of one and half a dozen of the other = equal
six of the best = a caning
sixth sense = intuition/understanding not based on any of the normal five senses

size
be (about) the size of it = describe something
how's that for size?/try that on for size = what do you think of that?
size somebody/something up = decide what somebody/something is like
  See also: **cut** down to size.

skate
get one's skates on = hurry
skate over = ignore/consider only superficially
  See also: skate on thin **ice**.

skeleton
skeleton staff = minimum number of people to work something
  See also: skeleton in the **cupboard**.

skid
put the skids on/under = hasten

skin
by the skin of one's teeth = only just
get under one's skin = be annoying
have a thick skin = be insensitive (to people's remarks)
save somebody's skin = rescue somebody
skin deep = superficial
skin somebody alive = punish somebody severely
soaked to the skin = very wet
  See also: here's skin off your **nose**; keep one's **eyes** skinned; no skin off one's **nose**; **slip** on a banana skin.

skip
skip it = forget/ignore it
skip off = go away/leave

skirt
piece of skirt = young woman

skittles
  See: all **beer** and skittles.

sky
sky high = very high
the sky's the limit = there is no upper limit
  See also: **mackerel** sky; **pie** in the sky; **praise** to the skies.

slagheap
on the slagheap = discarded/of no further use

slam
  See: shut/slam the **door** in somebody's face.

slang
slanging match = argument in which the parties insult each other

slap
slap and tickle = sex play
slap in the face = action that greatly discourages/frustrates
slap on the back = congratulations
slap on the wrist = minor punishment/scolding
slap-up = excellent/expensive
  See also: slap in the **face**.

slate
wipe the slate clean = cancel/ignore previous debts/misdemeanours
put something on the slate = buy something on credit
  See also: have a screw/slate/tile **loose**.

slave
slave-driver = somebody who makes people work very hard

sledgehammer
use a sledgehammer to crack a nut = use unnecessarily powerful
  forces/resources

sleep
get one's beauty sleep = have sufficient sleep to wake totally refreshed
lose sleep over = worry
put an animal to sleep = humanely kill an animal
put somebody to sleep = anaesthetize somebody (causing
  unconsciousness)
sleep around = be promiscuous

sleep in = oversleep

sleeping partner = associate who contributes money but takes no part in the running of a business

sleep like a log/top = sleep deeply/soundly

sleep off = recover while asleep

sleep on something = postpone making a decision about something

sleep together = have (regular) sexual intercourse

sleep with somebody = have sexual intercourse with somebody

  See also: let sleeping **dogs** lie; sleep **rough**.

sleeve

have an ace up one's sleeve = secretly retain something for use at the best time

have/keep something up one's sleeve = keep something secret (for later use)

  See also: in one's **shirt**-sleeves; **laugh** up one's sleeve; **roll** up one's sleeves; wear one's **heart** on one's sleeve.

slice

  See: best thing since sliced **bread**; slice of the **cake**.

slide

let something slide = neglect to do something

slight

not in the slightest = not at all

slink

slink/slip away = leave in a guilty/surreptitious way

sling

  See: sling one's **hook**; throw/sling **mud** at.

slip

Freudian slip = speaking the wrong word, which indicates an unconscious idea

give somebody the slip = evade/elude somebody

let something slip = say something accidentally, or miss an opportunity

slip of a boy/girl = young (slender) boy/girl

slip of the pen = mistake in writing

slip of the tongue = something said by mistake
slip one over on somebody = cheat/deceive somebody
slip somebody something = give somebody something unobserved
slip up = make a mistake
there's many a slip 'twixt cup and lip = do not depend on a plan until
  it is completed
  See also: **slink**/slip away; slip one's **mind**; slippery as an **eel**; slip
  through one's **fingers**.

slog
slog one's guts out = work very hard

slope
slope off = leave surreptitiously

slot
slot in = accommodate/fit (in)

slow
go slow = deliberately work slowly
in slow motion = much more slowly than usual
slow(ly) but sure(ly) = slow and effective (progress)
  See also: quick/slow off the **mark**; quick/slow on the **uptake**.

sly
on the sly = deceptively/secretly
  See also: sly **dog**.

smack
  See: smack in the **eye**.

small
feel small = feel humiliated, inferior
in a small way (of business) = with little capital/stock
it's a small world = what a coincidence
make small talk = have an unimportant conversation
no small = considerable/large
small-minded = lacking imagination/tolerance
small-time = doing something on a small scale
small wonder = as expected

See also: small **beer**; **look** small; small **fry**; (wee) small **hours**; small **print**; small **talk**; still small **voice**.

smart
look smart = hurry
See also: smart **Alec(k)**.

smash
smash-and-grab = robbery in which a thief breaks a shop window to steal displayed goods
smash hit = very successful book/song/show etc.

smear
smear campaign = systematic attempt to discredit somebody (using accusations in articles/speeches)

smell
See: smell a **rat**; smell of the grease-**paint**.

smile
be all smiles = be very happy
come up smiling = remain cheerful after coping with a difficulty
keep smiling! = do not worry!
smile on somebody = favour somebody
See also: wipe the grin/smile off somebody's **face**.

smoke
go up in smoke = quickly disappear
smoke somebody/something out = discover something/somebody, or force somebody out of hiding
put up a smokescreen = do something to hide one's intentions
See also: put that in your **pipe** and smoke it!; there's no smoke without **fire**.

smooth
See: smooth somebody's (ruffled) **feathers**; take the **rough** with the smooth.

snail
See: snail's **pace**.

snake
snake in the grass = somebody who is deceitful/untrustworthy

snap
snap at/up = eagerly buy/take
look/make it snappy = hurry
snap one's fingers at = treat with contempt
snap out of it = cease being depressed/moody etc.
snap somebody's head off = reply very abruptly/sharply

sneeze
not to be sneezed/sniffed at = not to be ignored/missed

sniff
sniff out = discover
  See also: not to be **sneezed**/sniffed at.

snook
  See: **cock** a snook.

snow
snowed in = unable to leave a building because of accumulated snow
snowed under = overwhelmed with tasks to do
  See also: cat's/snowball's **chance** in hell; **pure** as the driven snow.

snuff
snuff it = die

snug
snug as a bug in a rug = very comfortable

so
and so forth/on = et cetera
how so? = why?
is that so? = really?
it is so! = yes it is!
or so = approximately
so-and-so = somebody/something one dislikes (strongly), or
  somebody/something whose name one cannot remember
so be it = I accept/let it be
so far, so good = progress up to now is satisfactory
so-so = average/mediocre

so there! = exclamation of emphasis
so what? = what of it?
  See also: **ever** so; **just** so; so **much** for something; so to **speak**;
  without so **much** as.

soak
  See: soaked to the **skin**.

soap
get on one's soap box = firmly state one's (known) point of view
soap opera = long-running radio/television serial about the daily lives
  of a group of people
  See also: **soft** soap.

sob
sob story = account of somebody's misfortunes, related to obtain
  sympathy
sob stuff = sentimental account meant to arouse sympathy

sober
sober as a judge/stone-cold sober = completely sober
sobering thought = aspect/factor that makes one consider something
  seriously

sock
bless one's (little) cotton socks = expression of affection
put a sock in it = be quiet
sock it to somebody = speak in a forthright/impressive way
  See also: **pull** one's socks up.

sod
not care a sod = not care in the least
  See also: Murphy's/sod's **law**; **odds** and ends/sods.

soft
be soft on somebody = be (sentimentally) in love with somebody, or
  be lenient towards somebody
have a soft spot for = have an affection for
soften up = reduce resistance
soft job = occupation that is easy to do
soft option = an easy choice (among more difficult alternatives)

soft-pedal = deliberately fail to emphasize the importance of
  something
soft-soap = flatter/flattery
soft touch = somebody who is easy to convince/deceive
  See also: soft in the **head**.

soil
  See: dirty/soil one's **hand**s.

sold
  See: **sell**.

soldier
come the old soldier = act in a more experienced/superior way, or
  malinger
game of soldiers = something one does not want to do
soldier of fortune = somebody who (travels and) lives by his/her wits,
  or a mercenary
soldier on = persist in spite of difficulties

something
be/have something to do with = be associated with
make something (out) of it = cause an argument/fuss, or make
  something appear more significant than it is, or understand
make something of oneself = become successful
or something = or some other thing (largely meaningless)
see something of somebody = meet somebody
something like = approximately, or resembling
something like it = excellent
something of = to some extent
something of the kind = something similar
something tells me = I believe/suspect/think
you know something? = I'm going to tell you something (important)

son
every mother's son (of them) = everybody
son of a gun = (popular) man
  See also: like **father**, like son; his **father**'s son.

song
for a song = cheaply

make a song and dance about something = make a fuss about something
See also: **swan** song; **wine**, women and song.

soon

as soon as maybe = quickly/as soon as possible
no sooner said than done = done immediately
sooner or later = eventually
the sooner the better = as soon as possible
speak too soon = assume something will happen before it is certain

sore

stick out like a sore thumb = be very obvious
See also: (like a) **bear** with a sore head; sight for sore **eyes**; sore **point**.

sorrow

more in sorrow than in anger = sadly rather than angrily
See also: **drown** one's sorrows.

sorry

feel sorry for somebody = pity somebody
See also: better (to be) **safe** than sorry.

sort

after a sort = not totally
a good sort/not a bad sort = somebody who is kind/pleasant
bad sort = somebody who is dishonest/unpleasant
it takes all sorts (to make the world) = one should tolerate everybody
of a sort/of sorts = of a kind
out of sorts = (slightly) ill
sort somebody out = attack/reprimand somebody, or discover what is troubling somebody
sort something out = find a solution to a difficulty, or select from a miscellany
See also: **nothing** of the kind/sort.

soul

bare one's soul = reveal personal details/facts
God bless my soul!/upon my soul! = exclamation of surprise
not able to call one's soul one's own = be in somebody else's control/power

not a soul = nobody
the soul of = a good example of
sell one's soul for something = do anything to obtain something
soul-destroying = disappointing/onerous
soul-searching = analysis of one's own motives/reasons for doing
  something
  See also: keep **body** and soul together; **life** and soul; **life** and soul of
  the party; **own** somebody body and soul; with all one's **heart** (and
  soul).

sound
sound in wind and limb = physically fit
sound off = talk loudly
sound somebody out = attempt to find what somebody is
  planning/thinking
  See also: clear/sound as a **bell**; **safe** and sound.

soup
in the soup = in trouble
souped-up = with a more powerful engine

sour
  See: sour **grapes**.

sow
sow the seeds of = initiate/originate
  See also: **silk** purse out of a sow's ear; sow one's wild **oats**.

space
in the space of an hour/minute/moment = in an
  hour's/minute's/moment's time
  See also: **breathing** space.

spade
call a spade a spade = be very frank
doubled in spades! = even more so!
spade work = basic/initial work
  See also: **black** as the ace of spades.

Spain
  See: **castles** in Spain/the air.

span
  See: **spick** and span.

spanner
throw a spanner in the works = frustrate/sabotage

spare
go spare = become angry/emotional
spare tyre = fat round one's waist
to spare = more than needed
  See also: spare somebody's **blushes**; spare the **rod** and spoil the child.

spark
spark off = begin/initiate
make the sparks fly = cause an argument/trouble
  See also: **bright** spark.

speak
be on speaking terms with somebody = be casual friends with
  somebody
generally speaking = in general/on average
know somebody to speak to = know somebody casually
nothing to speak of = nothing worthy of attention
speak as one finds = for a point of view based on personal experience
speak for somebody = express somebody else's point of view
speak for yourself = I disagree with you
speak out = express one's views boldly
speak for itself = be self-evident
speak the same language (as somebody) = have the same views (as
  somebody)
speak up = talk more loudly
speak volumes = be significant
speak well of = praise
speak with a forked tongue = lie
strictly speaking = being exact/precise
to speak of = worthy of attention
  See also: **actions** speak louder than words; in a **manner** of speaking;
  plain speaking; **so** to speak; speak one's **mind**; speak/talk of the
  devil; speak/talk the same **language** as somebody; speak too **soon**.

spec
on spec = on the chance that something might happen

spectacles
pair of spectacles = batsman's score of zero in both innings of a
  cricket match
  See also: look at/see/view things through **rose**-tinted spectacles.

spell
spell something out = describe something in detail
under the spell of = fascinated/influenced by

spend
spend a bomb/packet = spend a lot (of money)
  See also: spend **money** like water; spend a **penny**.

spice
  See: **variety** is the spice of life.

spick
spick and span = neat/tidy

spike
on the spike = put aside for possible use later
spike a drink = add spirits to a weaker drink
  See also: spike somebody's **gun**s.

spill
  See: **cry** over spilt milk; spill the **bean**s.

spin
spin a yarn = tell an (untrue) story
spin something out = make something last longer
  See also: **flat** spin; make one's **head** spin.

spine
  See: send **shiver**s down/up one's spine.

spirit
be with somebody in spirit = think about somebody when one is
  unable to be with him/her
in high/low spirits = cheerful/miserable

moving spirit = somebody who initiates/is active in an undertaking
out of spirits = depressed/unhappy
public spirit = a feeling of wanting to benefit society
spirit away = remove secretly
take something in the right spirit = not take offence at something
the spirit is willing (but the flesh is weak) = one's desires cannot
  always be achieved physically

spit
dead spit of = identical to
spit and polish = fastidious/thorough cleaning
spitting image = exact replica
spit it out = say it
  See also: be spitting **feathers**; within spitting/striking **distance**.

spite
in spite of oneself = even though one would rather/should not
  See also: cut off one's **nose** to spite one's face.

splash
make a splash = attract much attention
splash-down = landing of a spacecraft in the sea
splash out (on) = spend much money (on)

spleen
vent one's spleen = display anger

splice
  See: splice the **mainbrace**.

splinter
splinter group = small group that has broken away from a larger one

split
do the splits = drop/sit on the floor with one leg forwards and the
  other backwards
splitting headache = severe headache
split on somebody = betray somebody (to the authorities)
split second = very short time
  See also: split **hairs**; split one's **sides**; split the **difference**.

spoil

be spoiling for something = be eager/keen for something
spoil-sport = somebody who spoils somebody else's enjoyment
 See also: spare the **rod** and spoil the child; spoil the **ship** for a
 ha'porth of tar.

spoke

put a spoke in (somebody's wheel) = place difficulties/obstructions in
 somebody's way
put one's spoke in = interrupt (to express a point of view)

sponge

sponge off/on somebody = scrounge (money) from somebody
throw in/up the sponge = give in/surrender

spoon

spoon-feed somebody = deny somebody independent action/thought
wooden spoon = prize awarded to somebody who does least well in a
 contest
 See also: **born** with a silver spoon in one's mouth.

sport

 See: **blood** sport; fighting/sporting **chance**.

spot

blind spot = gap in one's knowledge/understanding
high spot = best/most important
in a spot = in trouble
on the spot = in the place required, or immediately
put somebody on the spot = cause somebody difficulty
spot cash = ready money
spot check = random/surprise check
spot of = little
spot on = exactly correct
tight spot = difficult situation
 See also: have a **soft** spot for; **knock** spots off; **rooted** to the spot.

spout

up the spout = spoiled/ruined, or pregnant

sprat
  See: sprat to catch a **mackerel**.

spread
spread like wildfire = spread very rapidly
spread oneself = be indulgent/lavish
  See also: spread one's **wings**.

spring
spring a leak = let in water
spring somebody from custody/jail = arrange for a prisoner to escape/be released
spring something on somebody = surprise somebody
where did somebody/something spring from? = where did somebody/something suddenly appear from?
  See also: **full** of the joys of spring; no (spring) **chicken**.

spur
spur somebody on = encourage somebody to try harder
win one's spurs = achieve recognition
  See also: on the spur of the **moment**.

spurt
put a spurt on = go faster

spy
spy on somebody = secretly observe somebody
spy out the land = make a preliminary investigation

square
all square = equal/even/level
be (a) square = be dull/unfashionable
go back to square one = return to the beginning
have square eyes = suffer the effects of watching too much television
square bashing = basic training in the armed forces
square meal = meal that is nourishing/sufficient
square up with somebody = pay (a debt to) somebody
square up to somebody = face an attacker/critic
square up to something = face a difficulty/problem with resolution
square with = agree with

See also: **fair** and square; settle/square an **account** (with somebody); square **deal**; square peg in a round **hole**.

squeak
See: narrow **escape**/shave/squeak.

squeeze
in a tight squeeze = in (financial) difficulties

squib
See: **damp** squib.

stab
have a stab at = make an attempt at
See also: stab in the **back**.

stable
See: lock the stable **door** after the horse has bolted.

stack
See: stack the **cards** against somebody.

staff
staff of life = bread

stag
stag night/party = celebration (of a forthcoming wedding) for men only

stage
set the stage for = prepare for
stage fright = anxiety/nervousness felt before appearing in public
stage-manage = organize
stage whisper = loud whisper (that is meant to be heard by others)

stairs
below stairs = servants' accommodation
work below stairs = work as a servant
See also: by the **back** stairs.

stake
at stake = at risk
go to the stake for = accept criticism/unpleasantness for what one does/believes in

have a stake in something = make an investment in something
stake out = observe carefully/carry out surveillance
  See also: **pull** up roots/stakes; stake a **claim**.

stamp
stamp/on out = eliminate/put down
  See also: **rubber** stamp something; stamping **ground**; stamp one's **foot**.

stand
as matters/things stand = in the present circumstances
know how/where one stands = be aware of one's position/status
leave somebody standing = progress much faster than somebody else
make a stand against = defy/resist
on stand-by = in reserve and ready
stand alone = be unique, or be without help
stand aside/by = observe passively/fail to see
stand by = be ready for action, or be supportive, or observe passively/fail to see
stand corrected = accept that one has made a mistake
stand down = cease to be ready for action, or withdraw from a contest
stand fast/firm = be unyielding
stand for = represent, or tolerate
stand in for = substitute for
stand in somebody's way = prevent somebody from doing something
stand-offish = with a superior/unfriendly attitude
stand one in good stead = be available when needed
stand or fall by something = be committed to something (whether it succeeds or fails)
stand out = physically protrude, or be more noticeable than other things
stand/stick out for = persist in a request without compromise
stand over = supervise/observe closely
stand somebody up = fail to keep an appointment
stand to lose/win = be likely to lose/win
stand up and be counted = make one's views known to everyone
stand up for = champion/support
stand up to = resist

take a stand on = positively state (and be prepared to defend) one's point of view
See also: hold/stand one's **ground**; it stands to **reason** (that); last-ditch stand; not be able to stand the **sight** of somebody/something; stand a good/fair **chance** of; standing **joke**; standing on one's **head**; stand on **ceremony**; stand one in good **stead**; stand on one's **dignity**; stand on one's own (two) **feet**; stand/stick out a **mile**.

star

see stars = apparently see flashing lights (after a blow to the head)
star-studded = with many famous entertainers
star turn = high-quality performance/performer
thank one's lucky stars = regard oneself as very fortunate
See also: (one's star is) in the **ascendant**.

stare

See: staring one in the **face**.

stark

See: (stark) raving **mad**.

start

for a start/to start with/for starters = in the first place
get off to a bad start = begin something badly
get off to a good/flying start = begin something well
head start = initial advantage (in a contest)
make a fresh start/start from scratch = (re)start from the beginning
start life = begin one's working life
start out as = begin as
See also: **false** start; get/start off on the right/wrong **foot**; in **fits** and starts; keep/set/start the **ball** rolling.

state

get in(to) a state = become (emotionally) upset
state of the art = present status/stage of development
state the obvious = say something that everybody already knows
See also: in a state of **nature**; the state of **play**.

station

above one's station = above one's accepted position in life
See also: **action** stations.

statistics
vital statistics = (a woman's) measurements

status
status symbol = possession that indicates somebody's high position (socially)

stay
stay put = remain in one place/position
See also: stay one's **hand**; stay the **course**; stay the **pace**.

stead
See: stand one in **good** stead.

steady
go steady = not be excessive/extravagant, or have a regular friendship with somebody of the opposite sex
steady as a rock = very steady/reliable
steady on! = do not be so aggressive/angry/excessive

steal
steal somebody's heart = acquire somebody's love/affection
steal somebody's thunder = rob somebody of the chance to receive credit/praise
steal up on somebody = move unnoticed towards somebody
See also: steal a **march** (on somebody); steal the **show**.

steam
full steam ahead = at maximum speed
get (all) steamed up = become angry/upset
get up steam = summon up vitality
run out of steam = become exhausted
under one's own steam = by oneself/unaided
See also: **blow**/let off steam.

steel
See: **man** of iron/steel; steel one's **heart** against.

steep
a bit steep = unreasonable

steer
bum steer = false information/poor advice
steer a middle course = compromise (between extremes)
  See also: steer **clear** of.

step
in/out of step = conforming/not conforming
retrace one's steps = go back along the route just travelled
step by step = gradually/sequentially
step down = resign
step in = interrupt/intervene
step in the right direction = contribution towards what is
  desired/required
step on it = hurry
(ask somebody to) step outside = challenge somebody to a fight
step/tread on somebody's toes = offend somebody
step up = increase
take steps = take action
watch one's step = be (very) careful
  See also: **false** step; fill/step into the **breach; follow** in somebody's
  footsteps; step into somebody's **shoes;** step out of **line.**

Stephen
  See: **even** Stephen(s).

stew
get in(to) a stew = become agitated/upset
  See also: stew in one's own **juice.**

stick
dirty/rough end of the stick = unfair/harsh treatment
give somebody stick = harangue somebody
give something (some) stick = push something to its limit
on a sticky wicket = in a difficult situation
stick at something = persist in doing something
stick in one's craw/gullet/throat = be unacceptable
stick something out = endure a difficult/unpleasant situation
stick together = remain together (loyally)
stick up = rob, using firearms
stick up for = support

stick with which to beat somebody = (confidential/damaging)
  knowledge about somebody used to put pressure on him/her
wield a big stick = use authority/power to control somebody
  See also: **cleft** stick; come to a sticky **end**; get hold of the wrong **end**
  of the stick; have light/sticky **fingers**; put/stick one's **oar** in;
  stand/stick out a **mile**; **stand**/stick out for; stick in one's **throat**; stick
  in the **mud**; stick one's **neck** out; stick out like a sore **thumb**; stick to
  one's **guns**; something that sticks in one's **gizzard**.

stiff
  See: bore stiff/the **pants** off/to tears; keep a stiff upper **lip**; scare
  somebody stiff; stiff as **board**; stiff as a **poker**/ramrod; **worried** stiff.

still
still waters run deep = somebody can be more
  emotional/knowledgeable than he/she first appears

sting
sting in the tail = something unpleasant revealed only in the final
  outcome
take the sting out of something = reduce the severity/unpleasantness
  of something

stink
like stink = to excess/the maximum limit
  See also: **cry** stinking fish; **raise** a stink; smell/stink to high **heaven**.

stir
stir the blood = inspire one
  See also: lift/stir a **finger**.

stitch
a stitch in time saves nine = the correction of a minor fault promptly
  prevents the development of many other (possibly major) ones
in stitches = laughing very much/uncontrollably
not have a stitch on = be totally naked

stock
lay in a stock of = obtain a supply of
on the stocks = incomplete but in the process of being completed
somebody's stock rises = somebody's status/reputation increases

stock in trade = something that is standard/usual
stock up on/with = obtain/store a supply of
stock still = motionless
take stock of = review
    See also: **laugh**ing stock; **lock**, stock and barrel.

stocking
    See: **blue** stocking.

stomach
have a strong stomach = be difficult to disgust
have no stomach for = be most disinclined to
turn one's stomach = make one (feel) disgusted/sick
    See also: **butterflies** in one's stomach/tummy; on an **empty** stomach.

stone
cast the first stone = be first to condemn/criticize
leave no stone unturned = try every possible way (in a search)
stone dead = (completely) dead
stone deaf = completely deaf
stone me/the crows! = exclamation of disbelief/surprise
stone's throw = short distance
stony broke = with no money at all
    See also: get **blood** out of a stone; **fall** on deaf ears/stony ground;
    have a **heart** of stone; kill two **birds** with one stone; stone **cold**;
    stone-cold **sober**; stoned out of one's **mind**/head.

stool
    See: **fall** between two stools; stool **pigeon**.

stop
come to a dead stop = halt abruptly
come to a full stop = stop totally
full stop = and that's final
stop a tooth = insert a filling into a tooth
stop dead = come to an abrupt halt
stop off/over = interrupt a journey (to stay somewhere for a short
    time)
stop short of doing something = not go as far as doing something
    (dishonest/illegal/immoral)

See also: **pull** out all the stops; put an **end**/stop to; stop at/short of **nothing**.

store

in store = on its way
set/lay (great) store by something = value something (highly)
  See also: **cold** storage.

strom

bend/bow before the storm = yield to a (verbal) attack
storm in a teacup = disproportionally large fuss about something trivial
take somebody/something by storm = make a great impression on somebody/something
weather the storm = endure/survive throughout a difficult situation
  See also: any **port** in a storm.

story

cut a long story short = give an abbreviated account
likely story = unbelievable account (meant ironically)
same old story = repeated/boring account
story line = thread of a narrative/piece of fiction
success story = account of how somebody succeeds in life
tall story = exaggerated/unlikely account
that's (quite) another/a different story = that is (very) different
the story is/goes that... = the excuse/general opinion is that...
the story of my life = misfortune always happens to me
  See also: **cock** and bull story; shaggy **dog** story.

straight

get something straight = ensure that something is accurate/true
go straight = lead an honest life (after formerly not doing so)
know something straight off = know something without thinking
straight away/off = immediately
straight out/up = frankly/honestly
straight talk = frank/honest discussion
the straight and narrow = honest/moral way of life
  See also: (straight) from the **horse**'s mouth; keep a straight **face**; set the **record** straight; straight **answer**; straight as a **die**; straight from the **shoulder**.

strait
strait-laced = of a rigid/strict point of view

strain
  See: straining at the **leash**.

strange
be a stranger to = be unaccustomed to/unfamiliar with
little stranger = newborn baby
strangely enough/strange to tell = curiously/surprisingly
stranger things have happened = even more unusual things are
possible
  See also: stranger things happen at **sea**.

straw
choose/draw the short straw = be selected from among others for an
unpleasant task
straw in the wind = something trivial that may signify something
significant in the future
straw poll = sample of people's views
  See also: **clutch** at a straw/straws; **last** straw; make **bricks** without
straw; **man** of straw.

streak
be on/have a winning streak = win successively (at gambling)
do a streak = run naked in public
  See also: like greased/a streak of **lightning**.

stream
swim against the stream = hold a view opposite to most others

street
be on the street(s) = have nowhere to live
Fleet Street = the (London) newspaper business
go on the streets = become a prostitute
not in the same street as = not nearly as good/the same as
streets ahead = much better than/superior to
(just/right) up somebody's street = well suited to somebody
Wall Street = American big business
  See also: **Civvy** Street; in **easy** circumstances/on easy street; in **queer**
street; **man** in the street; the old **lady** of Threadneedle Street.

strength

at full strength = undiluted, or having the required
  number/complement
give me strength! = exclamation of annoyance/frustration
go from strength to strength = continue to improve
in strength = in force/large numbers
on the strength = as a member of the staff/workforce
on the strength of = because of (something demonstrated previously)
pillar/tower of strength = somebody on whom one can rely for
  help/encouragement
strengthen one's hand = make one's position better (in a contest)
  See also: **trial** of strength.

stretch

at a stretch = without stopping, or in the extreme
at full stretch = using maximum energy/resources
do a stretch = serve a prison sentence
  See also: by no stretch of the **imagination**; stick/stretch one's **neck**
  out; stretch a **point**; stretch one's **legs**.

stride

get into one's stride = attain one's usual rate of doing something
make great strides = make good progress
put somebody off his/her stride/stroke = spoil/interrupt what
  somebody is successfully doing
take something in one's stride = achieve something without
  difficulty/worry

strike

it strikes me = it occurs to me
strike an attitude = express a (strong/inflexible) opinion, or pose
strike camp = (take down tents and) move from a temporary resting-
  place
strike fear/terror into (the heart of) somebody = terrify somebody
strike home to somebody = have an impact on somebody
strike out in another direction = begin a new course in one's
  business/life etc.
strike somebody all of a heap = astonish/astound somebody
strike somebody off = remove somebody's name from a list/register

strike up = begin
strike while the iron is hot = act while the opportunity exists
wildcat strike = sudden unofficial strike (i.e. without trade union sanction)
   See also: **lightning** strike; strike a **balance**; strike a **bargain**; strike a **blow** for/against; strike a **chord**; strike a **light**!; strike a **pose**; strike (it) **rich**; strike (it) **lucky**; strike me **pink**!; strike **oil**; strike the right **note**; strike **terror** into somebody; strike while the **iron** is hot; within striking **distance**.

string
have somebody on a (piece of) string = control somebody
hold the purse-strings = be in control of money/spending
keep somebody on a (piece of) string = make somebody wait for a decision
string along with somebody = accompany/join in with somebody
string somebody along = retain somebody's affection/friendship (without returning it)
string somebody up = hang somebody
(all) strung up/highly strung = agitated/nervous
with no strings attached = without conditions
   See also: another/two string(s) to one's **bow**; **pull** strings; tied to one's mother's **apron** strings.

strip
strip off = get undressed
tear a strip off somebody = harangue/rebuke somebody

stroke
at a (single) stroke = in only one go
on the stroke of = exactly at
   See also: **put** somebody off his/her stride/stroke.

strong
(still) going strong = continuing to function well
somebody's strong suit = something that somebody is good/best at
strong-arm tactics = physical violence
   See also: (using) bad/strong **language**; **going** strong; have a strong **stomach**; strong **point**.

struck
be struck on somebody = like somebody very much
  See also: **strike**.

stubborn
stubborn as a mule = very stubborn

stuck
be stuck for something = be without something
be stuck on somebody/something = be attracted to or like
  somebody/something
be stuck with somebody/something = be unable to get rid of
  somebody/something
get stuck in = begin eating, or begin working (hard)
stuck up = snobbish, feeling superior
  See also: **stick**.

stuff
do one's stuff = demonstrate what one can do, or do what is expected
  of one
know one's stuff = be knowledgeable/skilful (in a particular subject)
stuff and nonsense = utter nonsense
that's the stuff (to give the troops) = that's just what is required
  See also: **bit** of skirt/stuff; **hard** stuff; **hot** stuff; **kid**'s stuff; **knock**
  the stuffing out of somebody; stuffed **shirt**.

stumble
stumble across = accidentally find
stumbling block = obstruction to progress

stump
be stumped = be at a loss/not know
stump up = find/pay some money
stump somebody = ask somebody something he/she cannot do/does
  not know

style
do something/live in style = do something/live in an extravagant
  manner
  See also: **cramp** somebody's style.

subject
be subject to = be conditional on, or be likely to be affected by
change the subject = alter the topic of conversation
subject somebody to = force somebody to experience/undergo

success
nothing succeeds like success = success once/in one area is likely to be
  followed by more success
  See also: success **story**.

such
such-and-such = somebody/something unnamed
such as it is/they are = it/they are poor/unsatisfactory

suck
suck up to somebody = fawn on/flatter somebody (in the hope of a
  favour)
  See also: **blood** sucker; teach one's **grandmother** to suck eggs.

sudden
all of a sudden = suddenly

suffer
on sufferance = tolerated (unwillingly)
  See also: not suffer **fools** gladly.

suffice
suffice it to say (that) = one need say only (that)

sugar
  See: sugar **daddy**; sugar the **pill**.

suit
suit oneself = (selfishly) do what one likes
  See also: **birthday** suit; **follow** suit; somebody's **strong** suit; suit-case
  economy; suit one's **book**; suit somebody down to the **ground**.

sum
sum total = complete total

summer
Indian summer = summery weather in autumn
  See also: one **swallow** doesn't make a summer.

sun
catch the sun = become sunburned
touch of the sun = illness/slight madness caused by overexposure to
  the heat of the sun
under the sun = anywhere/worldwide
  See also: make **hay** while the sun shines.

Sunday
Sunday best = one's best (formal) clothes
  See also: **month** of Sundays.

sundry
  See: **all** and sundry.

sunk
  See: **sink**.

supper
  See: **sing** for one's supper.

supply
in short supply = scarce

suppose
I don't suppose you could... = please could you...
I suppose so = I agree (reluctantly)
what do you suppose? = what do you think?

sure
a sure thing = a (near) certainty
be sure and/to = ensure that/be certain to
don't be/you can't be/you can never be too sure = one cannot be
  certain
for sure = certainly/definitely
make sure = ensure/make certain
sure as hell = certainly
sure-fire = certain
sure of oneself = confident
sure thing = emphatically yes
that's for sure = that is certain
to be sure = of course

See also: sure as **eggs** is eggs; sure **enough**.

surface
  See: **scratch** the surface.

surprise
catch/take somebody by surprise = confront somebody unexpectedly
much to one's surprise = causing one astonishment/great surprise

suspicion
above/beyond suspicion = not even considered as possibly guilty

swallow
one swallow doesn't make a summer = one good omen/sign does not
  make a good forecast
  See also: swallow one's **pride**.

swan
swan around = go around (selfishly) indulging in pleasurable activities
swan song = somebody's last performance/work

sway
  See: **hold** sway.

swear
swear black and blue = assert adamantly/emphatically
swear black is white = assert a falsehood
swear by = trust/rely on completely
swear like a trooper = habitually use swear words
swear somebody in = formally install somebody into an
  office/position
  See also: swear **blind**; sworn **enemies**.

sweat
in a cold sweat = apprehensive/frightened
no sweat = no bother/trouble
old sweat = somebody who is experienced/long-serving
sweated labour = people who work for very poor wages (and often
  for long hours)
sweat it out = remain throughout a difficult/unpleasant experience
sweat like a pig = sweat copiously
  See also: by the sweat of one's **brow**; sweat **blood**.

sweep
  See: make a **clean** sweep; sweep somebody off his/her **feet**; sweep
  something under the **carpet**/rug; sweep the **board**; sweep the **deck**;
  sweep/wipe the **floor** with.

sweet
all sweetness and light = apparently friendly and good-tempered
be sweet on somebody = be (slightly) in love with somebody
have a sweet tooth = like eating sweet foods
the sweets of = the rewards of
  See also: **short** and sweet; sweet **dreams**; sweet **nothings**.

swell
feeling swell = feeling happy/healthy
  See also: swollen-**headed**.

swim
go swimmingly = proceed successfully/well
in the swim = up-to-date/involved with the latest trends
swim against the tide = act/behave in a way that is opposite to most
  other people's
  See also: **sink** or swim.

swing
get into the swing of things = adopt an (existing) routine
go with a swing = occur successfully/without difficulty
in full swing = happening vigorously
  See also: no/not enough room to swing a **cat**; swinging the **lead**.

switch
be switched on = be aware (of current trends)
switch from/over = change

swollen
  See: swollen-**headed**.

swoop
at/in one fell swoop = simultaneously

sword
cross swords with somebody = have an argument/disagreement with
  somebody

double-edged sword = something that can cause damage in two
  different ways
sword of Damocles (hanging over one) = disaster that could happen
  at any time

symbol
  See: **status** symbol.

sympathy
in sympathy with = more-or-less in agreement with

system
all systems go = let us begin
get something out of one's system = reveal/get rid of something that
  has been occupying one's thoughts

T

T
to a T = exactly
See also: dot the i's and cross the t's.

tab
keep tabs on = continually check/watch/be informed
pick up the tab = pay the bill

table
drink somebody under the table = drink more (and remain conscious) than somebody else (who does not remain conscious)
turn the tables on somebody = seize the advantage from somebody by reversing the situation
See also: lay/put one's **card**s on the table; round-table **conference**.

tablet
keep (on) taking the tablets = reply to a crazy action/statement

tack
change tack = alter a course of action
See also: get down to **brass** tacks.

tag
tag along = follow or accompany somebody (perhaps when not wanted)

tail
keep/stay on somebody's tail = tenaciously follow somebody
tail off = diminish
turn tail = turn back and leave in the direction one came
with one's tail between one's legs = in a sad/ashamed manner
with one's tail up = carefree/happy
See also: hang on somebody's **coat** tails; in two **shake**s (of a donkey's/lamb's tail); like a **dog** with two tails; make neither **head** nor tail of; put **salt** on somebody's tail; **sting** in the tail; tail wagging the **dog**; **twist** somebody's tail.

take

be able to/can take it = be/is able to tolerate pain/trouble etc.

be taken with somebody/something = find somebody/something attractive

I take it (that) = I assume (that)

it takes one to know one = you are the same as the person you describe

take after somebody = resemble somebody

take it from me = believe me

take it from there = carry on without help/planning/supervision

take it or leave it = accept or refuse something

take it out of one = exhaust/tire one

take it out on somebody = direct one's anger/displeasure at somebody else

take off = suddenly improve/succeed

take one back = cause one to remember

take on the appearance of = resemble

take somebody for somebody else = mistake one person for another

take somebody in = cheat/deceive somebody, or admit somebody to one's home

take somebody off = imitate somebody

take somebody up on something = accept an offer

take something back = retract a statement

take something in = understand something, or include something

take something over = take control/possession of something

take something upon oneself = accept/take responsibility for

take something up with somebody = bring up/discuss a topic with somebody

take to something = come to like something, or adopt something (habitually)

take up with somebody = associate/make friends with somebody

See also: be taken **aback**; bring/take somebody down a **peg** (or two); caught/taken **short**; go take a running **jump** (at yourself)!; run/take the **risk**; take a **powder**; take **cover**; take **effect**; take **heart**; take holy **orders**; take it **easy**; take off one's **hat** to; take one's **cue** from; take one's **medicine**; take one's **time**; take **sides**; take somebody for a **ride**; take somebody on/to one **side**; take somebody's **mind** off something; take somebody's **name** in vain; take somebody's **place**; take

somebody's **point**; take somebody to one's **heart**; take somebody to
task; take something as **read**; take something into one's **head**; take
something to **heart**; take **steps**; take the **edge** off; take the **floor**; take
the **place** of something; take up **arms**; take up the **cudgels**.

tale

dead men tell no tales = one cannot be incriminated by somebody
who is dead
tell its own tale = be self-evident
tell tales about somebody = inform on/reveal confidences about
somebody
tell tales out of school = indulge in gossip
thereby hangs a tale = the account could be continued further
See also: **live** to tell the tale; **old** wives' tales.

talent
See: **bud**ding talent.

talk

do the talking = be spokesman
idle talk = gossip/useless conversation
know what one is talking about = be expert/knowledgeable
now you're talking! = what you are saying now is really relevant
pillow talk = conversation between lovers (in bed)
(make) small talk = (have a) trivial/polite conversation
sweet-talk somebody = flatter somebody (for gain)
talk about... = that is a perfect case of...
talk back to somebody = answer somebody in an impolite/rude way
talk down to somebody = talk to somebody as if he/she were less
intelligent/important
talking of... = now that subject has arisen...
talk of the town = something that everybody is discussing
talk somebody into/out of something = persuade/dissuade somebody
talk somebody round = persuade somebody
talk something over = discuss something (at length)
you can talk = you are not in a position to criticize
See also: **money** talks; **speak**/talk of the devil; talk **big**; talk **nineteen**
to the dozen; talk **shop**; talk somebody's **head** off; talk the hind leg

off a **donkey**; talk through one's **hat**; talk through the back of one's **neck**; talk to somebody like a **Dutch** uncle; talk **turkey**.

tall
   See: tall **order**; tall **story**; walk **tall**.

tan
   See also: tan somebody's **hide**.

tangent
go/fly off at a tangent = suddenly diverge from the path/subject

tap
on tap = available for (immediate) use

tape
have/get something/somebody taped = have a good knowledge of the
   nature of somebody/something
   See also: **red** tape.

tar
   See: spoil the **ship** for a ha'porth of tar; tarred with the same **brush**.

target
   See: **sitting** target.

tart
tart somebody/something up = make somebody/something
   superficially more attractive (in a tawdry way)

task
hard task-master = somebody who makes one work hard
take somebody to task = criticize/discipline somebody

taste
develop/have a taste for = acquire/possess a liking for
to taste = in the amount preferred
to one's taste = such as to give one pleasure
   See also: **acquired** taste; dose/taste of one's own **medicine**; in **bad**
   taste; leave a nasty taste in one's **mouth**; no **accounting** for taste;
   taste **blood**.

tat
  See: **tit** for tat.

tea
not for all the tea in China = not at all/ever
  See also: another **cup** of tea; nice (old) **cup** of tea; not one's **cup** of tea; **storm** in a teacup.

teach
that will teach one/somebody = what happened is (just) retribution for what one/somebody did
  See also: teach one's **grandmother** to suck eggs; teach somebody a **lesson**; you can't teach an old **dog** new tricks.

tear
dissolve in(to) tears = begin to cry copiously
reduce somebody to tears = make somebody cry
tear oneself away = force oneself to leave
  See: **bore** stiff/the pants off/to tears; **crocodile** tears; tear a strip off somebody; tear one's **hair** out; **wear** and tear.

teeth
armed to the teeth = carrying many weapons, or possessing as much as possible to give one an advantage
bare/show one's teeth = reveal one's intention to fight/resist
draw somebody's/something's teeth = cause somebody/something to be less of a danger
get one's teeth into something = make determined effort in doing something
give one's eye/back teeth for something = do anything to obtain something
gnash one's teeth = feel/show angry frustration
grit one's teeth = hide one's feelings
in the teeth of = against/in conflict with
make one's teeth chatter = cause the jaws to shake and the teeth to knock rapidly together
teething troubles = initial difficulties
  See also: **bit** between one's teeth; by the **skin** of one's teeth; **cut** one's teeth on; **fed** up (to the back teeth); in the teeth of the **wind**; **kick**

somebody in the teeth; **lie** in/through one's teeth; set one's teeth on **edge**.

telegraph
See: **bush** telegraph.

tell
as far as one can tell = as far as one knows/is aware
I can tell you = I assure you
I told you so = I predicted it would happen
tell me another = I do not believe you
tell on somebody = inform on somebody, or cause somebody to feel exhausted/strained
tell somebody (where to get) off = scold/reprimand somebody
(I'll) tell you what = I propose/suggest
there's no telling = one cannot know
to tell the truth = to be perfectly honest
what did I tell you? = what I said was true
you never can tell = it could happen
you're telling me = I agree
See also: **all** told; **live** to tell the tale; tell **apart**; tell its own **tale**; (you can) tell that/it to the **marines**; tell **tales** about somebody; tell **tales** out of school.

temper
keep/lose one's temper = conceal/show one's anger

ten
ten to one = it is very probable that

tender
See: leave somebody to the tender **mercies** of; of tender **age**; tender **trap**.

tenterhooks
be on tenterhooks = be (very) anxious about the possible outcome

term
in terms of something = define/describe with reference to something
on bad/good terms with = unfriendly/friendly with
See also: be on **speaking** terms with somebody; **blanket** term; **come** to terms with; **contradiction** in terms; on **easy** terms; terms of **abuse**.

terror
strike terror into somebody = make somebody very afraid/fearful
  See also: **holy** terror.

test
put somebody/something to the test = test somebody/something
  See also: **acid** test; stand the test of **time**.

tether
  See: at the **end** of one's rope/tether.

thank
have only oneself to thank for = be the sole cause of
I'll thank you to = please (used when annoyed)
thanks for having me/us = thank you for your hospitality
thanks to/no thanks to = because of/in spite of
thank you/thanks for nothing = I am not pleased
  See also: thankful for small **mercies**; thank one's lucky **stars**; **vote** of
  thanks.

that
and all that = and all (the rest of) that sort of thing
and/so that's that = that is the decision/result
at that = as well, or whereupon
in that = because/since
is that so? = expression of questioning surprise
(just) like that = without hesitation
that's about it = that is more or less all
  See also: **be** that as it may; **how**'s that for; that will **do**; that's **done**
  it!; that's the **way** it goes; you **do** that!

then
(every) now and then = occasionally
  See also: **there** and then.

there
so there = expression that emphasizes a (supposed) advantage
there and then/then and there = at that very time (and place)
there again = alternatively
there are (somethings) and (somethings) = there are good and bad
  examples of something

there you are = it is inevitable, or I said that would happen, or that is
  what you need/requested
there you go = there you are
  See also: (not) **all** there.

thick

a bit thick = slightly stupid, or unjust/unfair
in the thick of something = in the most active/dense part of
  something
thick and fast = many and often/quickly
thick as thieves = very close/friendly
thick as two short planks = stupid
through thick and thin = despite all adversity/difficulties
  See also: **blood** is thicker than water; box somebody's **ears**/give
  somebody a thick ear; have a thick **skin**; **lay** it on thick/with a
  trowel; **pile** it on thick; the **plot** thickens; thick/thin on the **ground**.

thief

set a thief to catch a thief = the best way to discover/outdo a
  wrongdoer is to use another wrongdoer
  See also: **den** of thieves; **thick** as thieves.

thin

thin edge of the wedge = insignificant start of a worsening situation
thin on top = balding
  See also: into thin **air**; lean/thin **time**; out of thin **air**; skate on thin
  ice; thick/thin on the **ground**; thin as a **rake**.

thing

a daft/silly/stupid etc. thing to do = a daft etc. action
a/the good/sensible/wise etc. thing to do = a good etc.
  action/decision
all things to all men = adaptable/suited to everybody
and another thing = moreover
do the handsome thing = be chivalrous/generous
for one thing = as just one example/reason
have a thing about = have a special affection for/interest
  in/obsession about etc.
it's a good thing = it is fortunate/lucky
make a good thing of something = make something
  profitable/successful

make a thing of something = overemphasize something

no such thing = on the contrary, or something different/non- existent

of all things = from all the possibilities

old thing = form of address to a colleague/friend

on to a good thing = involved in something beneficial/profitable

poor thing = object of pity/sympathy

sure thing = certainly

taking one thing with another = considering everything

the thing is. . . = the problem/question is. . .

the very thing = exactly what is required

(have) too much of a good thing = (do) something in excess

See also: all/other things being **equal**; all things **considered**; do one's **own** thing; **first** thing; **first** things first; **hearing** things; I've never **heard** of such a thing; **just** the thing; **know** a thing or two; **near** miss/thing; not **know** the first thing about; (just) **one** of those things; see/think **fit**.

think

get/have another think coming = be mistaken

good thinking = a good idea

I should think not/so = I agree that is incorrect/correct

I shouldn't/wouldn't think of doing something = under no circumstances would I do something

that's what you think = that is your opinion

think no end of = regard very highly

think no more of = forget

think something out/over/through = plan something mentally, or consider something (carefully)

think twice = consider carefully

think something up = devise/invent something

think-tank = group of specialists who meet to produce ideas/solutions to problems

think twice = consider carefully

who does he/she think he/she is? = he/she has an inflated opinion of himself/herself

See also: great **minds** think alike; not think **much** of; put on one's thinking **cap**; think **little** of it; think **nothing** of doing something;

think **nothing** of it; think on one's **feet**; think the **world** of somebody/something; **wishful** thinking.

this
this and that/this, that and the other = various trivial things
this is how it is = this is the situation

Thomas
See: **doubting** Thomas.

thorn
See: thorn in one's **flesh**.

thought
train of thought = sequence in which one's thinking runs
See also: **food** for thought; **penny** for your thoughts; **perish** the thought; **second** thoughts; **sobering** thought.

thousand
I believe you, thousands wouldn't = I (reluctantly) accept what you say
See also: **one** in a million/thousand.

thrash
thrash something out = discuss and resolve difficulty/problem

thread
pick up the threads = resume one's line of reasoning/way of life after a break
thread one's way = move between obstructions/through openings
See also: **hang** by a thread; **lose** the drift/thread.

three
See: three **Rs**.

thrill
thrills and spills = alternating success and failure
See also: thrilled to **bits**.

throat
at each other's throat(s) = fighting/quarrelling
words stick in one's throat = be unable to speak because of nervousness/reluctance

See also: **cut** one's own throat; **cut**-throat competition; **frog** in the throat; **jump** down somebody's throat; **ram** something down somebody's throat; **stick** in one's craw/gullet/throat.

throe
in the throes of = in the process of (usually something difficult)

throne
See: **power** behind the throne.

through
be through (with) = be finished (with)
through and through = thoroughly/totally
See also: **fall** through; **pull** round/through; **see** through somebody/something.

throw
throw a party = organize (and pay for) a party
throw a wobbly = have a tantrum
throw oneself at somebody = try to gain somebody's affection/love by openly demonstrating one's affection for him/her
throw one's weight about = be domineering (using one's authority/power)
throw somebody over = end a friendship/relationship with somebody
throw something in = add something (as an afterthought/gift)
throw something off = get rid of something
throw something open = make something accessible
throw something together = assemble/make something hurriedly
throw up = abandon/surrender, or vomit
See also: dive/throw somebody in at the deep **end**; throw a **spanner** in the works; throw **caution** to the winds; throw good **money** after bad; throw in one's **hand**; throw in the **towel**; throw in/up the **sponge**; throw **money** at; throw **money** away; throw oneself at somebody's **feet**; throw out the **baby** with the bath water; throw somebody out on his/her **ear**; throw somebody to the **dogs**; throw somebody to the **wolves**; throw something in someone's **face**.

thumb
give the thumbs up/down = give approval/disapproval

thumb-nail sketch = small, rapidly drawn picture, or brief description
twiddle one's thumbs = do nothing
  See also: all **fingers** and thumbs; **rule** of thumb; **stick** out like a sore thumb; thumb a **lift**; thumb one's **nose** at; **under** somebody's thumb.

thunder
go like thunder = progress quickly/vigorously
thunder box = lavatory
  See also: **blood** and thunder; **steal** somebody's thunder.

tick
give somebody a ticking off/tick somebody off = scold somebody
on tick = on credit
tick over = run gently (without needing attention)
what makes somebody tick = what motivates somebody
  See also: **half** a moment/tick.

ticket
that's the ticket = that is the correct/required thing
work one's ticket = obtain one's release from a job before the contract of service has expired
  See also: **just** the job/thing/ticket; **meal** ticket.

tickle
  See: be tickled **pink**; catch/take/tickle somebody's **fancy**; **slap** and tickle; tickle somebody's **ribs**; tickled to **death**.

tide
tide somebody over = help somebody to overcome a difficulty
  See also: **swim** against the tide; **time** and tide wait for no man.

tie
be tied up = be busy/occupied, or (inseparably) joined to, or confused by
tie somebody down = make somebody decide, or restrict somebody's freedom
tie in with = be logically associated with
  See also: have one's **hands** tied; **old** school tie; tie somebody (up) in **knots**; tie the **knot**; tied to one's mother's **apron** strings; with one **hand** tied behind one's back.

tiger
paper tiger = somebody who appears forceful/strong but is really feeble/ineffective

tight
on a tight-rope = finely balanced
  See also: in a tight **corner;** in a tight **squeeze;** keep a tight **rein** on; run a tight **ship; sit** tight; pull one's **belt** in/tighten one's belt.

tile
on the tiles = out (at night) enjoying oneself
  See also: have a screw/slate/tile **loose.**

till
  See: **catch** somebody with his/her fingers/hand in the till.

tilt
(at) full tilt = (at) speed
  See also: tilt at **windmill**s.

time
about time = the appropriate time, or late
ahead of one's time = with an idea/invention that is too advanced for one's contemporaries
all in good time = as soon as is/seems appropriate
any time = no thanks are necessary
at one time = at some time in the past
do time = serve a prison sentence
for the time being = meanwhile
from time to time = occasionally
gain time = create enough time to do something (by causing a delay)
half the time = often
have a time of it = have difficulties
have no/not much time for somebody/something = have a strong dislike for somebody/something
in good time = with time to spare
in one's own good time = at whatever time suits one
in one's own time = at whatever rate suits one, or in one's non-working time
in one's time = at some time in one's past

keep (good) time = synchronize, or display the time accurately
long time no see = it is good to meet you again
make good time = travel more quickly than expected
not before time = only just in time
one/two etc. at a time = singly or in specified groups
take one's time = do something at the (slow) rate one prefers
lean/thin time = time of difficulty (because of lack of money)
time after time/time and again = repeatedly
time and tide wait for no man = procrastination is inadvisable
time flies = time passes more quickly than one realizes
time is getting on = it is getting late
time was = there was a time (in the past)
  See also: a **stitch** in time saves nine; at the **same** time; **behind** the
  times; **bide** one's time; **big** time; **fall** on bad times; from time
  immemorial; have the time of one's **life**; **high** time; in the **fullness** of
  time; in the **nick** of time; **kill** time; **mark** time; **old** timer; **play** for
  time; **serve** time; **serve** one's time; there's no time like the **present**;
  time out of **mind**.

tin
  See: little tin **god**; put the (tin) **lid** on.

tinker
  See: not care a tinker's **cuss**/damn; not **worth** a tinker's cuss/damn.

tinkle
give somebody a tinkle = telephone somebody
have a tinkle = urinate

tip
tip somebody off = inform/warn/give a hint to somebody
tip the balance = be the factor that precipitates an action/decision
  See also: on the tip of one's **tongue**; tip of the **iceberg**; tip/turn the
  scales; tip somebody the **wink**.

tire
  See: **dog** tired; **sick** and tired of.

tit
tit for tat = repayment of a defeat/hurt by defeating/hurting the
  other party

to
to and fro = backwards and forwards
toing and froing = moving backwards and forwards (without making any progress)

toast
  See: **warm** as toast.

tod
on one's tod = alone

today
here today and gone tomorrow = ephemeral/present for only a short time

toe
on one's toes = alert/ready
tread on somebody's toes = offend/upset somebody by interfering with/usurping what he/she is doing
turn up one's toes = die.
  See also: from **top** to bottom/toe; toe the **line**.

toffee
can't do something for toffee = be unable to do something

together
together with = in the company of, or also/and

token
by the same token = moreover/similarly

told
  See: **all** told. See also: **tell**.

toll
take its toll = be very harmful

Tom
any/every Tom, Dick and Harry = anybody/everybody
peeping Tom = somebody who derives (sexual) pleasure by spying on others who are undressed/undressing

tomorrow

as if/like there's no tomorrow = as if it is the last opportunity (to do something)

tomorrow is another day = there will be another opportunity (said in consolation for a disappointment)

tomorrow never comes = what is not done now is unlikely to be done at all

See also: here **today** and gone tomorrow.

ton

See: like a ton of **bricks**; **weigh** (half) a ton.

tone

tone down = lessen the extremeness of

tongs

See: like **hammer** and tongs.

tongue

anything else while your tongue's warm? = have you anything else to say?

find one's tongue = begin talking (after being nervous/shy)

give somebody the rough side of one's tongue = talk to somebody in a harsh/scolding manner

give tongue to = begin talking about (enthusiastically/ vigorously)

have a tongue in one's head = be able to speak

have/with one's tongue in one's cheek = insincerely/not meant seriously

lose one's tongue = become speechless (through nervousness/shyness)

mother tongue = native language

on the tip of one's tongue = not quite remembered

wag one's tongue = talk indiscreetly/excessively

with one's tongue hanging out = be very thirsty

See also: **cat** get one's tongue; **civil** tongue (in one's head); have a **sharp** tongue; **hold** one's peace/tongue; **slip** of the tongue; **speak** with a forked tongue.

too

See: **none** too.

tool
down tools = stop working

tooth
 See: **fight** tooth and nail; have a **sweet** tooth; **long** in the tooth; **teeth**.

top
be/get on top of = dominate/overcome
be (the) tops = be (the) best
come out on top = succeed (eventually)
from top to bottom/toe = thoroughly/overall
take it from the top = start again at the beginning
on top of that = in addition to that
over the top = excessive
top of the pops = currently in favour
top somebody up = overcharge somebody
top something up = completely fill something that was partly empty
 See also: at the top of one's **voice**; **blow** one's top; **cap**/top it all; off
 the top of one's **head**; on top of the **world**; (not) out of the top
 drawer; **sleep** like a log/top; **thin** on top; top **brass**; top **dog**; top of
 the **ladder**; top of the **tree**; top the **bill**.

torch
 See: **carry** a torch (for somebody).

torn
torn between (two things) = in a dilemma
that's torn it = that has spoiled/ruined something
 See also: **tear**.

toss
it's a toss up = it is not certain
toss something off = make something quickly with ease (although not
 necessarily to a high standard), or drink something quickly
toss up = spin a coin to decide something
win/lose the toss = guess correctly/incorrectly which side of a tossed
 coin will show
 See also: **argue** the toss.

touch
finishing touches = final details (which complete something)

get in touch (with) = contact/communicate (with)

keep in touch (with) = maintain contact/communication (with)

lose touch (with) = be unable to communicate (with)

lose one's touch = lose the ability/skill to do something

out of touch (with) = not in communication (with), or lacking (latest)
  information (about)

touch and go = very uncertain

touch down = land, or score (at various football games)

touch somebody = persuade somebody to lend one money, or evoke
  an emotional response in somebody

touch somebody on the raw = say something that angers/embarrasses
  somebody

touch something off = initiate something

touch something up = make small improvements in the appearance of
  something

touch upon something = mention something briefly

See also: **easy** meat/touch; **common** touch; **Midas** touch; **soft** touch;
  touch **bottom**; touch **wood**; wouldn't touch somebody/something
  with a **bargepole**.

tough

See: hard/tough as **nails**; hard/tough **luck**; hard/tough **nut** to crack;
  (tough as) old **boots**; tough/ugly **customer**.

tow

have somebody in tow = have somebody with one

towel

throw in the towel = surrender

tower

See: **ivory** tower; pillar/tower of **strength**.

town

go to town = be extravagant/thorough

on the town = enjoying oneself with food, drink, entertainment, etc.

See also: **ghost** town; **man**-about-town; **paint** the town red; **talk** of
  the town.

traces

See: **kick** over the traces.

track
in one's tracks = where one is (located)
keep/lose track of something = have/not have knowledge about (the location of) something
make a track/tracks for = move in the direction of
make tracks = leave
(hard) on somebody's track = following/looking for somebody
on the right/wrong track = moving in the correct/incorrect direction
on/from the wrong side of the tracks = from a socially inferior background
on the track of somebody/something = looking for/pursuing somebody/something
track record = account of one's previous achievements
track somebody/something down = follow/look for somebody/something until he/she/it is found
See also: **cover** one's tracks; off the **beaten** track; one-track **mind**.

trade
trade something in = surrender something in part-exchange when buying something else
trade something off = exchange one thing for another/barter
trade on something = take (unfair) advantage of something (to gain sympathy)
See also: **jack** of all trades; **trick** of the trade.

trail
hard/hot on somebody's trail = following close behind somebody
See also: **blaze** a trail; **hit** the road/trail.

train
in train = happening (on schedule)
See also: get on/join the **gravy** train.

trap
tender trap = state of being in love
See also: **death** trap; **shut** one's face/mouth/trap.

traveller
See: **armchair** traveller.

tread
tread under foot = conquer
See also: follow/tread in somebody's **footsteps**; **fools** rush in (where angels fear to tread); skate/tread on thin **ice**; tread on **eggs**; tread on somebody's **corns**; tread on somebody's **heels**; tread on somebody's **toes**; tread **water**.

treat
treat somebody like (a piece of) dirt = show contempt for somebody
will do a treat = is (exactly) what is required
See also: **Dutch** treat; treat somebody like a **dog**.

tree
top of the tree = highest position in a career
See also: **bark** up the wrong tree; **family** tree; **money** doesn't grow on trees; not be able to see the **wood** for the trees; out of one's **mind**/tree; up a **gum** tree.

tremble
See: in **fear** (and trembling).

trial
trial and error = try to do something in various ways until the correct one is found
trial of strength = contest to determine the stronger/strongest
trial run = a test of something by doing/using it for the first time

triangle
See: **eternal** triangle.

tribute
be a tribute to = to recognize the worthiness of

trick
do the trick = do what is required
how's/how are tricks? = how are things going (with you)?
never miss a trick = do not fail to take advantage of an opportunity
trick cyclist = psychiatrist
trick of the trade = helpful inside/special knowledge associated with a trade

up to one's (old) tricks = displaying one's usual
(deceitful/mischievous) behaviour
See also: **bag** of tricks; **confidence** trick; **dirty** trick; you can't teach
an old **dog** new tricks.

trigger
trigger-happy = too willing to make use of weapons

trip
trip the light fantastic = dance
See also: **ego** trip.

Trojan
See: **work** like a horse/Trojan.

trooper
See: **swear** like a trooper.

troops
See: that's the **stuff** (to give the troops).

trot
on the trot = continually moving, or consecutively
trot something out = easily/habitually exhibit or say something

trouble
ask/look for trouble = be provocative (inviting a violent response)
get somebody into trouble = make somebody pregnant
go to the trouble of doing/take the trouble to do something = make a
special effort to do something
no trouble! = that will be easy!
there's trouble brewing/in store = difficulty/trouble is likely to occur
trouble one's head with = bother about
trouble-shooter = somebody brought in to solve problems
See also: **fish** in troubled water; **pack** up one's troubles; **pour** oil on
troubled waters; **teeth**ing troubles.

trousers
wears the trousers = (be a woman who) makes family decisions
See also: all **mouth** and trousers; **catch** somebody with his
pants/trousers down.

trowel

See: **lay** it on thick/with a trowel.

truck

have no truck with somebody/something = avoid
association/involvement with somebody/something

true

out of true = out of alignment
  See also: **come** true; **ring** true; (run) true to **form**; show oneself in
  one's true **colours**; **too** right!/true!; true **blue**; **well** and truly.

trump

turn up trumps = be efficient/kind and help somebody in difficulty
  See also: one's best/leading/trump **card**; trump somebody's **ace**.

trumpet

See: **blow** one's own trumpet.

trust

take somebody on trust = believe what somebody says without proof
take something on trust = accept something without checking
trust one to... = as expected, one has...

truth

arrive at the truth = find out (really) happened
home truth = true (but unpleasant) comment addressed to the person
  it concerns
naked truth = absolute truth
truth will out = the true facts will (inevitably) emerge
  See also: have a true **ring** to it; **home** truth; **moment** of truth; **ring**
  true; to **tell** the truth.

try

try it on (for size) = do something that is unlikely to be accepted to
  determine whether it will be accepted
try one's hand at = attempt to do something new/for the first time
try something (on) (for size) = try something to find out whether it fits/suits one
try something out = use something to find out whether it is
  suitable/works

tuck
take a tuck in = economize/reduce something by omitting part of it
tuck in(to) = eat heartily
tuck somebody in/up = make somebody comfortable in bed (by
   wrapping them tightly in the bedclothes)

tucker
   See: best **bib** and tucker.

tug
tug at one's heartstrings = appeal to one's emotions/sympathy.

turn
turn somebody in = hand over a criminal/fugitive to the police
turn somebody off = cause somebody to dislike somebody/something
turn somebody on = arouse somebody
turn something down = refuse an offer of something
turn something in = stop doing something
turn up = appear/reappear, or find
turn up for the book(s) = unexpected occurrence
whatever turns you on! = whatever interests you! (although it does
   not interest me)
   See also: come/turn up **trumps**; **do** a turn; not turn a **hair**; put/turn
   the **clock** back; **serve** its turn; tip/turn the **scales**; turn a blind **eye** to;
   turn a deaf **ear**; turn an honest **penny**/shilling; turn one's **hand** to;
   turn one's **head**/brain; turn one's **stomach**; turn on one's **heel**; turn
   on the **heat**; turn over a new **leaf**; turn the **corner**; turn the **tables**;
   turn to (good) **account**; turn to **advantage**; turn **turtle**; turn up one's
   nose at something; turn up one's **toes**; **U-turn.**

turtle
turn turtle = turn upside down

twice
once or twice = a few times/occasionally
   See also: once bitten, twice **shy**; **think** twice.

twiddle
   See: twiddle one's **thumbs.**

twinkle
in a/the twinkling of an eye = immediately/quickly

twist
round the twist = slightly mad
  See also: get one's **knickers** in a twist; twist somebody's **arm**; twist
  somebody round one's little **finger**.

two
put two and two together = deduce
there are no two ways about it = there cannot be two opinions about
  the matter
two's company (but three's a crowd) = two friends may resent the
  intrusion of a third person
two-time somebody = deceive one's (sexual) partner by
  simultaneously associating with somebody else

tyre
  See: **spare** tyre.

U

ugly
ugly as sin = very ugly
U-turn = reversal of direction/policy
  See also: tough/ugly **customer**; ugly **duckling**; ugly **rumour**.

unaccustomed
unaccustomed as I am (to public speaking) = I am not used to
  (speaking in front of an audience)

uncle
(well) I'll be a monkey's uncle = I am really surprised
Uncle Sam = (government of) the United States
  See also: **Bob**'s your uncle; talk to somebody like a **Dutch** uncle.

under
come/fall under = be grouped with
down under = Australia (and sometimes New Zealand)
take somebody under one's wing = guide/protect somebody
underr the weather = unwell
under somebody's thumb = dominated by somebody
under way = in progress
  See also: keep something under one's **hat**; take somebody under
  one's **wing**; under a **cloud**; under **age**; under **consideration**; under
  cover; under one's **breath**; under one's own **steam**; under somebody's
  nose; under somebody's **thumb**; under the **counter**; under the
  hammer; under the **influence**.

understand
come to an understanding = make an agreement
give somebody to understand = cause/lead somebody to believe
on/with the understanding that = on (the agreed) condition that

unknown
into the unknown = into an area about which nothing is known
  See also: unknown **quantity**.

unsound
of unsound mind = mad

unstuck
come unstuck = fail

up
be one up on = have an advantage
be/come up against = have to contend with
come up with = give/offer
it's all up with = there is no hope for
on the up-and-up = improving
up against it = be in difficulties
up a gum tree = in (serious) difficulties
up-and-coming = promising
up and doing = active/busy
up and down = first in one direction and then in the opposite one
ups and downs = times of good and bad fortune/health
up to a point = to a certain extent
up to somebody = the duty/responsibility of
up to something = able to do something, or involved in something
 dishonest/mischievous, or of the quality/standard of
up with somebody = at the same level as/equal to somebody, or be
 troubling somebody
up with somebody/something! = success to somebody/something!
up with you = get up/get out of bed
well up on something = well informed/knowledgeable about
 something
what's up with him/her? = what is troubling him/her?
 See also: be **one** up on somebody; **do** up; **end** up; in something up to
 one's **neck**; not up to **much**; one's **number** comes up; one's **number**
 is up; up in **arms**; up the **creek**; up the **pole**; up the **spout**; up the
 wall; up to **date**; up to no **good**; up to one's **elbows**; up to the **hilt**;
 up to the **mark**; up to the **minute**.

upper
on one's uppers = with very little/no money
 See also: gain/have the upper **hand**; keep a stiff upper **lip**; upper
 crust.

upright
 See: **bolt** upright.

upside
turn something upside down = confuse/jumble something

uptake
quick/slow on the uptake = quick-witted/slow-witted

use
come in useful = be of use in the future
get used to = become accustomed to
have no use for somebody/something = dislike/hate somebody
it's no use = it is hopeless/impossible, it is no good
make oneself useful = give help
make (best/good) use of something = use something to (best/good)
  advantage
no use to man or beast = useless
 See also: use one's **loaf**.

V

vacuum
create/leave a vacuum = leave a gap

vain
(all) in vain = ineffectively/unsuccessfully
See also: take somebody's **name** in vain.

valour
See: **discretion** is the better part of valour.

value
place/put/set a (high) value on = estimate the (high) worth of
See also: **face** value.

van
in the van = at the front

vanish
vanish into the blue/thin air = disappear completely

variety
variety is the spice of life = changes in one's activities/situation make
life interesting

veil
See: **draw** a veil over.

velvet
See: iron hand/fist in a velvet **glove**.

vengence
with a vengeance = excessively/thoroughly/violently

vent
give vent to = freely express
See also: vent one's **spleen**.

venture
See: **nothing** ventured, nothing gained.

verdict
  See: **open** verdict

verge
verge on = be close to/nearly

verse
  See: quote **chapter** and verse.

very
all very well = acceptable/all right
the very thing = just what is required

vested
vested interest = something that gives one a personal/selfish
  advantage

vex
  See: vexed **question**.

vicious
  See: vicious **circle**.

victory
Pyrrhic victory = success at such a cost it is rendered worthless
  See also: **landslide** victory.

view
come into view = in sight/visible
have in view = be planning/thinking about
in the long view = considering well in advance
in full view = completely in sight
in one's view = in one's opinion
in view of = because of/considering
take a long view = consider well in advance
with a view to = with the intention of
  See also: **bird**'s-eye view; **point** of view; take a **dim** view of; view
  with a beady **eye**.

villain
the villain of the piece = somebody who acts/behaves badly

vine
clinging vine = somebody who monopolizes one's attention/time

violet
shrinking violet = somebody who is shy

virtue
by virtue of (the fact that) = because of

vital
 See: vital **statistics**.

voice
at the top of one's voice = as loud as one can
give voice to = express (publicly)
have a voice in = be in a position to state one's opinion
in good voice = singing/speaking well
lose one's voice = be unable to speak
lower/raise one's voice = speak quieter/louder
voice crying in the wilderness = (somebody with a) minority point of
 view
wee/still small voice = conscience/reasonableness
with one voice = in total agreement/unanimously

void
 See: **null** and void.

volume
 See: **speak** volumes.

vote
put to the vote = obtain a decision by voting
vote of confidence = vote that determines whether a ruling body still
 represents the views of the majority
vote of thanks = request for appreciative applause/thanks
 See also: vote with one's **feet**.

W

wade
wade into somebody/something = unhesitatingly tackle
  somebody/something
wade through = move laboriously through

wag
  See: tail wagging the **dog**.

wagon
on the wagon = not drinking alcohol (although formerly doing so)
  See also: climb/jump on (board) the **bandwagon**.

wait
everything comes to he/him who waits = somebody who is patient
  will eventually get what he/she wants
wait and see = await a decision/the outcome
wait a minute/moment = I wish to say something, or please wait a
  short time, or exclamation of surprise
waiting in the wings = waiting for an opportunity
wait up = not go to bed (until somebody arrives)
(just) you wait = a threat (of discipline/punishment)
  See also: **lady** in waiting; **lie** in wait; play a waiting **game**; wait on
  somebody **hand** and foot.

wake
in the wake of = following after/behind
  See also: enough to wake the **dead**.

walk
walk all over somebody = be totally inconsiderate of somebody's
  dignity/feelings, or convincingly defeat somebody
walk away with/walk it = win convincingly/easily
walk off with = steal
walk on air = be extremely carefree/happy
walk tall = feel proud and confident
walk the streets = earn a living as a prostitute

walk through one's part = do what one has to do in an
indifferent/disinterested way
walk out on = abandon
walk out with = have as a boyfriend/girlfriend
See also: **cock** of the rock/walk; walk off one's **feet**; walk of **life**.

wall

drive/send somebody up the wall = make somebody very
annoyed/frustrated
go to the wall = become bankrupt
walls have ears = one might be overheard
(see the) writing on the wall = indication (that something bad may
happen)
See also: **back** to the wall; bang/knock one's **head** against a brick
wall; **fly** on the wall.

wand

wave one's magic wand = achieve something difficult as if by magic

want

be found wanting = be discovered lacking
for want of = because of an absence/lack of
somebody (just) didn't want to know = somebody was not interested
want for = need/require
you want to... = you should...

war

be in the wars = be (slightly) injured
carry the war into the enemy's camp = counterattack an opponent in
order to pursue one's aims/argument
on the warpath = (angrily) looking for trouble
war of nerves = conflict involving threats etc. but no actual fighting
See also: all's **fair** in love and war; **declare** war.

warm

warm as toast = comfortably warm
See also: warm the **cockles** of one's heart.

warrant

See: sign somebody's **death** warrant.

wart

wart

warts and all = including all blemishes/faults

wash

(all) come out in the wash = eventually have a satisfactory outcome

get lost in the wash = unaccountably disaoppear (while among other things)

it/that won't wash = it/that is an unconvincing reason

take in somebody else's washing = help somebody by doing part of his/her work

washed out = very pale, or abandoned (because of rain)

(all) washed-out/-up = failed/finished

See also: wash one's dirty **linen** in public; wash one's **hand**s of.

waste

go/run to waste = be wasted

waste not, want not = do not waste anything and a need will not occur

See also: **lay** waste; waste one's **breath**.

watch

be on the watch for = be observant for/look out for

watch it/out = be careful

watch one's step = take care

watch over = care for/guard

watch somebody like a hawk = observe somebody very closely

See also: a watched **pot** never boils.

water

make water = urinate

muddy the waters = (deliberately) confuse the issue

tread water = remain upright and afloat (by moving one's feet in the water), or bide time/wait

turn on the waterworks = cry profusely (and perhaps deliberately)

water something down = dilute something

water under the bridge = past event (and no longer important)

See also: **blood** is thicker than water; cast one's **bread** on/upon the waters; come **hell** or high water; **dull** as ditchwater; go through **fire** and water; **hold** water; in **deep** water; in **hot** water; keep one's **head** above water; like a **fish** out of water; like water off a **duck**'s back;

make one's **mouth** water; **milk** and water; of the **first**
magnitude/order/water; **pass** water; **pour** oil on troubled water;
pour/throw **cold** water onto something; spend **money** like water; take
to something like a **duck** to water; throw out the **baby** with the bath
water.

Waterloo
See: **meet** one's match/Waterloo.

wave
make waves = cause difficulties/trouble
on the same wavelength (as) = sharing an interest/opinion etc. (with)
wave aside = dismiss (as irrelevant/unimportant)
wave down = signal with the hand in order to stop a vehicle
See also: on the **crest** of a wave; wave one's **magic** wand.

way
by the way = incidentally
by way of = via, or as/for
get into/out of the way of doing something = adopt/break a routine
give way (to) = let past, or collapse/subside, or be followed by, or
  express/release one's emotions, or concede/submit
go a long way to(wards) = be very helpful in
go one's own way = act independently
go out of one's way = take trouble to
go the way of all flesh = cease to exist/die
have a way with one = have an attractive/friendly personality
have a way with somebody/something = be good at dealing
  with/using
have/get (everything) one's own way = do what(ever) one wants
have it both ways = have the advantage of two mutually exclusive
  options
in a way = in one respect
in/out of somebody's way = obstructing/not obstructing somebody,
  or within/out of reach
lead the way = go first
lose one's way = become lost
make one's way = go, or succeed
make way for = move aside (and leave room) for

there are no two ways about it = it is indisputable

way out = very fashionable/up-to-date, or not close to requirement
  See also: couldn't punch his way out of a **paper** bag; **elbow** one's way; **fall** by the wayside; in a **bad** way; in a **big** way; in the **family** way; **look** the other way; meet somebody **half** way; **mend** one's ways; **no** way; out of **harm**'s way; **parting** of the ways; **pave** the way for something; **pay** one's way; that's the way the **cookie** crumbles; **thread** one's way; **under** way.

weak

have a weakness for = have an (irresistible) fondness for

weak as a kitten = very weak

weak-kneed = easily frightened/intimidated
  See also: in a weak **moment**; soft/weak in the head.

wear

wear and tear = gradual deterioration through use

wear down = gradually reduce

wear off = diminish/fade
  See also: if the **cap** fits, wear it; wear one's **heart** on one's sleeve; wear the **trousers**; **worse** for wear.

weather

lovely weather we're having = we are having very bad weather (meant ironically)
  See also: **dirty** weather; fair-weather **friend**; keep a weather **eye** open; lovely weather for **ducks**; make **heavy** weather; **under** the weather; weather the **storm**.

weave

get weaving = begin moving/working

wedding

  See: **shotgun** wedding.

wedge

  See: thin **end** of the wedge.

weed
weed something out = remove something that is unwanted (from among others)
widow's weeds = (black) mourning traditionally worn by a widow

week
See: any **day** of the week; **dirty** weekend; knock somebody into the **middle** of next week.

weep
See: **cry**/weep buckets.

weigh
weigh (half) a ton = be very heavy
weigh in = join in enthusiatically/vigorously
weigh something up = consider/evaluate something

weight
See: **carry** weight; **pull** one's weight; **throw** one's weight about; worth one's weight in **gold**.

weird
weird and wonderful = strange but clever

welcome
be welcome to = be (willingly) allowed to
outstay one's welcome = remain too long
(as) welcome as the flowers in May = very welcome
you're welcome = I need no thanks/I was pleased to do it

well
be as well = be advisable/prudent
be well out of = be fortunate not to be involved in/with
do well out of = profit by

(all) well and good = acceptable
well and truly = thoroughly
well I never did = exclamation of surprise
well off = in a fortunate situation, or wealthy
well out of = lucky not to be concerned with
well up in/on something = well informed about something
  See also: **all** very well; **just** as well; well-**heeled.**

west
go west = cease to be of use/exist

wet
wet one's whistle = have a (alcoholic) drink
  See also: **talk** wet; wet behind the **ears**; wet **blanket**; wet the **baby's**
  head.

whale
have a whale of a time = enjoy oneself

what
and what have you/and what not = and so on
give somebody what for = punish/scold somebody
have (got) what it takes = have the necessary abilities/qualities
I know what = I have an idea/suggestion
know what's what = be experienced/prudent
or what = or what the cause/reason is
what about? = would you like? or what do you think about?
(well) what do you know! = exclamation of surprise
what in the world...? = (emphatically) why?
what of it? = what concern is it of yours?
what's all this?/what's up? = what is happening
what's-his-name = somebody whose name cannot be remembered
what's it to you? = what is your interest in it?
what's yours? = what would you like to drink?
what with = because of/owing to
  See also: and what's **more**; for what it's **worth**; **so** what?; what did I
  tell you?; what on **earth**?; what **price**...?; what's **cooking**?; what's
  eating you?; what's the **odds**?

wheel

behind the wheel = in control

set the wheels in motion = make a start to a (usually slow) procedure/process

take the wheel = take control

wheeling and dealing = doing business in a clever but often underhand way

wheels within wheels = complicated set-up in which small parts affect the other parts around them

  See also: **oil** the wheels; put a **spoke** in (somebody's wheel); put one's **shoulder** to the wheel.

when

say when = please tell me when I have poured you enough drink

where

where it's at = place of most excitement/interest

whet

whet somebody's appetite = stimulate somebody's eagerness/interest

while

worth somebody's while = worth somebody making the effort/spending the time

  See also: **once** in a while; while away the **time**; while the **going** is good.

whip

have the whip hand over somebody = have the advantage/control over somebody

whipping boy = somebody (likely to be) punished/reprimanded for somebody else's errors

  See also: **crack** the whip; fair **crack** of the whip.

whirl

give something a whirl = try something

whisker

by a whisker = by a very narrow margin

  See also: **cat**'s pyjamas/whiskers.

whisper

whisper
 See: **stage** whisper.

whistle
 whistle for something = ask for something but with no prospect of getting it
 See also: **blow** the gaff/whistle on somebody; **clean** as a whistle; **wet** one's whistle; whistle in the **dark.**

whit
 not a whit = not at all

white
 give somebody a whitewash = beat an opponent (at a game) before he/she has scored at all
 white as a sheet = very white
 See also: **bleed** (somebody) white; in **black** and white; hoist/show/wave the white **flag**; show the white **feather**; swear **black** is white; white-collar **worker**; whited **sepulchre**; white **elephant**; (great) white **hope**; white **lie**; white **man**; white man's **burden.**

whizz
 whizz kid = somebody who is intelligent/keen and progresses rapidly in his/her job

whole
 on the whole = considering everything
 See also: go the whole **hog**; the whole bang **shoot.**

whoop
 whoop it up = have a boisterous/enjoyable time

why
 whys and wherefores = explanation/(all) the details

wick
 get on somebody's wick = greatly annoy somebody

wicket
 See: **sticky** wicket.

wide
 See: **far** and near/wide; give a wide **berth** (to); off/wide of the **mark.**

widow

See: **grass** widow; widow's **weed**s.

wife

See: old wives' **tale**s.

wild

be wild about = be very enthusiastic about, or be angry about
See also: **out** in the wilds; **run** wild; sow one's wild **oats**; spread like wild **fire**; wild **goose** chase; wild **guess**; wild **horses** wouldn't.

wilderness

See: **voice** crying in the wilderness.

will

at will = when one wishes
with a will = with determination and energy
with the best will in the world = no matter how much one tries/wants
See also: willing **horse**.

willies

give one the willies = make one feel frightened/uncomfortable

win

win somebody over = persuade somebody (to give help/support)
win through = persevere and succeed
you (just) can't win = it seems one always fails
See also: carry/win the **day**; win by **default**; win **hands** down; winning **streak**; win one's **spurs**; win/lose the **toss**.

wind

get/have the wind up = become anxious/frightened
get wind of something = learn indirectly about something
in the teeth of the wind = with the wind against one/in one's face
in the wind = being planned (secretly)
like the wind = very quickly
put the wind up somebody = make somebody anxious/frightened
see how/which way the wind blows = postpone a decision until one has more information
take the wind out of somebody's sails = take away somebody's advantage/confidence

tilt at windmills = struggle against imaginary/trivial opposition
wind somebody up = deliberately make somebody agitated/anxious
wind something up = bring something to a conclusion
  See also: **broken**-winded (horse); **free** as the air/wind/a bird; get
  one's **second** wind; it's an **ill** wind; **sail** close to the wind; **sound** in
  wind and limb; **straw** in the wind; three **sheets** to the wind; throw
  caution to the winds.

window
window dressing = presenting something in the best possible way by
  revealing only its good features
window shopping = looking at goods in shop windows with no
  intention of buying

wine
wine and dine somebody = treat somebody to an expensive meal

wing
clip somebody's wings = reduce somebody's influence/power
spread one's wings = begin to act independently
take somebody under one's wing = guide/protect somebody
  See also: **waiting** in the wings.

wink
not have/sleep a wink = have no sleep at all
tip somebody the wink = give somebody (secret) advantageous
  information
  See also: a **nod** is as good as a wink to a blind horse; **forty** winks.

wipe
wipe something out = cancel/destroy something
wipe the grin/smile off somebody's face = reduce somebody's
  confidence/pride
  See also: sweep/wipe the **floor** with somebody; wipe off the face of
  the **earth**.

wire
get/have one's wires crossed = misunderstand (each other)
  See also: **live** wire.

wise
be wise to somebody/something = know about (the implications of)
  somebody/something
put somebody wise = inform somebody
  See also: be wise after the **event**; **none** the wiser; wise **guy**.

wish
wishful thinking = hoping for what is very probably unattainable
  See also: wish somebody **joy**.

wit
have/keep one's wits about one = be alert/careful
to wit = that is to say (as follows)
  See also: at one's wits **end**; **live** by one's wits; **scare** somebody out of
  his/her wits.

witch
witch-hunt = persecution of somebody whose beliefs/opinions are
  unaccepted by the majority

with
be with somebody = support somebody, or understand somebody
with it = aware of modern trends/fashion

without
  See: be without/have no rhyme or **reason**; without so **much** as.

witness
eye-witness = somebody who is present at and sees an incident
material witness = witness (in a court of law) whose evidence is
  crucial to the case

woe
woe betide one = one will be sorry
woe is me = I am (very) unhappy

wolf
throw somebody to the wolves = allow somebody to take the blame,
  or deliberately place somebody in danger/difficulty
  See: **cry** wolf; keep the wolf from the **door**; **lone** wolf; wolf in
  sheep's **clothing**.

woman
make an honest woman (out) of = marry
scarlet woman = adulteress/prostitute
See also: my **good** man/woman.

wonder
I shouldn't wonder = I would not be surprised
it's a wonder = it is surprising
I wonder if you'd mind (doing something) = please would you (do something)
no wonder = I'm not surprised
wonders (will) never cease = I am very surprised at what has happened
See also: **nine** days' wonder; **small** wonder.

wood
not be able to see the wood for the trees = be over-attentive to details and fail to realize/understand the main issue
out of the wood(s) = out of difficulty/danger
touch wood = hopefully/with luck
See also: **dead** wood; **neck** of the woods; wooden **spoon**.

wool
wool-gathering = day-dreaming.
See also: **dyed**-in-the-wool; pull the wool over somebody's **eyes**.

word
be as good as one's word = keep one's promises
break/keep one's word = fail to keep/keep a promise
famous last words! = so you claim/say!
have a word with somebody = talk briefly to somebody
have the final/last word = make the final comment in an argument
have words = quarrel
in a word = in (brief) conclusion
in other words = putting it another way
man/somebody of few words = somebody who says little
my word! = exclamation of surprise
not be the word for it = be an understatement
not in so many words = not exactly
operative word = most significant word

put in a good word for somebody = praise/recommend somebody
take the words out of somebody's mouth = anticipate what somebody
  is about to say
take somebody at his/her word/take somebody's word for it =
  believe somebody without question
word for word = exactly as spoken/written
words fail me = I am unable to find words to express my feelings
  See also: **action**s speak louder than words; by word of **mouth**; **eat**
  one's words; **exchange** words; from the word **go**; have a word in
  somebody's **ear**; **man** of his word; **mark** my words; **mum**'s the word;
  not get a word in **edgeways**; **play** on words; (just) **say** the word; the
  last word; words fail me; words stick in one's **throat**.

work

give somebody the works = let somebody have everything that is
  available
go to work on something = begin working on something
gum up the works = cause something to stop working
have one's work cut out = have a difficulty to be overcome
out of work = unemployed
set somebody to work = get somebody to start working
set to work = begin working
(all) worked up = anxious/excited
work like a horse/Trojan = work very hard
work of art = paint/sculpture or anything requiring great
  artistry/crafsmanship
work off = get rid of by exercising
work out = come to a happy/successful conclusion
work-out = session of physical exercise
work something out = calculate/solve a problem
  See also: all in a **day**'s work; **dirty** work; **donkey** work; **give**
  somebody the works; in running/working **order**; make **short** work
  of; **nasty** piece of work; the **business/works**; throw a **spanner** in the
  works; work like a **dog**; work one's **passage**; work one's **ticket**; work
  something to **death**.

world

a world of = very much
for (all) the world = for anything

for all the world like = exactly like

on top of the world = very happy

out of this world = very good/unusual

(all) the world and his wife = many people

the world is one's oyster = all the good things in life are available to one

think the world of somebody/something = be very fond/have a high opinion of somebody/something

what/why in the world? = emphatically what/why?

  See also: **dead** to the world; get/have the **best** of both worlds; have the world at one's **feet**; it's a **small** world; it takes all sorts (to make the world); **man** of the world; **New** World; not **long** for this world; not the **end** of the world; with the best **will** in the world.

worm

even a worm will turn = even somebody who is very tolerant/patient may one day decide not to be

worn

  See: worn to a **shadow**.

worry

no/not to worry = there is no need to worry

you should worry = you certainly have no reason to worry

worse

worse for wear = in a bad state because of prolonged effort/use, or drunk

  See also: **none** the worse for; worse **luck**.

worst

at (the) worst = regarding a situation in the least optimistic way

come off worst/get the worst of something = suffer more than somebody else

do one's worst = (try to) be as bad as one can

if the worst comes to the worst = if the most unpleasant thing possible happens

the worst of it is that = the most unfortunate/unpleasant thing about the situation is that

worth

for all one is worth = with all of one's energy/vigour
for what it's worth = if it is worthy of consideration (usually said by
  somebody who thinks it is important)
not worth a tinker's cuss/damn = worthless
  See also: worth one's **salt**; worth one's weight in **gold**; worth
  somebody's **while**; worthy of the **name**.

wound

  See: rub **salt** into the wound; **wind**.

wrap

keep something under wraps = keep something secret
wrapped up in = engrossed with
wrap something up = complete something
wrap up! = be quiet!
  See also: wrap somebody (up) in **cotton** wool.

wrist

  See: **slap** on the wrist.

write

write something off = accept that something is permanently lost, or
  destroy something
write something up = (neatly) write a description of
  See also: (see the) writing on the **wall**.

wrong

don't get me wrong = do not misunderstand me/do not take offence
  at what I say
get on the wrong side of somebody = cause somebody to dislike one
get something wrong = misunderstand, or make a mistake
go wrong = make a mistake, or cease to function/work properly, or
  become dishonest/immoral
in the wrong = culpable/guilty
two wrongs don't make a right = a second error/sin does not cancel
  the first
what's wrong with that? = why not?
  See also: get/start off on the right/wrong **foot**; get hold of the wrong
  end of the **stick**; not put a **foot** wrong; on the wrong side of the
  blanket; on the wrong **track**.

Y

yard
in somebody's own back yard = located near somebody/in the
 neighbourhood
like a yard of pump water = very thin
the Yard = Scotland Yard (headquarters of London's Metropolitan
 Police)

yarn
spin a yarn = tell a long (untrue) story

year
all the year round = throughout the year
getting on in years = becoming old
the year dot = a long time in the past
year in, year out = continuously (every year)
  See also: for **donkey**'s years.

yellow
have a yellow streak/stripe down one's back = be cowardly

yen
have a yen for = desire/want

yes
yes and no = answer that agrees in one respect but disagrees in
 another

yesterday
  See: not **born** yesterday.

yet
as yet = up till now

you
(strictly) between you and me = confidentially (with only us knowing)
you and yours = you and (all) your family
you and your something = something belonging to somebody else of
 which one disapproves

young

not as young as one used to be = getting older (visibly)

young at/in heart = with a young person's outlook although no
  longer young

you're only young once = the opportunities of youth are available for
  only a short time

  See also: young **blood**.

your

your actual = the real

yours truly = me

  See also: **what**'s yours?; **you** and yours; **you** and your something.

Z

zero
zero in on = accurately aim at

NOTES

NOTES

NOTES

NOTES

NOTES

NOTES

NOTES

ENGLISH SYNONYMS
★ Simple A-to-Z presentation for easy access
★ Comprehensive coverage in a convenient format
ISBN 0 245-54831-9

ENGLISH PUNCTUATION & HYPHENATION
★ Clear guidance for students, secretaries and editors
★ 13,000-word hyphenation dictionary
ISBN 0 245-60020-5